from the desk of
david housel ...

A COLLECTION OF AUBURN STORIES

BY DAVID HOUSEL

AUB RN
Network

HOST CREATIVE COMMUNICATIONS

Acknowledgements

There are many to thank and many to acknowledge. Special thanks must be given to *The Birmingham News, The Huntsville Times, The Opelika-Auburn News, Birmingham Magazine* and *The Auburn Plainsman* for allowing stories written for their publication to be used again in this collection. Dave Rosenblatt and Bev Powers at Auburn University Archives have been most helpful.

Particular recognition must be given to a whole cadre of student assistants in the Sports Information Office who diligently clipped, glued and "maintained" the scrapbook. Each no doubt wondered if their efforts would ever be recognized or appreciated. This book would not have been possible without their dedicated service to Auburn.

Thanks must go to Mike Hubbard for his many years of good work for Auburn and for me, and for his belief in this project. Special thanks also to Sherrie Morgan of Craftmaster Printers for her suggestions and her many hours of proofing when some of these pieces were first written and again when they were collected. When it comes to Auburn, hers is a labor of love.

This book would not have been possible without the loyal and dedicated efforts of Chuck Gallina, Jason Peevy and Ritch Saucer. Nor would it have been possible without the assistance and encouragement of my wife, Susan.

To these and to many others, some of whom believed in me when I did not always believe in myself, this is your reward. The road has not always been easy, but it has always been good. Thanks for helping along the way.

Photographs courtesy of: Auburn Athletic Department, Auburn University Photographic Services, Auburn University Archives, *The Talladega Daily Home*, Ed Jones and *The Huntsville Times*. The Heisman Trophy is pictured with permission of The Downtown Athletic Club, New York. Quotation on opposite page from *A Place of Springs*, by Viola Goode Liddell, ©1979 The University of Alabama Press. Used by permission.

ISBN 1-879688-07-7

Printed in the United States of America
First Edition

"I write of a passing scene, of a people needing love and understanding even while denying the need of anything, of a people whom I love not only for their great goodness and for their sometimes grievous faults but because they are my people and I am one of them."

Viola Goode Liddell
A Place of Springs

To Those Who Love and Those Who Care...

And Aren't Afraid to Show It...

Introduction

This book is a collection of stories, columns and news releases covering 24 years of Auburn and Auburn Football. Most have appeared in *Auburn Football Illustrated*, Auburn's game program, *The Birmingham News*, *The Opelika-Auburn News*, *The Huntsville Times* or similar publications. There is one exception, a reflection piece about my father, an Auburn man, written at the foot of his hospital bed the night he died.

With that one exception, this book is the story of 24 years of Auburn Football and life at Auburn. It is, to some extent, a book of Auburn people telling their story and the story of the place and time that brought them together.

These stories are presented in the time frame, form and order in which they were written. The temptation to edit and improve them to the style of a more mature, experienced writer, for the most part, has been resisted. If journalism is literature in a hurry and history as it happens, this is a history of Auburn and its people.

There are stories here that will make you laugh. There are stories that will make you cry. Many will touch your heart and remind you once again of the goodness, the possibilities of success or failure, and the humanity that is within each of us.

There are stories of winners here and there are stories of losers—losers who, through their dedicated and continuing efforts, were, in the end, triumphant. All, in their own way, shared their lives and their humanity with us, their fellowman.

This then, is a story of humanity at Auburn. As with all of us, it is the story of tragedy but, more often than not, triumph. It is their story and it is our story, because we, more often than not, shared their story and cheered them along the way.

I consider myself most fortunate to have been a part of it and to have the opportunity to tell this story—their story and our story—to you.

David Housel
May, 1991

Other Books by David Housel
Saturdays To Remember

Contents

From Farming to Pharmacy———————

A self-styled "rough and ignorant country boy" walked down the dusty unpaved streets of Auburn in 1918 to the Admissions Office of Alabama Polytechnic Institute.

It was a long-awaited moment for a young man leaving a place where "a nickel's worth of candy was a luxury" to face the world.

"What courses do you want to take, son?" a bespectacled admissions officer asked.

"What you got to offer?" the young man responded.

"How about pharmacy," was the reply.

"Is that all you got?" the youth groaned. "I've been farming all my life and I kinda wanted to get away from it here..."

Roy B. Sewell, the farm boy who became a self-made millionaire, got away from the farm all right, but he never got away from Auburn.

And it's Auburn's good fortune that he didn't.

Although Sewell, who is now president of one of the country's Top 10 clothing manufacturers had to quit school to work and never earned a degree from Auburn, his loyalty has been remarkable.

In addition to considerable financial support, Sewell has donated a flag pole for the football field, uniforms for the band and has served two terms as president of the Alumni Association.

But one of his donations to Auburn will far outlive the others, no matter how significant they are.

Roy B. Sewell gave Auburn the fight song "War Eagle." "Auburn didn't have a song to show the true Auburn spirit," Sewell recalled with a smile. "I wanted us to have one that would stir the listener's soul.

"I contacted Al Stillman on Broadway in New York," Sewell continued, "and tried to give him an idea of what Auburn was like and he came up with "War Eagle."

How did it feel when he first heard the Auburn band play its new fight song?

"I felt tremendously proud of it," he said, propping his feet on a desk piled high with mail and covered with miniature Tigers and War Eagles.

But as Sewell has not forgotten Auburn, Auburn has not forgotten Sewell.

The University has conferred an honorary degree on the Bremen, Ga. clothing manufacturer and ODK and the A-Club have made him an honorary member. The athletic dormitory is named Roy B. Sewell Hall.

Sewell smiled when listing his honoraries and said, "I didn't even know what a fraternity was when I was in school. Maybe they feel sorry for me now, or maybe they just see how much I love Auburn."

Sewell fondly remembers his two years at Auburn before he had to quit school to go to work.

"Ralph Draughon and I had several classes together," Sewell recalled. "We had English and geometry under Coach Mike Donahue and Ole Ralph was really smart.

"It was one of my biggest thrills when they made Ralph president," professed Sewell, "and the football team winning the national championship runs a close second."

Sewell is an avid supporter of Auburn athletic teams, but he is quick to add,

"Athletics are not the most important thing at Auburn. Education is the most important because education will stand by you even when you are too old to play."

Roy Sewell has seen Auburn grow from 1,700 students in 1918 to 13,400 in 1967, but he says, "It's still the same ole Auburn.

"Auburn has a Christian spirit. The good Lord made Auburn something special, " says Sewell, smiling, "and I thank Him every night for what he did for Auburn.

"Part of Auburn is that 'Never Give Up' spirit," Sewell continues. "There is always a better way to do something and we just have to find that better way. We can't stand still. We've got to find that better way."

Maybe Auburn helped Roy Sewell find that better way.

When he quit school, he began sweeping floors for his brothers who were in the clothing business. He eventually bought a small interest in the business, and in 1945, bought out his brother Warren.

"My brother is still my toughest competitor," Sewell says, smiling. "He can copy my styles, cut prices and give return privileges. How can you beat that?"

Roy Sewell will find a way.

He has too much Auburn in him not to find a way.

The Auburn Plainsman
November 10, 1967

Roy Sewell believed in Auburn and he believed in people. As much as he gave of himself to Auburn, he gave more to people. He helped hundreds of young men and women go to college who otherwise might not have been able to get an education. These young men and women are his greatest and most lasting legacy.

Lefty

Ralph Jordan would have made Auburn history even if he had not returned to his Alma Mater and become its most successful football coach.

A three-sport star in 1929-32, he was a football center, captain of the basketball team and the winning pitcher in the Southern Conference championship game. He remained at Auburn as an assistant football coach and head basketball coach following graduation.

As a basketball player, Jordan could be described as the Pete Maravich of the old Southern Conference which stretched from Virginia to Louisiana. In 1929, he was the conference's leading scorer with 111 points.

Now Jordan remembers, "In those days you had a wide open game when the team scored 40 points, and we won some in Alumni Gym by scores as low as 16-14, but they were as exciting as today's games. My 111 points looked big then, but Maravich gets that many in two games now."

The man who has won over 100 football games at Auburn still smiles broadly when he remembers that day in the early 1930s when he and his Auburn teammates met Florida for the Southern Conference baseball championship.

"I was a third-string pitcher," recalls Jordan. "This was the deciding game and our staff was pretty depleted. The coach walked up and said, 'Let's see your stuff, Lefty.'"

Waving his arms to describe his pitches, Jordan continued. "I threw my fastball which really looked like an annie-over, and my ole round-house out curveball and coach said, 'You got it, Lefty. Get in there.'"

Athletic director Jeff Beard recalls: "Shug just threw it up there and let them hit it, and did they ever hit it! Home plate was up at the corner of Drake Field where the tennis courts used to be (northeast corner of Haley Center). Florida would hit that ball and you would see it go over the rise and disappear toward the Field House (Petrie Hall).

"About that time, the centerfielder, Porter Grant, would come up with it. He saved Shug that day and late in the game, Shug was asking Porter for more help. The poor guy's suit was wringing wet already and his tongue was hanging out like a red necktie."

"I wasn't a very good pitcher," Jordan modestly admits, "but I did win the game 5-3 by hitting a three-run homerun."

At the prompting of Bill Beckwith, Jordan related how he decided to give up baseball one day.

"I'm not sure if I was pitching for the Selma Dewdrops or someone who paid me $1.50 to pitch, but I threw my fast ball as hard as I could once and hit a batter right between the eyes. It didn't even phase him. He just dropped the bat and trotted down to first base. I said if I couldn't throw any harder than that, then I'd quit," Jordan laughs.

Jordan graduated from Auburn in 1932. He was named assistant football coach in 1932, 25 days before his 21st birthday.

Jordan was named Auburn's basketball coach in 1934. His teams played its games in old Alumni Gym.

"They talk about a homecourt advantage in the Sports Arena," Jordan smiled, "well, they should have seen Alumni Gym. The seats were right on the out-of-bounds line and when you went up for a crip shot (layup), you would probably wind up halfway up in the crowd. The fans would literally throw you back on the court and you would take off again."

Beard recalls that the goals were right against the balcony walls and says, "It was really tough on opponents. They were not used to seeing people's legs dangling over the wall and feet banging against the side of the backboard. We tried to keep the feet back away from the backboard, but it was hard."

Jordan laughs when he tells about one big advantage Alumni Gym gave the Tigers.

"There was an area about the size of a desk top that was dead. When the players dribbled over it, the ball would not come back. We beat Georgia 31-30 one night because of that dead spot. We would see them dribbling toward that spot and when the ball hit the spot, we would grab it and run."

Jordan's basketball teams had no scholarship help, other than one Coke machine.

"The first aid any Auburn basketball player ever received," Jordan laughs, "went to Shag Hawkins, a player Bill Lynn and I believe could play in the league today. We had a soft drink machine near the coaches' offices and we gave Shag all of the money we made off the machine. It came to about $15 a month. We must have sold a lot of Cokes."

Most of Jordan's basketball players were also football players.

We would give them a couple of days off after the last football game and then we would start playing basketball. Our schedules were made during the Christmas holidays and we played teams like the Lanett Athletic Club in our games before Christmas."

Joel Eaves, Georgia's Athletic Director, and coach of Auburn's only Southeastern Conference championship basketball team, was a center under Jordan.

"Coach was then, as he is now, as fine a man to play for as you will find anywhere. He made the boys want to play for him," said Eaves.

"But I will never forget one night when we were playing a team we should have beaten by 50 points and were behind at the half. Coach Jordan cleared the dressing room except for the five starters and then he said, 'You all are pitiful. You couldn't beat Loachapoka, Wetumpka or Wedowee the way you are playing tonight.'"

Eaves said the Tigers went back out and won the game.

"That's as rough as he ever got with us," Eaves said.

Jordan's teams were always competitive. His surprising 1942 team went to the quarterfinals of the SEC tournament before losing to Adolph Rupp's Kentucky team 40-31.

We were leading 18-1 in the first half," Jordan says, smiling.

"We tricked them. We let them take the outside shots and played it tight inside. They were so surprised they couldn't even hit the rim for a long time."

Rupp and Jordan have been friends since their cage coaching days.

When I took over as head football coach and gave up basketball, Coach Rupp wrote me and said it was the worst mistake I'd ever make," Jordan laughs.

"He was also the only conference coach to congratulate us when we won the National Championship in 1957."

Rupp says Jordan is "as fine a football coach as he was a basketball coach, and associations with men like him make coaching worthwhile."

The basketball teams in Jordan's coaching days played as many as six games on the road in a row.

He recalls his "most terrible trip."

"We were going to Louisiana to play Tulane and Louisiana State. One of the players, J.P. Streetman, had a car and wanted to take it and collect three cents a mile expense money.

"We loaded up in J.P.'s car and two U-Drive-Its and headed out to Louisiana. Somebody stole J.P.'s car in Jackson, Miss. and we had to put the whole team in two U-Drive-Its.

"We drove into New Orleans and luckily one of the players bought a paper. In the excitement we realized we were supposed to play in Baton Rouge that night so we just packed back up and started out again."

Jordan says basketball teams of his day were lucky to get uniforms every three or four years and sweat suits lasted for "generations."

"Those were the days when you jumped center after every field goal," says Jordan, "and we seldom had any men over 6-2. And if anybody shot a one-handed shot other than a crip shot, the coaches would put him on the bench.

After a tour of duty in Europe during World War II, Jordan went to Georgia where he was assistant football coach and head basketball coach until 1950. He won more games, 18 in 1948, than any other Bulldog coach has won in a single season.

"We were playing St. John's in Madison Square Garden in my first game as Georgia's coach," recalls Jordan. "It was less than two weeks until the game and I asked Wally Butts, the athletic director, when we were going to get some war surplus mattresses out of Woodruff Hall so we could practice. He said, 'Shug, it's still two weeks until the game, isn't it? What are you getting so excited about?'"

St. John's won the game, but the most excitement came hours before the game started.

"The boys were so naive they went out in front of the ticket office and started selling their guest tickets. The whole team got arrested that afternoon, but we got them off in time for the game," Jordan recalls.

Jordan gave up basketball coaching for good on Jan. 1, 1950, but he is still an avid basketball fan. The game has changed, but some of the people haven't.

"Ed Pope was sports editor of the Athens Banner-Herald in 1946," says Jordan. "He was a genius, only 12 or 13 years old, but he was a die-hard Georgia fan. Georgia beat us 38-37 on Saturday night and the headline on Sunday morning said 'Georgia Routs Auburn 38-37.' All you could read about was Georgia."

"Ed is sports editor of a Miami newspaper now, and when we lost an even ball game to Miami 7-0 last fall, all you could read about was Miami. You wouldn't even know Auburn was in town for the game.

"I wrote him the next week and told him he hadn't changed a bit in over 20 years. He still doesn't know Auburn exists," Jordan said, smiling.

Jordan sees a lot of similarity in coaching basketball and football. It all gets back to people.

"Sports, individual sports included, teach a person emotional stability," Jordan believes.

"A man has to learn where his breaking point is," Jordan continues. "Every season, there's the guy you can whip everytime, there's the guy who whips you everytime and then there's the guy who fights you to a standoff with no one winning.

"All of this happens before thousands of people," Jordan says, "and the rules must be followed. It teaches a boy there are some things he can do and some he can't. Competitive sports help make men out of boys," says Jordan.

The Auburn Plainsman, February 29, 1968
Auburn Football Illustrated, November 9, 1968

He Left a Legacy

Dr. Ralph Brown Draughon, who died of a heart attack August 13 near the end of summer quarter, did not want to be president of Auburn University.

It was during his administration, however, the institution made its greatest progress.

"Ralph did not want to be president," recalled his wife, Mrs. Caroline Draughon, for whom Caroline Draughon Village, a married student housing complex, is named.

"His first love was teaching history," she continued, "and I think he really wanted to return to the classroom when President L.N. Duncan died in 1947. He certainly had no idea that he would be considered to fill the vacancy."

For a man who did not want to be president, Dr. Draughon's list of accomplishments for Auburn is remarkable. Shortly before Draughon's retirement in 1965, Dr. Paul S. Haley, who served on the Board of Trustees for almost 50 years, said Draughon was "the best president Auburn ever had."

And Haley had reason to make that statement. During Draughon's administration, Auburn almost doubled the size of its student body and achieved the largest enrollment of any college in the state of Alabama. All of its doctoral programs and many of its masters degree programs were begun under Dr. Draughon.

More than 50 major buildings, representing a capital outlay in excess of $30 million, were built and the Auburn Alumni Development program was launched, achieving its first goal of more than $2.5 million.

Auburn's faculty was upgraded so that 45 percent of the teaching personnel held the Ph.D. or other terminal degrees as contrasted to 12 percent in 1948, and more students graduated from Auburn while he was president than in all the years preceding his administration.

Dr. Draughon considered the development of a working relationship with Alabama his greatest achievement, according to his associates. Guided largely by Dr. Draughon's determination to aid education in Alabama, the state's two largest institutions began working together for better education for all of Alabama's youth.

Following Dr. Duncan's death in 1947, Dr. Draughon served as acting president for 18 months. In 1948, the Board of Trustees named him president, a post he held until his retirement in 1965. As president emeritus of the University, he maintained a simple office in the library and was writing a history of Auburn at the time of his death.

He did not like elaborate decor. He never allowed his Samford Hall office to be remodeled and he insisted on using the same desk used by his two predecessors. He would not even allow his offices to be air conditioned.

"He loved Samford Hall the way it was," his wife remarked, "and he was reluctant to change anything about it."

Dr. Draughon was an avid sportsman, but even on his trips to escape the pressures which surround being president of a growing university, he still thought about Auburn.

Former Dean of Faculties, M.C. Huntley, Draughon's close friend and fishing companion recalls a relaxed Ralph Draughon.

"Ralph loved to fish, but even when he was on Lake Martin, he would still have his mind on his work at Samford Hall. He worked very hard to upgrade Auburn's faculty and secure the funds for the library. And much of that work was done in a boat in the middle of Lake Martin. He was always thinking of ways to improve Auburn."

Dr. Draughon had not expected to be appointed Auburn's president in 1948, and in 1965, he was surprised again when the state legislature agreed to name the new University library in his honor.

They also voted to name a married students housing complex for his wife Caroline, and an associate recently recalled the Draughon's momentous day.

"Dr. Draughon was tickled to death that the library had been named for him, but suddenly he turned to his wife and said, 'Why, they just named one building for me and 12 for you. That's not fair!' "

Dr. Draughon was a supporter of Land-Grant colleges and universities like Auburn. He believed these schools, more than any other institution, enabled the common people to get an education.

Draughon, according to Huntley, "lived, breathed, ate and slept Auburn," but when retirement came, he was ready to let the new president, Harry M. Philpott, run the show.

"Ralph said it was a 'new day' when Dr. Philpott moved into the office," related Mrs. Draughon, "and he seldom went back to Samford Hall. He just wanted to stay at home and enjoy growing roses."

"When Dr. Draughon cut loose as president, he cut loose," said President Philpott. "He was perfect. If I needed him for advice, he was always available, but he never interfered."

Dr. Draughon had no intention of growing old quickly in retirement. In fact, he vowed "to stay away from barbershops and restaurants, since men grow older a lot quicker if they sit around talking about the old times."

At the time of his death, the former president was eagerly looking to the day when the Auburn Tigers started fall football practice. Dr. Draughon was a frequent visitor at the Tiger practice field. He sat on the ground and passed the time chewing grass or smoking cigarettes.

Dr. Draughon attended football practice with a purpose. More than once he recommended plays to Coach Ralph Jordan. Some of the plays he recommended were illegal and others had no chance of working, but Draughon was still eager to help the Tigers' football fortunes.

His peers recognized Draughon's great love for college athletics as they chose him to serve two years as head of the Southeastern Conference's Presidents Committee, a committee composed of the presidents of member institutions. He also served on the conference's executive committee.

"Dr. Draughon had a great sense of humor," remembered Jeff Beard, Auburn's Athletic Director. "He always sat in the press box and he never attended a game in Cliff Hare Stadium without needling me about the lack of an elevator so he would not have to climb the stairs."

Dr. Draughon made no efforts to hide his feelings at a football game nor in the office, and one of the people who knows the moods of Ralph Draughon best is Jim Smith, chauffeur and butler for many Auburn presidents.

"You could always tell when things weren't going well for Dr. Draughon or the college," Jim recalled. "He would come down the stairs in the morning without a word. He'd look over the rims of his glasses, but he wouldn't say a thing. Sometimes he would be in deep concentration when we would travel and other times he would be laughing and talking all the time."

'Fesser Draughon,' as he was called, "was an honest man," said Smith. "You could rely on what he said."

"When he would go home for lunch, he would expect a pack of Chesterfield cigarettes and a glass of buttermilk to be waiting on him," Smith recalled. "Sometimes during the dinner hour, he'd asked for the milk and a new pack of cigarettes for the rest of the day.

"But no matter what might be happening," concluded Smith, " Dr. Draughon was always talking about Auburn. He sure loved this place."

But where did Ralph Draughon's love of Auburn originate? Where and how did it begin?

"It was instilled in him when he was young," said his wife. "He must have always loved Auburn."

Roy Sewell, a 1918 freshman classmate of Draughon's recalled, "Times were really hard for Ralph and everyone else in those days, but nothing was going to stop him from getting an education."

Draughon, with the help of his family in Hartford, worked his way through college and earned a BS degree in 1922. He was a teacher and a principal in several state high schools for a while, but in 1931, he and his bride, the former Caroline Marshall, returned to Auburn and he began teaching in the history department.

He became executive secretary to President Duncan in 1937 and ran the University while the Trustees were searching for a new president following Dr. Duncan's death in 1947.

Dr. Draughon had no idea he might be offered the presidency of his alma mater. He brought some of the nation's leading educators to Auburn for interviews with the Board, and when the big day came in 1948, he still was not prepared for the announcement Gov. James E. "Big Jim" Folsom made at a press conference.

Folsom announced that Draughon was the choice of the Board, and the new president stepped to the microphone.

"Thank you very much, Governor and gentlemen of the Board of Trustees..."

There was a pause as emotion overwhelmed Dr. Draughon. He could not continue, but he had to say something. Finally, he managed to force out some words "...I think we'd all better go and eat."

And, as one faculty member said at Dr. Draughon's retirement, "He inherited a polytechnic institute and left his successor a university."

The Auburn Plainsman
September 20, 1968

Captain Crunch

Auburn fans can "Thank the Lord" that Mike Kolen, number 54, decided to come to Auburn.

"Eight schools were recruiting me," recalls Kolen, "and I didn't know where to go. There were relatives and friends who wanted me to sign with each school, but I wanted to do what the Lord wanted me to do. I prayed a lot about it, then signed with Auburn, and I'm convinced I did the right thing. There's no other place like Auburn."

And War Eagles are convinced there's no other linebacker like Kolen, captain of the 1969 Tigers. In the estimation of coaches and teammates, Kolen is an All-American in every respect. An All-SEC performer last year, Kolen was Auburn's leading tackler and a four time winner of the "Headhunter" award which is awarded to the leading tackler in each game.

Kolen not only makes a lot of tackles, he makes the kind that are remembered - especially by ball carriers. His teammates have nicknamed Kolen "Captain Crunch" and with good reason. "When Mike hits people," says 1968 All-America David Campbell, "there's a big C-R-U-N-C-H. He passes the hardest lick I've ever seen—or heard. Another of Kolen's teammates admits he had "rather hit any two other players twice than hit Kolen once."

Even Coach Ralph Jordan marvels at Kolen's hitting ability. "Mike is the hardest-hitting linebacker I've seen in 38 years of football playing and coaching. He has the unique ability to uncoil on a ball carrier even if he's not in a balanced position."

It should not be surprising that Kolen's Christian faith played an important role in the linebacker's decision to come to Auburn. It is a motivating factor in Kolen's daily life.

Captain Crunch draws a parallel in playing football and living a Christian life. "A Christian has got to be totally committed to Christ," says Kolen, "and a football player should be totally committed and dedicated to football."

President of Auburn's chapter of the Fellowship of Christian Athletes (FCA), Kolen, a popular youth speaker, is busy in the off season with speaking engagements throughout Alabama and Georgia.

"Speaking to young people is a great opportunity," says Kolen. "Christ has changed my entire life, including football, since I rededicated myself to Him.

"For a long time, I really didn't enjoy football. Like most freshmen, I was homesick and in my sophomore year, I didn't feel like I was getting anywhere on the football field or going anywhere in life. Then I realized I was living my life for Mike Kolen and not for Jesus Christ. I rededicated my life and reoriented my goals. Since that time my life has gone a lot smoother on and off the football field."

Kolen has the rare distinction of being a captain on Auburn's football team two years in a row. In 1968, he was alternate captain. This year he is captain. He regards this as " the greatest honor I've ever received. It's a tremendous honor to represent the type men we have on our football team.

"As captain, I must set an example for other players to follow, and I've got to keep them inspired. I try to handle it on an individual basis. If a player gets whipped on one play, I tell him to get his head up because they won't be able to do that again. A football player, like anyone else, must have confidence in himself."

Captain Kolen's dedication and leadership ability spread through the whole team.

"You can't help but be inspired with Mike on the field," says Campbell. "He's like electricity. He always seems to find the switch that ignites the team, especially the defense."

If being elected captain is his biggest honor, Kolen regards Auburn's 28-14 upset win over Tennessee last season as his biggest thrill as an athlete.

"We had a great team spirit that night. Everybody was working as a complete unit, the way a team should. Everyone was fired up and it was great after the game, but all this happened last year. We've got to worry about 1969 now."

Kolen has already achieved athletic stardom. He knows the way to the top, so what advice would he give youngsters who might want to become a college football star?

"Youngsters should start playing football as soon as they can. I started playing in the third grade in the Termite League. They should try to build their bodies physically, of course, but they should not neglect to build character and high morals. All three are important to the successful athlete."

Throughout his football career, Kolen has enjoyed line play the best.

"I've never wanted to play anywhere but on the line, and I've always liked defense best. I've always enjoyed trying - not always doing, mind you - but always trying to stop the ball carrier."

Son of Mr. and Mrs. Robert E. Kolen of Birmingham, Captain Crunch will graduate in June with a degree in Business Administration. After graduation he hopes to play professional football and work in the insurance field in the off season. Kolen married the former Nancy Washburn of Opelika last March and they now live in Auburn's Caroline Draughon Village, an apartment complex for married students.

Football, schoolwork, and FCA related speaking engagements take up most of Captain Crunch's time, but he still likes to play tennis and slip away for a fishing trip occasionally. Kolen fishes for bass and crappie in the backwaters of Lake Martin. "Fishing is a great sport," he says. "It's good to get out in the fresh air, enjoy the scenery, throw that ole purple worm out on a steep ledge and wait for that big fish to bite." Kolen also likes to read, with religious books taking preference.

Kolen, starting his 13th straight Auburn game today, still remembers the toughest spot he's been in as an Auburn Tiger. It was in the 1967 Miami game.

"We were playing down there and the game was really rough. Gusty Yearout was playing ahead of me, but got hurt in the second quarter and I had to play the whole second half. Man, I was scared. I would have made a jack rabbit look cool and collected that night!"

Kolen's spectacular play in the second half earned him his first "Headhunter" award. The highlight of his play that night was a crunching tackle of Miami's star running back, Vince Opalsky. Opalsky had been running almost at will through the Tiger defense, but on a third and two situation, Kolen and Opalsky met head-on. The collision, heard around the Orange Bowl, brought "Oohs" and "Ahh's" from the crowd. When the players unpiled, Kolen trotted back to the Tiger huddle and Opalsky was being helped off the field. Coach Jordan said Kolen's tackle was the hardest lick he had seen in his 38-year association with football.

Kolen may have been scared that night in Miami, but since then, opposing ball carriers have been more than a bit concerned.

Only his size, 6-3, 216 pounds, would indicate that Kolen is an All-America football player. A modest person, Kolen could easily be mistaken for a young Baptist minister, but few, if any, ministers can tackle the way Kolen can. No one could have a greater dedication to his Christian faith.

Auburn's Mike Kolen, number 54, is more than just a number.

Auburn Football Illustrated
Auburn vs. Wake Forest
September 20, 1969

Mike Kolen, Captain Crunch, went on to have a successful pro career with the Miami Dolphins. He was on the 1972 Dolphin team that went undefeated and won the Super Bowl. The Mike Kolen Award is presented each year to Auburn's leading tackler in recognition of Mike Kolen's leadership and his contribution, both tangible and intangible, to Auburn Football.

King of the Quarterbacks _____

Pat Sullivan, at home, is very unheroic. He lounges around in shorts, faded tee shirt, barefooted. His apartment has a noticeable absence of football mementos, only one small statuette on the edge of a table. Notebooks and textbooks lay at strategic points.

He sweeps the floor, sets the table, washes dishes, occasionally changes the baby, and helps his beautiful wife Jean with all the household chores except one, taking out the garbage. He hates to do that.

Thus, the life of Pat Sullivan, husband, father, student, is not a great deal unlike any other married student husband—unless you consider those golden autumn Saturday afternoons collectively known as "football season." This soft spoken resident of Willow Street in Auburn, Alabama, then becomes Pat Sullivan, quarterback par excellence, and leading contender for 1971's coveted Heisman Trophy. Thousands of football fans jam stadia across the Southland for a first-hand view of Sullivan and football history in the making. Hundreds of thousands more search the airways for radio or television word of Pat Sullivan, billed by all as the greatest quarterback in Auburn history, and by many as perhaps the greatest in the annals of Southern football.

No Auburn player has captured the confidence of Auburn men and women, the imagination and fancy of Southern football followers as has this young man from Birmingham who led Auburn to 17 victories in the last two years and rewrote the Tigers' record book in the process.

By the time Pat finishes his regular season Auburn career against Alabama November 27, the Tiger record book could easily be by-lined "By Pat Sullivan". Already he has gained 4,747 yards, almost 1,000 yards more than Travis Tidwell's record, and Sullivan's yardage has come in two years, just half the time it took Tidwell to make his mark.

In 1970 alone, Sullivan led not only the SEC but also the nation in touchdown responsibility (26), passing percentage of completions (.590), yards gained per play (8.57, a new NCAA record) and total offense (285.6 yards per game).

In addition to making every All-SEC team, Sullivan made numerous All-America teams. He was named the Outstanding Player of the Gator Bowl's 35-28 Auburn victory over Archie Manning and Ole Miss. Perhaps Pat's highest honor came from the Southeastern Conference coaches who picked him as the SEC's Outstanding Player for 1970.

His own coach, Ralph "Shug" Jordan says, "Pat is the most complete quarterback I've ever seen. When he's in the game there's not one thing your offense is not capable of doing."

Alabama's Paul Bryant echoes Jordan's praise of Sullivan: "He does more things to beat you than any quarterback I've ever seen."

The most important records and accolades for any quarterback, however, are team records, and Auburn's offense, rolling over and through opponents like Patton's Third Army rolling through France, has averaged 35 points and almost 500 yards total offense a game under Sullivan's field generalship. Needless to say, Auburn is no longer considered primarily "a defensive team." The Tigers are offensive juggernauts, and last year's team was the most explosive in the history of the SEC.

Impressive credentials are but an outward sign of greatness. What quality or qualities distinguish Sullivan from all other quarterbacks? What makes Pat Sullivan great? Was he ordained by some mystical spirit, or did his magnificence come from human attributes?

Those who know Sullivan, the quarterback, best, those who play with him and coach him, believe Sullivan's greatness comes from his unyielding confidence in himself and his teammates. This confidence, they say, is contagious, and more than once it has been Sullivan who has sparked Auburn on the comeback road.

Dick Schmalz, a receiver who played with Sullivan at Birmingham's John Carroll High School and now at Auburn gives one example:

"We were behind 10-0 early against Tennessee. It was my first game to start and I was all nervous and jerky. Pat came into the huddle. He looked at each of us and said, 'Men, it looks like we're going to have to score some points today, so let's block, run our routes, and get to it.' His calm confidence erased all of my anxieties, and after that, we all felt like it was just a matter of time until we went ahead if we all did our jobs."

Go ahead, Auburn did. The Tigers beat the Vols 36-23, handing them their only loss of the 1970 campaign. And it was Sullivan who, late in the game with Auburn leading by only six points, 29-23, ran a quarterback draw more than 40 yards to get field position and insure the win for the Tigers. He has confidence and he has ability.

Wallace Clark, Auburn's fullback for the past two seasons, adds to Schmalz's observations:

"I've never seen Pat worried, not even when we're behind. Concerned, yes; worried, no. He knows how to win; how to come back when he gets behind, and he always keeps the pressure on the other team when we get the upper hand. Being behind only makes Pat watch himself more."

Pat's contagious confidence was manifesting itself even before he played his first game for Auburn. This boy was supposed to be pretty good. Would he be the redeemer of Auburn's offensive fortunes? Would he be able to make the crucial play, to pick up a crucial yard here, the crucial foot that would win the big games and turn 6-4 seasons into 8-2, 9-1, maybe 10-0 seasons?

A rumble stirred. Auburn people thought so.

The early part of Sullivan's freshman career indicated he was good, but to see just how good, Auburn fans had to wait until the final game against the Alabama freshmen in Tuscaloosa.

Down 27-0 in the second quarter, Auburn fans were already looking for excuses. They could find none. After five years of Alabama victories, their bag of excuses was about empty. But Sullivan wasn't thinking about excuses. He lofted a long bomb to speed demon Terry Beasley, even then his favorite target, and the Tiger Cub offense was off to the races, races they finally won by a 36-27 score. It was Auburn's first football victory over their cross-state rival in five years, and if Auburn fans were happy that day, perhaps it's a good thing they didn't know what was to happen on a cold November day two years later in 1970. They couldn't have stood it.

A record crowd attended the Auburn A-Day game the next spring. Sullivan's team won 26-0, but it wasn't impressive and questions began to mount again. What about Sullivan? Sullivan didn't wait long to answer the question.

His first outing as Auburn's varsity quarterback brought a 57-0 win over Wake

Forest. The score was important, but the most indicative part of the "new-look Auburn," the "Sullivan-look," came on the first play of the game.

Sullivan dropped straight back, looked long, and lofted a pass far downfield to Terry Beasley, the other part of Auburn's dynamic duo, who was running free behind the Deacon secondary. The pass was incomplete, but the fans stood up and cheered, cheered loud and long. It was that instant that the "bomb" became more of a weapon than a threat in the Auburn offensive arsenal.

The next week against Tennessee, Auburn lost late 45-19. In the fourth quarter it was 24-19, but key pass interceptions led to the Vol's embarrassingly wide margin of victory. Sullivan, in his first big game, had five passes intercepted on the Vol's Tar-tan turf which has a reputation for causing passes to go awry. It would have been enough to shake the confidence of most youngsters, but Sullivan was not typical of "most youngsters."

Coach Jordan had decided to have a man-to-man talk with his young quarterback before practice Monday, just in case Sullivan needed to have someone restore his confidence. Before Jordan could speak to him, Pat walked up and said, "Don't worry about me, Coach. I'm okay," and trotted on to practice.

Auburn defeated Kentucky 44-3 and Clemson 54-0 the next two outings, and finished with an 8-2 season and a Bluebonnet Bowl bid. In a nose-to-nose confrontation with John Reaves, Florida's sensational sophomore quarterback, Sullivan came out on top 38-12. The first year of the seventies brought another 8-2 record and another bowl bid, but Auburn fans will best remember this particular year for what happened in the waning shadows of November 28 at Legion Field.

Auburn, with an injury-mauled defense, was playing Alabama and Bear Bryant's Crimson Tide jumped to an embarrassing 17-0 lead in the first quarter. Beasley was hurt and out of action. Surely a comeback was too much to expect from anyone, even Sullivan. Auburn fans reached for their bag of excuses, but Sullivan wouldn't let them have it. He had reserved it for Alabama again. Sullivan's confidence was a key factor and it was evident on the sidelines.

As Beasley sat on the bench, trying to regain his bearings, Sullivan walked up to him, flicked his red hair, and said, "Hurry up and get ready, Beas, we're going to beat them just like we did when we were freshmen."

It was 17-7 when Beasley returned, and when the scoreboard beeped the game's conclusion, Auburn had beaten Alabama 33-28, in what must surely be one of the greatest, if not the greatest game in Auburn football lore.

Pat called most of the plays in the victory over Alabama as he does in most Auburn games. "We just decide on the game plan and present it to him," says chief offensive coach Gene Lorendo. "Pat is always prepared for any eventuality. He spends a lot of extra time watching films, studying the defense, and asking questions."

While Beasley is his favorite receiver—he caught 52 for 1,051 yards and 11 touchdowns in 1970, Pat has confidence in his other receivers and does not hesitate to call on them. "I knew he'd throw to me if I was open," says Alvin Bresler, a 1970 receiver, "and so does everyone else. This helps morale."

The running backs know too that Sullivan will give each man ample opportunity to run the ball and taste a share of the glory during the season.

As Schmalz puts it: "Whatever Pat does, you know it's for the good of the team. He's the most self-less person I've ever known."

Schmalz has touched another aspect of Sullivan's greatness: a hat size that refuses to increase no matter how profuse or great the accolades. No matter what honor he accepts, Sullivan accepts it "not for myself, but for the Auburn football team."

When he went to Nashville to accept the 1970 SEC Player of the Year Award, Sullivan had to miss a day of Gator Bowl preparations. On returning, with Coach Jordan's permission, he called the team together, and said, "I want to apologize for missing practice yesterday. You all read the papers and you know where I was. I'm sorry I had to go during practice, but I want you to know that I didn't accept that award for me. I accepted it for you. Any praise or credit I get, doesn't belong to me. It belongs to you, and I thank you for letting me be your representative."

The Auburn Tigers responded with a rousing cheer and in the spring elected him captain for the coming year, an honor which Sullivan treasures more than all the others that have come his way. "This," he says, "shows that the team has put their utmost confidence in me. I have to maintain their confidence and trust."

Their trust in him and his confidence in them is one reason Sullivan was dropped behind the line of scrimmage only three times last year.

The Sullivan mystique is not reserved only for the football field. He has been tapped for many campus leadership honoraries, and scholastically, Pat, a business major who hopes to own his own firm someday, made a 2.8 out of a possible 3.0 spring quarter.

Rod Carlson, who had Pat in his economics class, has his own idea on what makes Sullivan great not only in the classroom, but also on the field.

"He has a tremendous belief in himself and a respect for other people. Not too many people of his ability maintain this sense of respect for others, but I've never heard Pat say a derogatory word about anyone. He's almost 'boyish' about it," says Carlson.

"Pat respects people for what they are and for their potential," Carlson continues. "That's a rare attribute for an athlete. He is keenly aware that his athletic opponent, while he may not have a good record, can, by virtue of his position, hurt you. The fellow may not have made the play all day, but this might be the one time he does. That attitude makes Pat a great athlete and his respect for other people makes him a great person."

Confidence, ability, humility, respect. Those, according to those who know him best, are what make Pat Sullivan a great quarterback. But how did he develop those qualities? How did he happen to choose the Blue of Auburn rather than Alabama's Crimson or Notre Dame's Blue and Gold? And what about the coming season? And the Heisman? Does Pat think he will win it?

The Pat Sullivan football story began many years ago, when Pat was in the sixth grade, and it began very inauspiciously—he quit.

His first coach, Brother Christopher ST., had put him at center, and Pat just didn't like playing center. Also, he happened to be younger than all the other boys out for the team.

A year later, and a year older, Pat came back. This time, Brother Christopher, having noticed Pat's speed and ability to throw a ball during baseball season, decided to try Mr. and Mrs. Jerry Sullivan's son at quarterback. He's been there ever since.

"It was obvious from the start," recalls Brother Christopher, director of the Magic City's Toy Bowl Program, "that Pat was an athlete of college calibre. He had the right mental attitude and success never went to his head. It was somewhat embarrassing at times. I'd be on the sidelines trying to figure out what should be done, but Pat had already figured it out himself. He was real smart."

Mr. and Mrs. Sullivan never forced their son to participate in sports. They only "encouraged him when he wanted to go out for the teams," and, in Pat's case, that meant a lot of encouragement. He loved almost every sport, football and baseball taking the upper hand, and he wanted to excel in whatever he did.

"We always congratulated him on his success," recalls his father, "but we always cautioned him that he, like everyone, was subject to a bad game. We just took him as he was and was thankful for all of the good things that came his way. It's still that way."

At age 12, Pat Sullivan, who "always liked Auburn," saw his first Tiger football game. The young athlete sold cokes to get in the 1962 Auburn-Georgia Tech game, which Auburn won 17-14.

"That was a great game," Sullivan smiles. "I'll never forget Jimmy Burson (Auburn halfback) scoring on the first play from scrimmage. I almost stopped selling Cokes right then."

It was early in his senior year that Auburn and Sullivan had their first important contact. "Coach Lorendo had come to see John Carroll play," says Pat, smiling, "and I was walking off the field when this big man came up and said he was Coach Lorendo from Auburn and congratulated me on what he said was a fine game. I was flattered. That was the first time I knew Auburn knew who I was and was really interested in me."

Pat met his wife Jean shortly after graduation when John Carroll and Auburn teammate David Shelby got the two together on a blind date.

"I didn't really know who Pat was," laughs Jean. "I'd read a little about him in the paper. I knew he played football, but I didn't know how good he was. It wouldn't have made any difference anyway."

Pat and Jean were married in the summer of 1969 and Jean soon found that being married to a hero has its drawbacks as well as benefits. There's a tremendous demand for a hero's time, and Jean readily admits, "I don't always look forward to it, but when I go with him, I have a great time. I enjoy meeting different people like Pat does."

The shapely brunette especially enjoys one part of being a hero's wife. "Every boy should have someone to look up to, and when that someone is your husband, you get a great thrill down deep inside just seeing those big admiring eyes gazing up at your husband."

"Those admiring eyes," as Jean calls them, place an added responsibility on Pat. "You have to think about those people looking up to you," observes Pat. "What's right for most people my age, may not be right for an athlete, especially when there are youngsters looking to you to set an example."

And if there is any doubt about Pat Sullivan's popularity with the youngsters, go back to Auburn's A-Day game. For more than an hour and a half after the game, Pat stood on the sidelines signing autographs, on programs, paper sacks, anything kids could get their hands on. Jean stood patiently by the entire time.

Jean does her part to help Auburn's football fortunes, too. She makes sure their "lucky" gold blanket, which Pat takes to the athletic dorm each night before a home game, is ready each Friday. She gives up the car, too. Pat takes that, like the blanket, for good luck. And finally Jean and Joan Beasley, Terry's wife, go to the games together each weekend. That's lucky, too, or so they say.

Now all that remains for the Sullivans and Auburn is the 10-game 1971 schedule, and, almost surely, another bowl game before Pat launches a pro career. What does Pat foresee for Auburn this fall? "Everyone will be after us because of our high preseason rating," he predicts. "We won't surprise anyone, and it will be up to us to live up to what people expect out of us. We had some key losses, but our boys have a lot of ability. With a little luck, we could be okay."

And so it is with Pat Sullivan, Auburn's quarterback par excellence. Because he doesn't wear a white hat, you wouldn't know he's a hero. To his classmates, Sullivan is just another student. To his neighbors, he is the fellow down the street who likes to grill hamburgers. To his brothers, Joe, 11, and Bill, 6, he's a big brother, not a hero, even though they both wear No. 7 Auburn jerseys. To baby daughter Kim, he's a father.

Sullivan is very much the unheroic type at home and in the classroom, but on the football field it's a different story.

And it's not a bad story for a lad who once quit football, but came back out and may carry a Heisman Trophy home.

And what about the Heisman, "Will you win it, Pat?"

"I'm very honored to be considered for such an award, but winning the Southeastern Conference Championship is more important to me. That's our team's ultimate goal. If our team wins, everything else will take care of itself."

Birmingham Magazine
August, 1971

Pat Sullivan won the 1971 Heisman Trophy and became the first player from a school where John Heisman coached to win the trophy that bears Heisman's name.

September's Song ———————————————————

Make no mistake about it.

This has been a wonderful week to live in Auburn and experience once again this city's annual September metamorphosis which accompanies the fall breeze's first daring dashes across hot September afternoons.

It has been the kind of week that brings a placid reassurance that, amid the madness, everything is going to be all right, the kind of reassurance that comes to a kid when he realizes that tomorrow's adventures and those of the next day and the next will be just as good and just as much fun as those of today and yesterday.

There is a permanence about Auburn's September revival each year. The names and faces change, but, with the return of the students, Auburn is reborn each fall again and again, just like it has been every year since there has been an Auburn.

In 1971, it began last Saturday when multi-colored car tags from across the Southeast marked the arrival of the girls participating in sorority rush. The girls—younger and more beautiful than ever before to these observant eyes—tried to hide the excitement from their eyes and their walk, but they failed. Failed just as their parents failed to hide their sadness and concern as arm load after arm load of "essentials" were carried to the dorm room. Their little girl, their baby, a young lady now, was going off to college. The parents did not smile. As much as they tried, the girls couldn't stop smiling. Life goes on.

Many of Auburn's churches, shifting back to the fall time schedule, were filled Sunday morning, and at Auburn Methodist, Charles Britt regained his mid-quarter form a bit early this year.

Not far away the Phi Gams were painting their house again. The KA's were painting, too, all preparing for fraternity rush which began Wednesday, but they found time for a little football. One brother, an aspiring intramural Pat Sullivan, leisurely tossed a few passes to an intramural Terry Beasley counterpart. The SAE's, as usual, were painting their lion white. Again.

Up at Toomer's Corner, the pulsating rhythm of drums rumbled over the Loveliest Village. Bill Walls and the Auburn band were beating out the rough spots in Auburn's 1971 drum cadence, the one used today.

The lights in Langdon Hall's inner sanctum burned long after the drums were put away for the night as Plainsman editor John Samford and his staff began preparations for their first issue, due to hit the campus Thursday, the day after classes start.

Down the road a piece, Mildred and Barbara stoked their pizza ovens at the War Eagle Supper Club, and The Tiger once again did a boomtown business in beer. The students were indeed back.

Last night rush was over and the squealing girls—soon to be Auburn women—raced across campus to their new sisters' waiting arms. Their peach-cheeked counterparts, already the audacious swaggering Auburn man, walked masculinely "over to the house" to his new Auburn family. More business for The Tiger.

No one gave much thought to the disappointed and bidless girl or boy who had no where to go but back to the room. But they shall learn, as others before them learned, the most valuable lesson of all—this crisis too shall pass. Life will go on.

This was Auburn's week that brought us to today's event, what *"The Game Today"* is all about: Auburn-UT Chattanooga. During the week, it was agreed by many more than one, "Maybe it was a good thing the Tigers didn't play last week. Look at all those upsets: Southern Cal, Georgia Tech, Florida, LSU and Vanderbilt almost lost to UT-Chattanooga."

UT-Chattanooga. The narrow 20-19 losers to Vandy are now in Cliff Hare Stadium to test Auburn's pre-season ratings, ratings which become fact or fiction today.

They will test the Tigers' defense, rated "questionable," with an intimidating ground game featuring fullback William Martin who gained 105 yards last week, and to win they must also stop the Auburn offense.

More than 36,000 of you joining us today are season ticket holders and your seats stretch from the North to the South end zone through the West stands and spill over into the East stands. You have been waiting for Auburn Football 1971 to begin for weeks. We have enjoyed the pre-game week. Let us detain you no longer.

Auburn Football 1971 is about to begin.

Auburn Football Illustrated
Auburn vs. UT-Chattanooga
September 18, 1971

This scene is re-created each September. With each new re-creation of Auburn come new names and new faces, each discovering Auburn—their Auburn—for the first time. There has never been an Auburn like their Auburn. There has never been a time like their time. They may not say it, but they think it, they feel it and they believe it with all their hearts.

And they are right. This is their Auburn. This is their place and it is their time, just as it was once our place and once our time. They bring with them—and to us— a sense of excitement, a sense of awe, a sense of wonder and a sense of confidence and reassurance. Life does indeed go on. And most of it is good.

Cliff Hare

"Athletics make men strong; study makes men wise, and character makes men great."

This statement, inscribed on the annual Cliff Hare Award, gives an insight into the person of Clifford Leroy Hare, the man for whom Auburn's Cliff Hare Stadium was named.

To remember Cliff Hare solely for his athletic contributions to Auburn would be to honor an incomplete memory. While he loved athletics, it was not his first or only interest. His first concern was for the complete man, a man who was knowledgeable in any realm of academic endeavor.

Cliff Hare was such a man. He often quoted Shakespeare to his chemistry classes and frequently discussed philosophical issues with students and Auburn townspeople.

He was an avid follower of not only Auburn football, but Southern football, serving as president of the Southern Athletic Conference in 1932. He was chairman of Auburn's faculty athletic committee for many years. At home he liked to work in his flower garden and occasionally play golf or tennis.

Cliff Hare believed that the complete man would seek ways in which to serve his fellow citizens. In addition to his faithful service to the Methodist Church, Dean Hare served on the city council and as mayor of Auburn.

Each year, the Cliff Hare Award, presented by Hare's children, is given to the senior, who, in addition to distinguishing himself athletically and scholastically, exhibits in great degree the qualities of leadership, integrity and courage.

Connie Frederick and Alvin Bresler, both football players, have been selected for this award, the highest honor an Auburn athlete can receive, the last two years.

Cliff Hare was born in 1869 in Lee County. He received his BS from Alabama Polytechnic Institute in 1891 and his MS in 1892. It was in 1892 that he was a member of Auburn's first football team, an aggregation of students and instructors, gathered by Dean George Petrie. This team traveled to Atlanta in February of 1892 and beat Georgia 10-0 in the South's first intercollegiate football game.

Dean Hare studied at the University of Chicago and received his MA from the University of Michigan in 1903. He returned to Auburn as an instructor of chemistry and assistant in the state chemical laboratory. In 1932, he was named dean of the school of chemistry and pharmacy, and state chemist. He remained dean until his death in 1948.

The stadium, known as Auburn Stadium, was officially dedicated Cliff Hare Stadium on November 5, 1949, ten years after it was built. Originally seating 7,290 the stadium has been enlarged five times and now seats more than 61,000.

Auburn Football Illustrated
1971 Season

Cliff Hare Stadium was renamed Jordan-Hare Stadium in 1973 and now has a capacity of more than 85,000.

Mr. Spirit

At 6-2, 289 pounds, Archie Deavers is not lacking in size.

And he's not lacking character, desire, pride, determination, intestinal fortitude, or just plain guts. Use whatever football term you choose to describe those intangible qualities that enable a man to scoff at the percentages and emerge a winner. Whatever you call it, Archie Deavers has it.

No, Archie Deavers is not an Auburn football player, and he never will be. Archie is Auburn's "Mr. Spirit." In two years the Birmingham student has never missed a pep rally or a football or basketball game, but he has yet to see one. Archie Deavers, you see, is totally blind.

Glaucoma stole Archie's sight when he was seven, before he could see an Auburn Tiger team play, but no one, not even those who have seen every game, loves Auburn more than Archie Deavers.

At Auburn, and at Knoxville, Archie, helped to the microphone by one of Auburn's prize-winning cheerleaders, stood in front of the Auburn cheering section, his hands lifted high over his head, and led cheers, big cheers. His glassy gray eyes could not see the action, but his ears could hear the results.

When the cheering lags, as it did in the fourth quarter with Auburn leading Chattanooga 53-7, head cheerleader David Roberts knows on whom to call. He calls for Archie.

"Archie is a tremendous asset for our student body spirit," said the personable Roberts. "He inspires a crowd. The students respect him for what he is accomplishing despite his handicap. Archie Deavers brings out the best in people."

Archie was not sought out from Auburn's 14,000 students to be "Mr. Spirit." He, like all winners, stepped to the front and presented himself. His lack of sight did not keep Archie from trying out for cheerleader last spring. Although Archie thought he had "as good a chance as anyone" to be selected, it was obvious that a person without sight could not perform the tedious tasks demanded of an Auburn cheerleader.

It was just as obvious that Archie Deavers could not be simply written off as another tryout. A special position, "Mr. Spirit," was created by the cheerleader selection committee and Archie was given the position.

Archie uses the old "I-could-hardly-believe-it-when-they-told-me" cliche when he recalls the moment he learned of his honor, but when Archie says it, the cliche is stripped away. It becomes sincerity. "Yes," Archie says, "it was the greatest thing that has ever happened to me."

Archie has been pretty great for Auburn.

As Mr. Spirit, Archie tries to "keep the students pepped during the week by talking about the game between classes and over WEGL, the campus radio station." Officially considered an alternate cheerleader, Archie, who must provide his own transportation to out of town games, says "It's not too hard to keep mentally prepared after a game like last week's Tennessee game."

The 21-year old son of Mr. and Mrs. Rupert Deavers, Archie, who went to Talladega School for the Blind, Jefferson State and now Auburn, is a senior in Secondary Education. He wants first to "repay Auburn for what Auburn has done for me," then to become a teacher. The oddsmakers aren't giving a line on his making it. Archie has already beaten the odds too many times.

And the Auburn football team—and fans too—can remember Archie Deavers. When your back is against the wall, their ball, first and goal on the two, or when the odds are against you, first and 10, 86 yards and a tough opponent away from a game winning touchdown, you need only look to the Auburn student body for assurance that anything is possible. The "War Eagles" and the "Hold That Lines," all help, but the presence of Archie Deavers helps more.

Archie Deavers is, indeed, Mr. Spirit, a representative of not only the Auburn Spirit, but that greater spirit which fosters the Auburn Spirit, that indomitable human spirit that will not yield.

Auburn Football Illustrated
Auburn vs. Kentucky
October 2, 1971

That Archie Deavers was black made his story even more remarkable. Efforts to reach Mr. Spirit have been unsuccessful.

"You're So Right, Carl..."

"Good afternoon and welcome to the Auburn Football Review...."

Ten Sunday afternoons a year, Carl Stephens, host of the weekly television show reviewing the Tigers' game the previous day, begins the program in that fashion.

There's nothing special about it, unless you happen to be sitting in the television room at Sewell Hall watching the replay with about 30 members of the Auburn football team, and it's more special when they don't know you're there and have no idea that their comments will be printed in the Auburn football program just six days later.

The names, in most cases, have been omitted to protect the guilty, but who is going to protect me from the football team, Coach Jordan and Carl? No one, I'm afraid, but on with the show:

"The Auburn Football Review is brought to you by South Central Bell and now here's your host Carl Stephens along with Coach Ralph 'Shug' Jordan...."

"Good afternoon and welcome to the Auburn Football Review...."

"Good afternoon, Carl...."

"Ah, gee, Coach doesn't get any potato chips again this week...."

"Carl, we didn't show a lot of enthusiasm...."

"You tell'em about it, Coach. Tell'em exactly what you told us at half...."

"Rick Chastain making the tackle for Auburn...."

"Oooooh, ahhhh. Good lick!"

"Rick Chastain made a great play on that, Carl."

"All right 'Tain. Aattaway to go 'Tain...."

"Kentucky fumbles, Auburn recovers...."

"Who's that rah-rah guy in there jumping up and down?"

"Looks like Brown."

"Nah, that's not Brown...."

"James Owens makes the first down for Auburn."

"Go, Big-O, Go...."

"There's the draw play as we call it...."

"As we call it, heh, heh, heh...."

"So it's fourth down and Gardner Jett is in to try a field goal...."

"Oh, me, here it comes...."

"A bad snap foiled the field goal attempt and Kentucky takes over...."

"Look at Jett...."

"Hey, who snapped that ball? Did you snap that ball, 'Crack' (Spence McCracken)?"

"Did you snap that ball?"

"Nah, I didn't snap it. I didn't have anything to do with it."

"Ah, come on, 'Crack,' you snapped that ball...."

"Nah, it wasn't me....it was Tom Banks!"

(The center who actually snapped the ball, laughed, but did not come to McCracken's rescue.)

"Hey, Henley, you really got hit...."

"Yeah, he knocked my butt off...."

"Someone missed a tackle over there...."

"Someone? Who's someone? Is that you, Beck?"

"There was a fine crowd on hand yesterday, Coach...."

"You're so right, Carl...."

"Well, you're right, Carl...."

"Auburn University's writer in residence, Madison Jones, has just had his fourth book published...."

"Gone With the Wind."

"Tickets for the Blood, Sweat, and Tears performance will go on sale...."

"When did they start selling tickets to practice?"

"If we had lost, that wouldn't be so funny...."

"Well, Coach, what did you say at the half...."

"Leading 10-0, Coach, what did you say at the half...."

"Well, Carl, if I told you exactly what I said in the dressing room, they'd probably run me, you and everybody off the air...."

"You're so right, Coach...."

"Well, whatever you told them must have worked...."

"You're so right, Carl....It did work."

Auburn Football Illustrated
Auburn vs. Southern Mississippi
October 9, 1971

Carl Stephens, hosted "The Auburn Football Review" with Coach Ralph "Shug" Jordan for 13 years. He is now director of programming for WSFA-TV in Montgomery. He continues to serve Auburn as the public address announcer for Jordan-Hare Stadium and for men's basketball games in Eaves-Memorial Coliseum. He still smiles when someone says, "You're So Right, Carl..."

The "Other" Receiver _____

Dick Schmalz.

Who is Dick Schmalz?

Oh, you mean Dick Schmalz, Auburn's other receiver.

Dick Schmalz, Auburn's fifth-year senior from Birmingham is just that to most football fans, but to those persons who really count, Ralph Jordan, Pat Sullivan, the Auburn football team, and probably most important to Schmalz himself, Karen Harter, the girl he will marry April 15, Dick Schmalz is more than just "Auburn's other receiver."

To Jordan, Sullivan, and the Auburn football team, Schmalz is probably one of the most underrated players in the SEC. Without him, they say, Auburn football 1971 would not be where it is at this moment.

To Karen, however, Schmalz is "just a wonderful person who happens to be a good football player."

While they see him from different perspectives, they all agree that Schmalz is worthy of more recognition than he has recieved.

Dick, who injured a knee his sophomore year and missed the entire 1968 season, came back for his fifth year anticipating more of the same things held by the 1969-70 seasons, a lot of playing time, several key receptions, and not much recogonition by anyone other than the coaches and players.

The year started out in just that fashion. He was the victim of a mistake in the Auburn football press brochure. Page one featured a picture of an Auburn player making a running catch to the Tennessee 12-yard line, a catch that set up the go-ahead touchdown in Auburn's 36-23 1970 victory. The cutline said it was Terry Beasley making another great catch. But it wasn't Beasley, it was Dick Schmalz.

Only through careful inspection of the receiver's facial features could it be determined that it was Schmalz's 89 on the player and not Beasley's 88. For Schmalz, it appeared that 1971 would be no different from 1970. He would continue playing in the shadow of someone else.

Secretly Schmalz may have liked it that way. He doesn't like publicity because he embarrasses easily. The 6-1, 190 pound senior from Birmingham emphasizes his modesty by revealing, "My face turns red when I hear my name called on the stadium loud speaker." And as he says it, his face turns a light crimson.

But if Schmalz or anyone else thought the error in Auburn's press brochure was indicative of the season he would have, they were wrong, very wrong.

Several games into the 1971 season Schmalz was Auburn's leading receiver, ahead of the All-America Terry Beasley, and in the 10-9 win over Tennessee it was Schmalz who thrilled a regional television audience with three straight clutch catches for 23, 22, and 12 yards as Auburn marched 86 yards against the clock to claim a victory over the ninth-ranked Vols.

Some self-styled experts would attribute Schmalz's 1971 success to the double, often triple coverage given Beasley. That may be partially, but not wholly true, and Pat Sullivan, the Heisman Trophy contending quarterback, tells why.

"Dick works hard to get open," says Sullivan, "and he manages it by making moves the average receiver would not make. Dick doesn't have the speed of Terry, but he certainly has the ability to get open in the clutch situation despite heavy traffic.

"And once Dick is open," continues Sullivan, "his tremendous hands enable him to make catches many other receivers would miss. Anyone who says Dick Schmalz is just an average receiver is wrong. And so is anyone who says Dick is having a good year because of the coverage given Terry. No one can deny that attention to Terry helps, but Dick's presence helps Terry, too.

"You have to have people like Dick to win," continues Sullivan. "He's a tremendous competitor, and, in my book, that's the best thing you can say about an athlete."

Sullivan has been known to have a pretty good book on what it takes to be successful in athletics, and Schmalz has written a major portion in that book. Both Pat and Dick went to Birmingham's John Carroll High School, and their birthdays are one day apart, Schmalz being a day older. Dick came to Auburn a year earlier than Pat, and, in Schmalz's senior year, the Sullivan-Schmalz combination was one of the most terrifying in the Magic City.

Beasley echoes Sullivan's praise of Schmalz: "With Dick having such a good year, the secondary and linebackers can't afford to ignore him. If they do, they will be making a fatal mistake."

Ralph Jordan is on the Schmalz band wagon, too. "We knew we had to find a complement receiver to Terry, and all that Pat and Terry have said about Dick is true. He's been a great asset to our football team.

"One of the things that makes Dick such an asset to our team is character. Dick Schmalz is one of the finest young men you'll find anywhere, and it has been attitudes like those exemplified by Dick Schmalz that have carried this football team this far."

Sullivan has a few words about Schmalz the man, too. "If I have a son," says Pat, "I'd want him to be like Dick Schmalz. What more can you say about the man?"

No one could agree with Coach Jordan and Sullivan more than Karen, the Indianapolis, Indiana lass who will become Mrs. Dick Schmalz. She thinks her man is "just wonderful."

"He's one of the most understanding people I've ever known," smiles Karen, a lovely brown-eyed brunette who has a quick wit, personality, and a good sense of humor, the qualities Schmalz admires in a girl.

Karen, a member of Alpha Delta Pi sorority, continues, "He always listens and never jumps to conclusions about anything, and he's so modest. He wouldn't let me show my own brother a story about the Tennessee game. Dick made me leave the paper in the car."

A fiancee of a football player is, of course, deeply involved in the sport, and so is Karen, but she always follows the guidelines laid down by Dick. "If we win, I don't say much. If we lose, I don't say anything, and, if Dick drops four passes, well, he just told me to 'be ready!'"

But Karen, according to her roommate Judy Buckhalt, "really doesn't think Dick will drop four passes in a game," so she's not too worried about being ready.

And what about Schmalz? What does he think about his newfound success this fall?

"Well, I'm still the 'other receiver,' but I don't mind that as long as the first one is Terry Beasley. I've been fortunate this year, being able to make the right move at the right time, and I just thank God for the good fortune I've had this year.

"One thing about this year," smiles Schmalz, somewhat sheepishly, "I don't embarrass quite as easy as I did before."

It's no wonder.

The name Dick Schmalz has become a familiar sound on the Cliff Hare Stadium loudspeaker—almost as familiar as that of Terry Beasley.

Auburn Football Illustrated
Auburn vs. Southern Mississippi
October 9, 1971

Dick Schmalz and Karen Harter never married, but both are presumably grateful for the times they shared together. Schmalz, a successful Birmingham real estate developer, is happily married to the former Jane Nix Dann from Decatur.

The Auburn Grille

Those who know the Verbillis family of Auburn, Andrew, Rose, and the children, Jean, John, and Lewis, know them as proprietors of The Auburn Grille.

Even their friends, which number into the hundreds of Auburn alumni, faculty, and students, are unaware of the role the Verbillis family played in preparation for today's game with Clemson and each Auburn football game.

Andrew, Rose, and the children have been doing their part for Auburn football for almost three years and in that time, Auburn has won 22 games, including the last seven straight. Their "part" is to prepare Coach Ralph Jordan's "pre-game" meal.

To a football player, a pre-game meal is steak, egg, applesauce, baked potato, toast, honey, and tea or coffee served at 9:30 a.m. the day of the game. To Coach Jordan, a pre-game meal is a quiet dinner with friends at The Grille on Thursday night, the last day of rough work for the team. All that remains before kickoff is Friday's brief work-out, staff meeting and office hours.

The Grille, located on North College Street, just off Toomer's Corner is a simple restaurant consisting of 17 dark brown booths lining the wall, a row of five tables in the center and a short counter on the left. Just behind the counter is a giant coffee urn and a mountain of coffee cups.

The tables, possibly the same ones that have borne the elbow weight of Auburn townspeople and students since The Grille began in 1936, are draped with yellow tablecloths, new in the spring, but now discolored and faded, finally showing signs from the continual swipe of wet rags as one coffee club—the most notorious one being the El Toro Club, called El Toro for obvious reasons—makes way for another spontaneous gathering of Auburn townspeople and students.

Everything and everybody in the University, community, state, nation, maybe even everything in creation are cussed and discussed from time to time by a multitude of coffee drinkers that varies only with the University calendar and their class schedules.

Through and over it all 14 hours a day, seven days a week, there is Andrew, the slim Greek whose English may be as good now as it was the day he first came to Auburn.

In short, The Auburn Grille is traditional collegiate atmosphere, Auburn's version of "the table at Mory's" just a short hop from "the place where Louis dwells," those places someone immortalized in "The Whiffenpoof Song," itself synonymous with homecomings everywhere.

It is to this place that Coach Jordan and his gracious wife Evelyn come each Thursday to enjoy a quiet meal with their close friends, Joe Sarver, Executive Secretary of the Auburn Alumni Association, and his wife Molly.

The Sarvers are in charge of selecting the menu each week, but that's just a formality. The main course is seafood, dictated by the success of Auburn football teams since the Thursday preceding last fall's Alabama game. Seafood is also a Jordan favorite.

Andrew, Rose, and the family have the table near the back prepared and waiting when the Sarvers arrive, always preceding the Jordans. There is no fanfare when the

Jordans arrive. They speak to the Verbillis family and proceed to their table. Hardly anyone notices the Jordans' arrival, but, on occasions a freshman may glance up at the right time and have something to write, possibly even call, home about.

He's had supper with Coach Jordan—at least in the same place.

It's been that way for almost two years and six games now. It will be that way this Thursday night when the Jordans start their football weekend at The Grille, far from Saturday's teeming crowd.

Auburn Football Illustrated
Auburn vs. Clemson
October 23, 1971

The Grille is still an Auburn tradition. Two generations of owners have come and gone since the Verbillis family moved from Auburn in the mid-seventies, but The Grille remains an Auburn landmark, two doors down from Toomer's Corner.

In His Own Time, a Legend —————————

Terry Beasley's introduction to Auburn people was an inauspicious one. It came in the state high school track meet in the waning shadows of a warm May afternoon in 1967.

Beasley had just run in the mile relay for the first time. He ran the last leg in record time and with that record came a state championship for Robert E. Lee High School of Montgomery.

As Beasley stepped up to receive the Wilbur Hutsell Award which went to the meet's outstanding performer, Auburn people applauded.

When asked if he had anything to say, Beasley looked at the crowd through glimmering eyes and stammered a bit before saying, "Just...just War-r-r Eagle!"

Once again, the Auburn crowd responded, this time with a loud roar. Maybe this Beasley kid would come to Auburn and run track. That would be nice.

Well, Beasley did come to Auburn, and he did run track. In fact, he set an Auburn indoor record with a 6.1 60-yard dash, but Auburn won't remember this son of a Montgomery fireman because of his winged feet on the track.

They will remember Terry Paul Beasley for his exploits on the football field. Like visions of sugar plums on Christmas Eve, memories of Terry's over-the-head catches, his darting dashes around defensive backs and his rapid bouncy, mechanical-like footwork will ease their way into the minds of Auburn people again and again as the years go by. Time will not fade the memories of Beasley. It will only enhance them. In other words, Beasley, in his own time, is a legend.

That Beasley would become a track star is remarkable. That he would become an All-America football player is amazing, for this is the same red-haired kid that doctors said would never play the game again.

This decree came after Beasley had sustained a series of what would normally be crippling injuries. First, as a seventh grader there was a badly bruised kidney. Beasley was down, but not out. Next came a shattered arm. Again Beasley was down, but not out. Along the way there was a torn hamstring muscle. Then came a crushed leg. Beasley was down again, and this time the doctors ruled him out.

But Terry would not accept their ruling. He appealed it to a higher authority on Beasley, Terry himself. Beasley could not, rather would not, accept the fact that he was irrevocably banned from the sports he loved so well. Terry Beasley "down" is one thing, Terry Beasley "out" is another thing. Something his junior high coach told him kept coming back again and again until Beasley realized its full meaning. That "something" Beasley remembered was a verse to the poem, "It's All In A State Of Mind." The "Beasley verse," says,

> Life's battles don't always go
> To the strongest or the fastest man;
> But sooner or later the man who wins
> Is the man who thinks he can!"

Terry Beasley, the little hospital case, not only thought he could win; he knew he could win, and that was the beginning of Terry the Great or Terry the Terrible depending on which side of the field you're on.

Beasley went on to become one of the premier receivers Robert E. Lee ever produced, winning a scholarship to Auburn, and he has continued that Beasley tradition here.

Any attempt to list the Beasley records other than to say, "He holds them all," would be useless. With each pass reception, Beasley sets another record. He is that good.

Beasley has not forgotten those who have helped him achieve his present station of greatness. He credits Lee and James Ray, another of his early football coaches, with showing him at an early age what athletics can mean. Providing spiritual guidance along the way has been Rev. Ralph Smith of Montgomery. Before each of his high school games, Beasley would stop by Rev. Smith's house for a "little talk."

Speed is another factor in the Beasley success story. Many Auburn people say Beasley can "bulldog a deer," and, while he's never tried it, Beasley says, "If I can't, my brothers can."

Speed, so to speak, "runs" in the Beasley family. His older brothers Wayne and Johnny were famous for their fleet feet in high school and his younger brother, 13-year-old Jerry, is carrying on the family name as a running back for Capital Heights Junior High in Montgomery, which, at present, is undefeated this season.

"I've only seen Jerry play once," says Terry, "but Mamma (Mrs. Kilby Beasley) says he runs just like me. I think he is faster than I was at his age."

There's another family that plays a role—the most important role—in Beasley's life: his own, wife Joanne and baby daughter Wendy. "I've got an extra incentive to be a good football player," Beasley smiles, "that little girl. I want her to hear about what a good player her daddy was, not what a lousy one he was."

Terry need not worry about that. Wendy's daddy's name is already enshrined in Auburn football annals forever. He has taken care of that himself. He did it because he is a winner, the kind of man who thinks and says, "I can." And then proves it.

That's Terry Beasley, Auburn's greatest receiver.

Auburn Football Illustrated
Auburn vs. Florida
October 30, 1971

When Terry Beasley finished his Auburn career in 1971, he held virtually every Auburn receiving record. Twenty years—two decades later—most of them still stand.

Sullivan, Beasley and Musso_____

Look, if you will, to the north end of Legion Field. Ten years ago, before the north stand was constructed, temporary bleachers marked the end of the playing field.

Stretching behind those bleachers was a grassy plain, sloping upward to an ominous black scoreboard. Surrounding it all, a hundred or so yards away from the field, was an aging, ivy-covered brick wall.

It was over that wall, in 1961, that All-America Johnny Musso entered his first Auburn-Alabama football game.

For Pat Sullivan, Auburn-Alabama football began in 1962, the same year college football first came into the world of the little dark-haired Coke seller who would one day become the King of College Quarterbacks.

For Terry Beasley, Auburn-Alabama began as it did for so many other youngsters, with a nationally televised game in 1964.

Today marks the end of their era.

But how did it begin, and did they ever visualize this championship day, a battle of unbeaten Auburn and unbeaten Alabama, coming to pass, even in their wildest childhood dreams?

"I was thrown out four times before I finally made it in," says Musso, smiling. "When I did get in, I was overcome by the crowd and the excitement. My two brothers—they climbed the wall with me—were Alabama fans, so I yelled for Alabama, too, but it really didn't make much difference to me then. I had a sister who had gone to Auburn, and I kind of liked Auburn, but everybody else was for Alabama so I yelled for Alabama, too.

"After they put barbed wire on the fences," Musso said, smiling again, "we used to crash the gate. We would either get in front of an older man and point back at him like he was our father, or we would just wait until we had a clear shot at the gate and get a running start. Those tactics don't work now. They make it too tough for a kid to get in these days.

"No," he says, "I had no idea that I'd ever play football, much less college football for Alabama that day in 1961."

Pat Sullivan missed the first half of his first Auburn-Alabama game in 1962. He was selling Cokes in an East Stand concession booth.

"Some family friends ran a concession stand," recalls Pat, "and helping them was the only way I had to get in the game. After the half, I went out in the stands and watched the game. I've never missed another Auburn-Alabama game since then. I had to sell Cokes to get in the game. I usually didn't sell many Cokes, but I saw a lot of football.

"I was amazed at the people in 1962," Sullivan recalls. "I had never seen Legion Field full or seen so many people at one place. I couldn't believe the enthusiasm of the Auburn people.

"College was a long way off in 1962," Sullivan continues. "I wanted Auburn to win, but I was mainly concerned with my junior high season."

Living in Montgomery instead of Birmingham, Beasley was not exposed to the vices inherent to a boy getting into a sellout football game.

"I really didn't have a favorite," Beasley says of the 1964 TV game, "but when I saw my first one in person, in 1967, I was committed to Auburn and it really hurt to see us lose that one 7-3 in the rain.

"In 1964," he says, smiling, "all I was worried about was high school football. Auburn and Alabama football was something you watched on television or read about in the papers."

When Johnny Musso, Pat Sullivan and Terry Beasley saw their first Auburn-Alabama game, all they wanted to do was play football—junior high football. The dreams and aspirations would come later, and, through hard work and dedication, those dreams and aspirations became reality.

Today, they pass into history. They will not go quietly. They will burst from the present to the past amid the roll of stirring drums, the blare of trumpets and the cheering of thousands.

Soon they will belong to the ages.

Auburn Football Illustrated
Auburn vs. Alabama
November 27, 1971

Pat Sullivan is now an assistant football coach at Auburn. Terry Beasley is in the golf cart business in Wetumpka and Johnny Musso has a seat on the Chicago Board of Trade.

Growing Up in Boligee

Boligee, Alabama, located near the banks of the Tombigbee River in west Alabama is what you might call, "a wide place in the road," but the river, the "Big Tom," saves the community from that label. It has a greater claim to fame.

Boligee, to fishermen throughout the area, is "one of the best places to put in on the river."

There wasn't much for a young boy growing up in Boligee to do when he got tired of fishing. He had about three choices: walk, play basketball, walk some more.

So Henry Harris, like all Boligee boys, black and white, fished, walked, and played basketball. In Henry's case, he primarily walked and played basketball. "My buddies and I used to walk all the time," recalls a smiling Harris. "We would spend a whole Sunday afternoon just walking and shooting basketballs."

Henry still likes to take long walks—he lists walking as a hobby—but basketball is demanding a much larger portion of Henry's life than just Sunday afternoons. Basketball, and the pursuit of basketball excellence, has been a major part of his college career.

Harris, of course, is captain of Auburn's 1972 basketball team, and it is on this 21-year old senior's speed, maneuverability, and quickness that much of Auburn's hopes for the current season reside.

Henry still feels the effect of knee surgery following last season but he is optimistic, "It has swollen a bit in the first two games," he admits, "but it will come around as we play more games."

Thus far, Harris has scored 630 points going into this season, good enough to rank in Auburn's top 25 all-time scorers. Offense is just one phase of the game, however, and Coach Bill Lynn is as quick to praise Henry as Henry is to pick up an offensive player. "He's like a cat," says Lynn. "He can stay with anybody. Henry's valuable to our team offensively, defensively and as a leader. He is a good rebounder too."

The Harris method of basketball began as it did with most Boligee boys, in the backyard, but to Henry, basketball may as well have been part of being born.

"I don't remember when I first started playing," he says. "Basketball has always been something we did."

Harris graduated from the backyard league to Greene County Training School where he scored more than 3,000 points in a four- year career on his way to making two high school All-America teams.

Basketball shared Harris' interest with football at Greene County as he quarterbacked his team to an undefeated regular season and a high state ranking.

It was at Greene County that Henry came in contact with two of three people who were to mean a great deal to his athletic career, Coach P.H. Pettway and Coach A.W. Young Jr. "Coach Pettway got me started in organized ball," says Henry, "and Coach Young pushed me."

The third person Harris considers as a MVP, "Most Valuable Person" to his athletic career is his younger brother Carl. "Carl played against me day in and day out," he says.

Carl, the baby boy of the six-child Harris family, is now playing for Bessemer's

Abrams High School. The Harris family moved from Boligee soon after Henry came to Auburn, but Henry still affectionately calls Boligee "home." It always will be.

"My mother wanted to move before she did," reveals Henry, "but I didn't want to leave so she stayed until I graduated from high school."

Harris, of course, will be remembered as the first of his race to receive a Southeastern Conference athletic scholarship in the state of Alabama, the man who broke the color barrier in Alabama.

That's fine with Henry, but to him, "It just wasn't that big a deal. To me and the other players and the coaches, I was just another basketball player."

If Henry had his choice, he'd want to be remembered as "a basketball player who cared for other people."

That's the reason he has chosen vocational rehabilitation as a career following graduation. "It will give me a chance to help those less fortunate than me," says Henry, "and there's no greater feeling than helping someone in need."

That's not a bad way to be remembered, for Henry Harris, or anyone else.

Auburn Basketball Illustrated
December 13, 1971

Henry Harris was not destined to live a long life. He died in 1974 from injuries received in a fall while working in Madison, Wis.

Jeff Beard—a Patriot

Jeff Beard may not like this story.

As he put it when he announced his retirement, "I came in without fanfare and I want to go out the same way."

In Jeff Beard's case that would be impossible because a leader is stepping down. The man who directed Auburn to athletic heights once thought unattainable is retiring. Such an event merits and will receive fanfare.

Coach Beard's retirement is no secret now as it was last February when he tried to announce it. "Tried to announce it"— that's exactly what he did—try to announce it, but he could not.

Memorial Coliseum's VIP meeting room was crowded with the Auburn athletic staff, some of whom had been with him since the beginning back there in 1951. They had been with him all the way, from the depths of despair to the pinnacle of glory.

He walked in, looked at his staff now called before him and tried to say something humorous—something about not realizing the staff had gotten that big and that cutbacks might be necessary. He looked at the staff again. He started to speak, but emotion broke his voice.

"I just can't do it," he said. "I just can't do it."

Tears trickled down his face as he turned and walked out of the crowded meeting room into the solitude of his office.

His friend and companion of many years, Ralph Jordan, stood up. "What Jeff was trying to tell you, what he called us together for," Jordan said in a sad, low voice, "is something he, the Doctor (President Philpott) and I have known for sometime. Jeff is retiring July 1."

Those words outlined the final chapter of a relationship that had spanned two decades and the most successful years in Auburn athletic history. The end was in sight. Jeff Beard's tenure as athletic director would be over in four months.

For 21 years, Jeff Beard had been the leader of Auburn athletics. He had been the "Kingfish."

"I've never had a vacation," he would say later, "not because I couldn't take one, but because I was always too busy."

Now, at 62, Jeff Beard was going to take a long vacation and enjoy the golden years of life. He and his wife, Maiben Beard, would piddle around their farm up the road a piece in Chambers County, play a little golf, fish a lot, but primarily they would spend a lot of time with their children and grandchildren. Now there would be enough time to do all they had always wanted to do.

As Bill Easterling, sports editor of *The Huntsville Times* wrote, "Auburn didn't lose an athletic director. She lost a limb. A vital organ. A patriot."

Since the day Coach Beard announced his retirement, his accomplishments and contributions have been chronicled again and again. Here, for the record, they are listed once more:

More than 40,000 additional seats in Cliff Hare Stadium, Memorial Coliseum, Sewell Hall, Hutsell Track, a financially-sound athletic program and, most importantly, a composite team record of 1,442 victories against 670 defeats in all sports.

This is the tangible evidence of Jeff Beard's 21-year labor of love and devotion, but perhaps his greatest accomplishment was one of morale.

He brought Auburn back from the worst kind of despair, a depression of spirit, a hopelessness of heart that permeated every aspect of Auburn's athletic program.

Soon after he became athletic director, he approached a university committee with a proposal to upgrade Auburn's athletic facilities. Their first question was, "How much will it cost?"

"Less than $1,000," Beard told them, "and we'll pay for it out of next year's gate receipts."

"Nonsense," the committee replied. "The athletic department never has had any money and it never will."

Negative attitudes such as that did not deter Jeff Beard.

"When Jeff contacted me about coming back as head football coach," recalls Jordan, "he didn't try to paint a rosy picture. We knew the road ahead was a rough one. And a lot of Auburn people didn't think Auburn men could do the job. They thought you had to be from Notre Dame or somewhere like that."

"We've been friends and teammates a long time," Beard told Jordan. "We've been through a lot together. It's going to be tough. I haven't got anything to offer you, but blood, sweat and tears, but we can make it, Shug. *We can make it for Auburn...*"

And make it they did.

Bowl games, national and conference championships, sellout crowds, you name it—and not just in football either. In every sport, if it is good, it has probably happened at Auburn during the Beard era.

And finances?

Coach Beard took care of that, too. The athletic department's track record at the bank was so good that some of the department's financial resources were diverted to other campus programs.

This was the Beard era, and it was all coming to a close that February day when Ralph Jordan had to make an announcement his old friend could not make.

Coming to an end? Not quite.

Leadership like that of Jeff Beard is not a common quality. It is a rare commodity held in high regard. Recognizing this, many sports figures, including a friendly adversary, Paul Bryant at Alabama, urged him to take the job as Commissioner of the Southeastern Conference. Coach Beard refused. "I've promised Maiben I wouldn't," he said, "and I won't."

Even if he had consented to take the job, there is no guarantee he would have gotten it. Dr. Philpott was president of the Southeastern Conference and he was Auburn's president.

"If Jeff Beard is going to work anywhere," he said, "it's going to be at Auburn. He wouldn't have it any other way and neither would I."

When Jeff Beard stepped down to assume the title of athletic director emeritus, he wanted to fade into an orange and blue sunset without fanfare. Perhaps he thought he could do that, but he can't.

"Jeff doesn't realize how much people think of him," a close friend once confided. "He never received the credit he deserved while he was athletic director. Now that he is gone, maybe all Auburn people will recognize what he has done and give him the credit he has deserved all along."

That, in summation, is what this story is about and what this day is about. Today Auburn pauses to show Jeff Beard just how much he is really appreciated—if it is possible to do that in one day, at one time.

Jeff Beard has made his position clear. He would prefer to sit quietly in Seat 55 in the press box, his seat of the last 18 years, and talk with the press and bowl scouts.

But Auburn has called him back, called him back to honor him not for what he accomplished for himself, but for what he accomplished for Auburn.

There is a sad note to this occasion, however.

"Mamma," as he called his wife, will not be here. She died last spring following a lengthy illness. Had she been here, this would have been her day, too, for she was at her husband's side, both of them, putting Auburn first for 21 years.

It is fitting that this recognition should come at an Auburn-Georgia game. It was Jeff Beard who set about getting this ancient series moved from Columbus' small Memorial Stadium to a home-and-home series where 60,000 instead of 30,000 fans, can see the game every year.

He also brought the Georgia Tech and Tennessee games home to Auburn. Georgia Tech came two years ago. Tennessee will come year after next.

Leading athletic figures from across the country would gladly help Auburn honor Jeff Beard, but they were not invited. This is a special occasion. Jeff Beard is a family man and this is a family affair—Auburn people honoring one of their own for his contributions to our University.

The people here today are Jeff Beard's people, Auburn people. They are the ones saying "Thank You" today.

The highest most meaningful honor Auburn can bestow on one of her own is to dedicate the Alma Mater to him. This is an honor that can not be bought, sold, bartered for or borrowed. It can only be freely given and freely accepted. It is given only to those individuals who, through their love, loyalty and dedication, have earned it. Jeff Beard is such an individual.

Jeff Beard is an emotional person. Today will be an emotional day, but that's all right, too. No one checks the time a man's heart takes from him. No doubt Jeff Beard's mind and heart will travel back across the years today, through his days as an Auburn athlete, as an assistant track coach, business manager, camera man and to that day in 1951 when he first sat behind the athletic director's desk in the old Field House.

He will think about the early days when he had to borrow money to meet the athletic department's debts. He will think about echoing stadiums and fans cheering first downs instead of touchdowns. He will think about grass banks for overflow crowds, about 62,000 people in Cliff Hare Stadium. He will think about 0-10 seasons and 10-0 seasons. He will think about national championships and conference championships.

He will think about Memorial Coliseum and compare it to the old Field House. He will think about how nice it is to play Georgia Tech in Auburn—and win.

Auburn has come a long way in the last 21 years. Most of the fans here today have never known anything but good Auburn times. Some will remember the bad times—the dark times and discouraging days before Jeff Beard went to work.

Jeff Beard retire without fanfare?

Impossible.

Auburn has too much to thank him for.

He, more than any other person, made Auburn's athletic program what it is today.

Ladies and Gentlemen: Garland Washington 'Jeff' Beard—an Auburn man. A Patriot.

Auburn Football Illustrated
Auburn vs. Georgia
November 18, 1972

Jeff Beard's greatest dream and one of his major goals as athletic director, was for Auburn to have a home schedule in football—to have a stadium good enough and a program good enough to bring all of the Southeastern Conference teams to Auburn.

That dream came true on Dec. 2, 1989 when The University of Alabama became the last SEC team to come to Auburn for a varsity football game. That day may have been the happiest day of Jeff Beard's professional life.

His smile in the press box indicated as much, and there was never any doubt in his mind that Auburn would win the game. "It's meant to be," he said.

Anatomy of a Surprise

What made Auburn a good football team?

What makes the scrawny little kid down the street a competitor, ready to take on all challengers—and win?

What turned what was supposed to be a mediocre team into a good one, a 9-1 team that beat undefeated Alabama, a team with a Gator Bowl berth?

Where and when did it all begin? How did it happen?

For Auburn, 1972, determining where and when it began is easier than determining "what" did it. "The "what" varies with each player and each coach. The "where," "when" and "how" are the common denominators.

On April 22, 1972, a clear cool spring day, the Auburn Tigers saw their goal, realized their potential, and a 9-1 season was born. From that day forward, it was a matter of just how high Auburn would go, although no one but the team knew it.

The 9-1 year did not come as a flash of light from on high or as an instant of brilliance. It was just the opposite. It came during a long agonizing afternoon of football practice, practice while other Auburn males were off with their girls at Chewacla, playing golf or just goofing off.

It came on a day when Auburn coaches took their best 11 offensive players and put them against their best 11 defensive players. The object was simple—to see who was best.

The offense had only three plays and within two series of downs, the defense knew what was coming, and the offense realized they knew. For hours and hours, more than 145 plays, the equivalent of two ball games, maybe more, the tailback ran off-tackle, up the middle or around end. When the tailback didn't carry the ball, the quarterback did, around end. There were no passes and no punts, just three plays, over and over again.

It was matter of pride and competition. Each player had to ask himself if he was good enough to beat that man across the line from him, then prove it.

Finally, in the waning of a long practice, the offense began to put together a few sustained drives. The defense would eventually stop them, but not before they had made two or three first downs. The first shades of confidence in Auburn's new ball control offense were developing.

"It was a rotten day," recalls Mike Neel, Tiger captain. "I can't remember how long we stayed out, but I remember how tough it was. After we went through that day, I think the whole team realized we could go through anything."

Randy Walls and other players agree with Neel that April 22 was the day the Tigers began their climb to glory, but it did not just happen.

That day was a calculated plan by Coach Ralph Jordan and his staff. Without such superstars as Pat Sullivan and Terry Beasley, Jordan, who would later become Coach of the Year, knew his team must control the football. The defense was supposed to be good, but the offense would have to control the ball and keep pressure off the defense. The two teams that beat Auburn in 1971, Alabama and Oklahoma, had controlled the ball. This year Auburn would control the ball and with it, the ball game.

Jordan and his staff set about finding the players who could and would lineup head-to-head and whip the men in front of them.

Perhaps offensive coordinator Gene Lorendo had the toughest job of all. Within months he would have to transform his entire offensive strategy from a passing pro-style offense to a bitter ground game where each down and each yard was invaluable. The offense would have to get tough, nose to nose.

"Pap" Morris would have to tell his offensive linemen, "Forget what you've learned the last three years about keeping people out. From now on, we're going to move them out ourselves."

As the offense toughened, so did Paul Davis' defense. The more Ken Bernich, Bill Newton and others tackled Terry Henley, the more prepared they would be to tackle the Mississippi State, Tennessee and Ole Miss backs. The more Benny Sivley and Bob Newton fought off their own blockers, they better they became.

For two weeks, the offense and defense battled each other, without a punt, without a pass, without anything more than a block from the fullback. Just run and tackle, run and tackle.

It was during these two weeks of hell, each day meaning 145-160 snaps—the equivalent of two or more whole games—that the men who would make up Auburn 1972 grew together as a team. They were molded into a unit that would be so essential to the success of the 1972 campaign.

"We were all in it together," recalls Walls. "There were no superstars, just a team going through it together."

"It was a real credit to the younger boys," says Neel. "Their attitude was great and they were willing to do whatever needed to be done."

The rugged spring training came as no surprise to the football team. Shortly after the Sugar Bowl, Jordan had issued what is now fondly called "The Haircut Rule" which set standards on athletes' hair lengths.

"We knew the coaches meant business when they came out with that. That was the first step toward getting us mentally prepared for a tough spring," one player said. "Coach Jordan told us that if we thought the haircut rule was too tough, we'd better not come out for spring training because we hadn't seen anything yet."

"A lot of the outside students didn't understand Coach Jordan's concern with our hair," he continued, "but we did. I haven't heard many outsiders complaining about our business this season."

As spring training neared an end and the offense and defense continued to complement each other, Ralph Jordan called his tired forces together, and he told them a story.

No one remembers exactly what the story was. It had something to do with someone asking a manager, a trainer or a coach what was the best football team his school ever had. The man replied, "The one coming up."

The story has been forgotten, but the point remains. Auburn's best football team was not the last one (1971). It would be the one coming up, 1972.

That motto became each player's war cry and rallying point from that day forward.

Neel prophesied the glories to come to the A-Day crowd as Sullivan and Beasley, their numbers retired, departed. Not that he and the other players didn't like Pat and Terry; they did, but it was up to them—each and every one of them—to win now, and win they would, even if nobody but their coaches thought so.

A shrewd football observer might have noted something good that sweltering A-Day afternoon. Offensively, both the Orange and the Blue teams converted a vast majority of their key third down plays. The winning team converted seven of nine third down situations, some of them third and six situations, and they made them running the football.

Still, however, no one believed in these Tigers. Throughout the summer, they saw themselves relegated to the lower half of the Southeastern Conference. Two and eight, one magazine predicted. Another said one win and nine losses. Ed Shearer of the Associated Press wrote their epitaph: "The biggest change in the Southeastern Conference power structure will be the demise of Auburn..."

"...the demise of Auburn." The Auburn Tigers put these things in their hearts and pondered them.

They returned for fall practice in August in top physical condition. They were ready to go about their business of winning football games they weren't supposed to win. A renewed desire and determination was evident to all around them.

No petty injuries hampered this team. At one time, all three starting defensive backs, Dave Beck, David Langner and Johnny Simmons were nursing sore shoulders or other injuries, but they were not in the training room. They were on the field practicing.

That scrawny kid down the road aways was getting ready to be a winner.

The Southeastern Conference Skywriters were polite when they came to Auburn, but Auburn knew how the writers really felt about football on the Plains this year and they tried to convince them they were wrong.

President Harry M. Philpott said he hoped the skywriters had "come not to bury Auburn, but to praise us." Coach Jordan told them the Tigers would be more powerful than in recent years. The Skywriters smiled at Philpott and Jordan, but when Dave Beck told them, "We'll go undefeated if we can find a quarterback in the first two games," the Skywriters rushed to Buddy Davidson, the Sports Information Director, and asked when the last time Beck's sanity had been checked.

"Now," Davidson laughs, "they are asking themselves why they didn't print the story."

The Mississippi State game neared. Football observers thought Auburn had conceded a schedule advantage to State by playing early instead of later in the year. Indeed, they had, but Auburn was prepared to physically whip Mississippi State.

Friday night prior to the game, Coach Jordan, following tradition, gathered his team around him in the end zone. "I'm proud of you," he told them, referring back to the hard days of the spring, and, "wouldn't be afraid to put you up against any team in the country right now."

Brave words for a coach whose team was supposed to win no more than two games, but Jordan believed even if no one else did.

The next night Auburn, with only five offensive plays, beat Mississippi State 14-3, and in the dressing room, each player said over and over, "We're on our way. We're on our way..."

The early Tiger strategy was evident. Get the ball, punch out two, three or four first downs, punt and put the opposition in a hole. "A punt and a prayer," Jordan called it, and it worked for Auburn as Auburn beat Chattanooga, Tennessee and Ole Miss.

Tennessee was the crucial game. "We knew we could win," Neel recalls. "From the start of spring training we knew we were going to beat Tennessee somehow."

And they did it with a punt, a prayer and a rugged defense.

Neel recalls that Jordan again told the team he wouldn't be afraid to take them up against anyone. This time he was specific. "Even Nebraska," he said.

"We were ready to go," Neel smiles "maybe, just maybe, that same afternoon."

The offense scored 19 points against Ole Miss, but, in the closing minutes, it was the defense that had to win or lose the game. They won it by stopping the Rebels inside the Auburn 10-yard line.

"We were nervous," says Danny Sanspree, "but after what we had been through in the spring, we knew we could stop Ole Miss or anybody if we had to. After the spring we thought we could do anything."

Then came LSU, and a 35-7 loss at Baton Rouge. Injuries, strep-throat and breaks offered excuses, but the Auburn Tigers did not want them. "We just got beat," said Johnny Simmons as he prepared to leave Tiger Stadium that night. "It's just like a day at practice. We've got to learn from this one and get ready for the next five."

Before the next five were over, Simmons and his teammates yearned for another shot at the Bayou Bengals.

The Georgia Tech game was next, and never was the Auburn defense and offense more complementary. Trailing 14-10 in the fourth quarter, the defense stopped Tech on a crucial third down and short yardage situation. The offense took the Tech punt and quickly drove down the field for the winning touchdown and a 17-14 lead.

The defense intercepted a Tech pass and set up another score late in Auburn's 24-14 win, a win in which the Tigers had come from two touchdowns behind.

The offense had gained complete confidence in the defense in the Tennessee game and the defense had complete confidence in the offense after the Tech victory. Everyone believed in David Beverly and Gardner Jett, so the Auburn football team, trust and faith, was now complete.

FSU, Florida, Georgia and Alabama—all victories—followed, and in the end, Jordan proclaimed this team, the predicted have-nots of the SEC, as his favorite team in 22 years of coaching Auburn football.

They had overcome the odds.

This, then, is the "Where," the "When," and the "How" of Auburn's successful football campaign, but how about the "What?"

What made this Auburn team a good team?

Perhaps the "What" is best summed up in Jordan's "Seven D's of Success: Discipline, Desire to excel, Determination, Dedication, Dependability, Desperation and Damn it anyway—do something."

"When finesse and everything else fails," Jordan told them, "work, work, work, press on and you will ultimately come out a winner."

Each player and coach, at some point in his life learned the value of hard work.

Mike Neel learned it at a backyard basketball goal trying to be as good as his brother Rick.

Randy Walls learned it as a high school freshman throwing the football all summer and then being a quarterback the next fall.

Bill Newton and Roger Mitchell may have learned it through long rough days on the practice field, non-scholarshippers earning a scholarship.

Ralph Jordan learned it as a boy growing up in Selma and as a college graduate trying to get a job during hard times.

Perhaps an incident involving Terry Henley, the team's leading rusher, and Jordan best typifies Auburn Football, 1972.

During a long spring workout, the offense had the ball on the defense's 30-yard line. On first down, behind good blocking, Henley darted and dodged for an 11-yard gain.

The offense whooped it up, "Attaway to run, Terry. Way to go!"

Jordan stepped into the huddle, looked at Henley, and said, "What's everybody so excited about? A good back would be in the end zone pitching the ball to the official."

On the next play, without good blocking, Henley broke four tackles, eluded several more and rammed 19 yards for a touchdown. Once in the end zone, he turned and pitched the ball to the official and grinned at Jordan.

He had learned the difference between a good back and a very good back.

Watch him or check the films. Everytime he scores, he'll pitch the ball to the official...a reminder of what Jordan called "a good back."

What made Auburn a good football team?

Desire, determination, just plain work and "want-to."

Nationally, they call it the Spirit of '76 for 1776.

At Auburn, they call it the "Spirit of '72" for the Auburn Tigers, 1972.

The Birmingham News
December 17, 1972

The 1972 Auburn team defeated Colorado 24-3 in the Gator Bowl and became only the second team in Auburn history to win 10 games in a single season. The other was the 1957 team, the national champions.

New Game in Town ─────────────────

In the beginning, there was Jones, Woodruff, Ware and Lacy. Whitaker, Hall, Hardie and Donahue.

Names. Just names.

But these are the names of the men who formed Auburn's first varsity basketball team. The year was 1906, just 15 years after James Naismith "invented" the only completely American game.

Their record was a highly commendable 4-1-1. They beat Tulane 27-7, Atlanta 28-17, Georgia Tech 26-6 and Mercer 64-8.

The only loss was to Columbus 18-16 and there was one tie, a 14-14 draw with Birmingham. Auburn might have won that one in overtime, but Auburn "had played five men against six and Capt. Jones properly refused to submit to further sacrifice of work to unfair decisions."

Officials were a problem then, too.

Mike Donahue was the coach and the win over Tech was especially pleasing to the little Irishman and to the Auburn student body. It came over John Heisman, who had gained fame coaching football at Auburn.

There were class teams in these days, too, and, in the winter of 1906, the Senior class had the best team of all. The Seniors beat the Juniors 12-6 and the Sophomores 12-10. Players dressed in knee length pants, stockings and a basketball shirt that would be standard even today.

Basketball was a social event in these days as men came to the games wearing bow ties, derby hats and carrying walking canes.

The ladies? They came in wide flowing dresses with broad colorful hats perched on their heads.

"We have reason to be proud of ourselves," wrote the *Glomerata* of that year. "The enthusiastic reception of this sport at Auburn is a noticeable feature of the year. The fellows crowded the 'gym' and supported the team well every game."

By 1929, Donahue and the founders of Auburn basketball were gone, but a new man had arrived on the scene.

A fellow by the name of Jordan. James Ralph Jordan was his name. His friends called him "Shug."

Shug was quite a basketball player. In 1929, he was the leading scorer in the old Southern Conference. He had a deadly two-hand set shot. He was later captain of the basketball team.

When he wasn't playing basketball, Jordan played a little football and in 1932, just 25 days before his twenty-first birthday, Jordan was hired as an assistant football coach. It was becoming obvious even then that he would stay around Auburn for awhile.

He was named head basketball coach in 1934. His teams played in the old Alumni Gym (located where the Union Building cafeteria now stands). The home court, in those days, was more than an advantage. It was part of the game plan.

"We knew about this one particular dead spot in the floor," Jordan laughs, "and we would try to force the opposition to dribble over this spot. About the time they'd hit the dead spot, we'd grab the ball and away we'd go. We beat Georgia 31-30 one night because of that dead spot," he laughs.

There were other things about Alumni Gym that caused problems. Things such as people.

"The seats were right on the out-of-bounds line," remembers Jordan, "and when you'd go in for a crip shot, you'd probably land half-way up in the crowd. It didn't matter. They'd just throw you back out on the court and you'd take off again. That was part of playing at Auburn."

But the people around the court were not the only problem. The ones above it were a problem too.

The goals were right at the balcony walls and that caused Auburn's opponents some problems shooting the ball. They weren't used to seeing legs dangling over the wall and banging against the backboard.

"We tried to get people to keep their feet off the other team's backboard," grins Jordan, "but it was hard. We didn't have much success. They wanted to be a part of the game and there's no doubt they were."

It was under Jordan that Auburn took the first step toward scholarships for basketball players. One must crawl before he can walk, however, and Auburn's first step toward basketball scholarships was little more than a good crawl.

"The first financial aid any Auburn basketball player ever received," reveals Jordan, "came from a Coke machine. We had a Coke drink machine near the coaches' offices and we gave a player named Shag Hawkins all the money we made off the machine. It came to about $15 a month. In those days, that was a lot of Cokes."

One of Jordan's players was destined to become Auburn's most successful basketball coach, surpassing only Jordan himself. His name was Joel Eaves, and it was under Eaves that Auburn won its only Southeastern Conference basketball championship. That came in 1961 when Snow White, as Eaves was called, and the Seven Dwarfs went 19-3 using Eaves' special shuffle offense.

They had almost won the title a year earlier when they won 30 straight games over a two-year span, also an Auburn record. All of the Eaves' years were, of course, in what has become affectionately known as "The Barn." Officially it was the Sports Arena, but the 2,500 seat cracker box was synonymous with Hell around the Southeastern Conference. Not many teams, not even mighty Kentucky, and Adolph Rupp could come into the Barn and win with regularity. Not in those days.

These were the days of noise and pretty girls. They were synonymous. When a girl—a real beauty—walked in, the noise from the predominantly male student section would reach such a crescendo that the game would have to be halted. If she was a real beauty, the boys sometimes picked her up and passed her overhead to the top row of the student section, much to the chagrin of her frustrated and helpless date. It was all in fun and everyone recognized that, even the girl and her date.

These were the days of Boogaloo Benny, the floor sweeper, and of the students counting cadence while he swept—hup, two, three, four...hup, two, three, four....The days of standing in line for hours—just waiting to see the Tigers play basketball. These were the days of good Auburn basketball. Winning Auburn basketball. There are more to come too.

Auburn Basketball Illustrated
Auburn vs. Virginia Tech
December 8, 1973

Dedication Day

At 1:02 p.m., Governor George C. Wallace, Mrs. Wallace, Dr. Harry M. Philpott and Ralph "Shug" Jordan entered Cliff Hare Stadium.

Jordan was nattily attired in sky blue trousers, striped sport coat, and white shirt. His good luck khaki jacket of the past had been forsaken for today.

He walked to the 15-yard line with the Wallaces and Philpott. They proceeded on to the reviewing stand at midfield, but Jordan stopped and paced nervously between the 10 and 30 yardlines, watching his Auburn football team loosen up.

At 1:10, the Auburn band entered from the North end of the stadium playing "War Eagle." As they formed the words "Jordan-Hare," Wallace, his wife Cornelia, and Philpott clapped their hands to the music. Jordan signed autographs.

At 1:11, Philpott stepped to the microphone. Jordan stood behind Wallace's wheelchair. As the president began speaking, Jordan walked nonchalantly to the back rail and faced the crowd.

Philpott introduced the descendants of Cliff Hare and members of the Jordan family who were sitting on the front row. He introduced the governor.

Wallace rolled himself to the microphone. "Henceforth," he said, "this stadium shall be known as the Jordan-Hare Stadium."

There was loud applause. Jordan dropped his head and ran his left hand through his hair.

"Today," the governor continued, "we honor a man who has been of great benefit to the athletic program of this great university. Every young man and woman who has come in contact with him knows how to play the game of life a lot better.

"His honor, integrity, impeccable character and his coaching record make him a legend in his own time."

There was a 20-second ovation. The crowd stood as Jordan approached the microphone.

"I am delighted and happy to be here," he said. "I hold in my hand a ticket to the 1939 Auburn-Florida game. It sold for $2.50. On the back there is a certificate stating that those who wish may contribute another $2.50 to the stadium fund. We were very proud of the stadium we dedicated that day," he said. "It held 7,900 people."

A chuckle murmured through the 56,000 people in the stands.

"I was a young assistant coach in 1939 and I remember the first spade of dirt that was turned in this stadium," Jordan said. "I am highly honored, deeply grateful and appreciative to the people who have helped me down through the years and led to this day.

"I knew 'Fesser Cliff Hare well," he continued. "I used to take my eligibility slip to him every year. We spent many afternoons together talking about football. The Jordan part is real proud to have our name up there with 'Fesser Hare."

He stepped back. The crowd was on its feet again, applauding.

Cornelia Wallace kissed him on the cheek.

Two state troopers escorted him to the dressing room as the band played "Glory, Glory to Ole Auburn..."

The Birmingham News
October 6, 1973

That's the way it was the day and the moment Cliff Hare Stadium officially became Jordan-Hare Stadium. Auburn defeated Ole Miss 14-7 to cap a perfect day for Auburn and for the Jordans.

Jordan and Hare

The man they call "'Fesser Hare" liked to sit on his front porch on over in the shank of the evening and watch the sun set behind the trees across Gay Street.

Those were the good old days, the days when there weren't many cars to disturb the solitude of Gay Street and Cliff Hare's broad front porch was a good place to sit, talk, and pass the time of day. People from all walks of Auburn life came to see the old 'Fesser and spend a leisurely afternoon. He knew a little about almost everything. He had been on the city council, a member of the waterworks board, a trustee in the Methodist church, a faculty member at API, and he was still an avid sportsman. He didn't get to hunt quail as much as he used to, but he never missed listening to an Auburn football game. Age had not changed that.

Folks who knew him well knew that he loved his God, his fellowman and Auburn. They knew, too, that he hated stray cats, Alabama, missed extra points and fumbles.

The house is gone now. Where the stately old southern home once stood, now stands an efficiency apartment complex housing 250 college boys. Only the concrete depression of the Hare driveway remains. The man is gone too. He died in 1948, at the age of 79.

But, as William Saroyan once wrote, "The person of a man may go, but the best part of him stays. It stays forever." So it is with Cliff Hare. His influence lives on in those who know him. One of those is Ralph Jordan, the man honored today, the man whose name now joins that of Hare as the name of Auburn's football home—"Jordan-Hare Stadium."

It was a much younger Ralph Jordan who used to park his two-seat Studebaker by the magnolia tree in the Hare yard, go up, and spend the afternoon talking with 'Fesser. The older Hare was also dressed up, usually in a light seersucker suit. He smoked a pipe and, occasionally, a cigar. He liked to sit in a spring rocking chair. His visitors, Jordan included, would sit in the swing or in one of the conventional rockers on the porch. As they talked, they could hear the sound of a clock ticking down the hall.

These were dark days for the young Jordan, fresh from World War II. He and other Auburn assistant coaches had been given a hero's sendoff. They had received something less than a hero's welcome home. There had been a coaching change and the young assistants who had been assured of a job when they returned were considered excess baggage by the new regime.

"Never lose faith," 'Fesser Hare told the young assistant coach. "Never lose faith and keep working."

"No matter how much he disagreed with a decision—and he disagreed with the situation at Auburn then—I never heard him say a derogatory word about anybody," recalls Coach Jordan. "If 'Fesser disagreed with a person's decision, he'd let that person know, but he would never interfere with that person's authority to make the decision.

"He was an intensely loyal man. He knew that loyalty is a two way street. Be loyal to others and they will be loyal to you. He despised disloyalty."

The old professor believed that loyalty and hard work would, in the end, be rewarded. That's what he told the young assistant coach. That's what he told all those who knew him.

"Looking back on it now," smiles Jordan, "I guess we were just two lonely men talking about old times on the front porch. He was old, lonely, and in declining health. I was a lonely young assistant coach. Those afternoons we spent together—there must have been 15 or 20 of them in the course of a year—have meant a great deal to me."

All the talk was not serious, however. There were good days to reminisce about, too, days to remember with a smile, a chuckle and, perhaps, a tear.

The two men, quite naturally, talked about football.

Hare had been a second string quarterback on Auburn's first football team in 1892. Jordan had been a star center in the early '30's. Together they forged a link with Auburn football's past, present, and future.

"'Fesser Hare told me how he and Dr. Sanford—for whom the stadium in Athens is named—used to come to Auburn every year after the Auburn-Georgia game in Columbus and divide the money," recalls Coach Jordan. "They would sit down in the Hare kitchen, take the money out of an old cigar box, spread it across a marble table top and say, 'A dollar for you and a dollar for us,' until the game proceeds were divided equally between the two schools."

Hare had his own ideas about football, too. He went into a frenzy when Auburn fumbled and there was no excuse, he said, for missing an extra point. 'Fesser Hare believed in a strong kicking game and some of that rubbed off on Coach Jordan.

"'Fesser used to say, 'If the kicking game wasn't important, they wouldn't call it football,' and I agree.

"Cliff Hare was a great man," remembers Coach Jordan, "a scholar, quiet and unpretentious, but a scholar nonetheless. He was a Southern Gentleman, too, in every sense of the word. He used to escort his wife to the Presbyterian Church, then go on to the Methodist Church himself. That demonstrates his loyalty too.

"I wouldn't take anything for those hours we spent together."

Like the writer says—"The best part of a man stays. It stays forever."

A part of Hare will forever stay with Jordan.

In more ways than one.

Auburn Football Illustrated
Auburn vs. Ole Miss
Dedication Day
October 6, 1973

At Home With the Jordans

Three large pecan trees shade the Jordan home. There is a small white bench in the backyard, a brick wall, too, and a barbecue grill, now standing dormant in the autumn breeze. All are extensions of the man of the house. They belong to him. They are indicative of the man himself.

To millions across the country, the man is Ralph Jordan, one of the most successful men ever to coach the game of football. To his family and close friends, he is something altogether different. To them, he is the man who likes to cut his own grass, the man who used to shoot two-hand set shots with his son in the backyard, the man who calls a repairman rather than tinker around the house, the man who likes butterbeans, sliced tomatoes, roast beef—anything but chicken. He had enough of chicken on the banquet circuit back in 1951 when he was getting the Auburn program started.

This is the other side of Ralph Jordan the football coach, the side the public fan doesn't know.

He came to Auburn in 1951. They didn't like football coaches in Auburn then. Coaches never stayed over two, maybe three years. Jordan was different. He stayed four years, then had his contract renewed for five more years, then five more, and five more. Ad infinitum.

He had a chance to leave in 1955. The Philadelphia Eagles made an attractive offer. He turned it down. Why? "I like Auburn," he said. "Auburn is my cup of tea."

With that, Ralph Jordan permanently declared Auburn his home. It was proclaimed to the world when he and Mrs. Jordan planted those pecan trees in the backyard. "When a college football coach does that," wrote the late Benny Marshall, "he plans to stay awhile."

Other things have been added to the Jordan backyard, too, things that are, in their own way, a part of the man. There was a large barbecue pit constructed, but it has long since given way to a gas grille. It is here that the man called "Shug" performs some of his greatest feats. "A backyard gourmet." That's what his son calls him.

The white bench is from the old Alumni Gym, many years a casualty to the omnipotent thing called progress. "We gave that old bench a lot of wear when I was basketball coach," the man says.

There is a story behind the brick wall, too. Some of the bricks came from the old Alumni Gym where the man played and later coached Auburn basketball. Others come from the old Albert Hotel, once a landmark in his hometown of Selma.

He is a student of history. These are small reminders—mementoes if you will—of the rocks from which he was hewn. He is not one to forget the past. Only from the past, he believes, can you understand the future.

There are other signs too, signs such as the immaculate lawn around the Jordan's fashionable-but-comfortable ranch style home. The duty of keeping up the lawn belongs to the head coach.

"He loves to ride the lawnmower," his wife says. "He won't let anyone else near it. Cutting the grass is just like a ball game to him. He has a schedule to go by. He knows when to cut it, how long it takes to cut it, and how long it takes to sweep it.

Each time he putters around the yard on that lawnmower, he tries to set a new time record. It's his way of relaxing."

He relaxes with his dogs, two basset hounds, Beau and Talley. He and Mrs. Jordan like to take them for walks. There are two Siamese cats, too. They like the man also. All animals do.

So do people, the postman, the paper boy, the repairman and the neighbors. All like to have a friendly chat with the man.

Ralph Jordan is not a flamboyant man. "Not very exciting," is the way he once described himself to two student journalists. And, compared to some men of his profession, he is not. Rather than check with his stockbroker in New York or his lawyer in Birmingham at lunch, this man likes to go home at lunch, have a glass of tea and take a nap when time permits.

He may not be "exciting," but one thing he is—solid—solid like a rock.

Over it all stand the pecan trees, planted 18 long years ago. They symbolize the man, the other side of the man, known only as coach to millions.

Auburn Football Illustrated
Auburn vs. Ole Miss
Dedication Day
October 6, 1973

Following a Dream _____

Bill Newton, to most of us, is the guy who blocked those two punts against Alabama last year, those two punts in a row.

Bob Newton is Bill Newton's brother—it was the other way around before those two blocked punts—and he, Bob, was in on the blocked extra point, the one that ultimately proved to be the difference. Auburn 17-Alabama 16.

To most of us, this is Bill Newton. This is Bob Newton. Forevermore they will be linked and associated with one of the greatest Auburn victories ever.

To most of us maybe, but not to Burladine Newton.

To her, Bill and Bob Newton are two ordinary little boys, little boys who used to bite each other in fights over a sand bucket, little boys who used to slip off to "fish" in the Sipsey River and bring home finger-size perch for her to "clean and cook."

To Mrs. Burladine Newton, Bill and Bob Newton are anything but big, rough, tough football players. They are her little boys, and they always will be her little boys. Nothing will ever change that, certainly not a football game, not even one as important as the Auburn-Alabama game.

Their father, Lew Allan Newton, died from a stroke in January, 1965, when the boys were only 12 years old. The job of raising the two youngest boys—Bill is six minutes older than Bob—fell on Mrs. Newton. It would not be an easy task. She knew that, and she knew, too, that she would have some help.

The Newtons are a close-knit family. The older boys, Cliff and Joe, almost out on their own, would help. So would a daughter, Barbara. But the main responsibility would be with their mother and she would not fail them.

Bill was always the smaller, more tender-hearted, of the two. Bob, always big for his age, started "courting" at 14 and his mother often drove him to see his girlfriend.

She was determined that her boys would not miss any opportunities because she had to act as a mother and father to them. As it turned out, they had opportunities they might not have had if their father had been alive. One of them was football.

"Daddy never was much for athletics," recalls Bill. "He didn't even want Joe to play basketball. After Joe got a scholarship to Auburn, Daddy eased up some on basketball, but not football.

"Another older brother, Robert, went out for football," Bill smiles, "and Daddy went and got him."

Lew Allan Newton never could see the value of football, especially in the fall. The Newtons were a working farm family and he thought the boys needed to be home.

After Lew Allan died, the Newtons quit farming. Mrs. Newton started selling insurance and that opened the football door for Bill and Bob. If her baby boys wanted to play football, that's what she wanted them to do.

Thus the road that would eventually lead to Auburn, to the two blocked punts and to today's game began.

Bill and Bob contributed greatly to the athletic success of the Fayette County High School Tigers, and, when their playing days were over, Sam Mitchell of the Auburn coaching staff, was there with a scholarship in hand, only he held one scholarship, not two. It was for Bob, who, in the opinion of college scouts, had more potential to improve in college than Bill.

It was an emotional moment. Tears were shed by all, including the battle-hardened coach. A scholarship for one twin, nothing for the other. Nothing but a mother who loved him and a brother who loved him, who loved him so much that, even though he was on full scholarship, promised to work so that Bill could come to Auburn. A chance is all Bill Newton ever wanted and, with the support of his mother and brother, he had that chance.

Bill Newton took that chance and, in the best interest of the American dream, he succeeded.

Years later, after the two blocked punts, he asked a reporter, "Why do they still write about me winning a scholarship? It's not that big a deal."

"Maybe not to you," answered the reporter, "but think what an inspiration your story—the blocked punts and all—is to other people who have hopes and dreams. You have proven that dreams do come true."

And that he had. And, that he had.

The Newton twins came to Auburn in 1970. Their mother followed a year later as housemother of Sigma Pi fraternity.

Although it is not among her official duties as housemother, Mrs. Newton has become the Sigma Pi tour guide for all of Auburn's out-of-town games. At the Tennessee game, for example, she led an entourage of 17 Sigma Pi's to Knoxville.

But Burladine Newton is more than just a housemother to the Sigma Pi's. She is a mother to her own sons and unofficial mother to the Auburn football team.

"When they're sick, when they want to talk, when they just want to get away from it all, a lot of the players come to see me," she says with obvious pride and pleasure. "They call me 'Mamma,' too, just like Bill and Bob do."

"It's always been that way," says Bob. "Our friends have always felt at home with Mamma. They will go in, take their shoes off, get something to eat out of the refrigerator and make themselves right at home."

"I wouldn't have it any other way," says Mrs. Newton smiling.

But time waits for no man, and soon, Mrs. Newton will be forced to have it another way.

After today's game, only the Sun Bowl remains, and the Newton story, the Auburn part of it at least, will be over. Only two more chapters to be written.

Then, for the first time, Bill and Bob Newton will go their separate ways. Life will never be the same for them or for Burladine Newton.

Their mother—always "Mamma" to them—will stay in Auburn, but her door will always be open to them and to their friends.

That part will never change.

They will always be her two little boys.

Auburn Football Illustrated
Auburn vs. Alabama
December 1, 1973

Burladine Newton moved back to Fayette in 1980, where she is growing old with grace and dignity. Bob lives in Birmingham and Bill is back home in Fayette, "on the home place" as his mother—his "Mamma"—calls it.

D-Day, June 6, 1944 ————————————

(Editor's Note: Thirty years ago today, the greatest invasion in military history was launched. Ralph Jordan, later to lead Auburn to its greatest football era, was part of the huge landing force. Today, he recalls some of his thoughts on that momentous day.)

For months now, Captain Ralph Jordan and the 1st Engineer Special Brigade had practiced for the invasion of France. They would board a ship, start across the channel, then double back and land on the beaches of Southern England. Any one of those feints could have been the real thing. They knew that and so did the Germans.

There was something strange, however, about the landing exercises of June 5, 1944. They were called off. Heavy seas was the reason given. Yet, Captain Jordan's outfit was ordered to remain aboard the ship.

"Gee," said one of the men near Jordan. "Why don't they let us go on back to the staging area if the weather's too bad. Why take a chance?"

The question was never answered. The premonition Jordan had when breaking camp a few days before had come to pass. "This was it. The real thing. D-Day. The invasion of Fortress Europe." No one had to tell them. They knew.

There was a pensive quietness about the men of the 1st Engineer Special Brigade as they rocked silently on the murky waters of the English Channel. They thought of home, of family, of good times and of what lay ahead.

Ralph Jordan thought about his wife, Evelyn. Their anniversary was just five days away. He wondered where he would be when that day came. He thought about his two daughters, Susan and Darby. He wondered what the future held for them. He thought about Selma and Auburn. And, thought about the Germans.

You never quite get used to an invasion, no matter how many times you have been through it and Jordan had been through it many times. He had hit the beaches of North Africa in 1942. A year later, he and other members of Patton's new 7th Army were "born on the high seas and baptized in blood" on the beaches of Sicily. But this one—D-Day—was different. This was to be the granddaddy of them all.

There was more emotion about this one. All of the other invasions had been working toward this one great moment.

For months now, Jordan had worked to bring all elements of his outfit together and keep them supplied. For four months he had known the place of the invasion, but he had not known the day or the time. Now he knew that.

The show was on for June 6.

Under the cover of night, the ships carrying Jordan's brigade crept slowly into the channel. It moved north, past the Isle of Wight. Usually they turned left here, back toward England, but this time they sailed on, due north. Then came the slow sweeping right turn toward the continent, toward France and the waiting Germans.

Finally, the ship's captain told them officially what they had all known for some time. "This is the captain speaking," he said. "Today, June 6, is D-Day. H-hour is 6 a.m. Elements of the 1st Engineer Special Brigade would land on Utah Beach east of Cherbourg at H plus two hours."

The night passed quietly. No one slept, but no one talked. There was no need.

At dawn Ralph Jordan gazed at the greatest naval armada the world has ever known. More than 4,000 vessels had edged their way toward France during the night. Overhead 11,000 planes provided air cover. Giant barrage balloons prevented the Lufwaffe from staffing the Allied armada.

Ahead lay Hitler's impregnable Fortress Europe. Men were already fighting and dying there. The 82nd and 101st Airborne Divisions had dropped behind enemy lines during the night. They waited there for the troops coming in from the sea. Those troops were dropping into landing crafts for the short journey to the beach.

Jordan knew the plan. He knew it well. Ahead he could see flames and belching smoke. He could see the giant German guns, 88's they were called, firing from the Normandy beaches. He wondered how much good the Allied naval bombardment had done.

Finally the word came down. Time to go. Time for the 1st Engineer Special Brigade and Ralph Jordan to get back into World War II. They left the ship at H plus one hour and 30 minutes. Forty-five minutes later, Auburn's future football coach was scurrying for cover on Utah Beach.

The Allied bombardment had not done much good. The German bunkers were too thick. Machine guns, mortars and 88's dropped death on the beaches. The mortars gave warning before they hit. The deadly 88's did not. It was one of these, the 88's, that wounded Jordan.

It exploded near him and rivetted his left arm with shrapnel. It was a painful wound, but it was not serious enough, in Jordan's opinion, to return to the ship. Utah Beach, despite enemy fire, had to be secured and prepared to accept more men and machines from England. There was work to be done, so Jordan stayed.

Four days later, just before his wedding anniversary, the metal was removed from his arm.

It has been 30 years since Captain Jordan, now Coach Jordan, landed in Normandy. He has not been back. He has no desire to return.

In the intervening years, he has seen the elements of D-Day in a hundred football dressing rooms across the country—the planning, the preparation, the human drama of young men going into battle. Not as serious as D-Day, perhaps, but, in its own way, serious enough.

Ralph Jordan has not forgotten June 6, 1944. No man who has walked through the valley of such a shadow ever will.

The Birmingham News
June 6, 1974

Ralph Jordan never returned to the beaches of Normandy. Though he went to Europe several times, Utah Beach was not one of the places he chose to visit. He had walked the valley of the shadow. There was no need to return.

Beginning of the End

AUBURN—It began on a Sunday night, just over 25 years ago.

It was 11:30 p.m., February 25, 1951, when Dr. Ralph B. Draughon walked out of Auburn's presidential mansion and announced that Ralph Jordan had been selected Auburn's head football coach. He was selected by a 3-2 vote of the search committee.

Thus began the greatest athletic era in the school's history. In the next 24 years, Alabama Polytechnic Institute would grow into Auburn University, win 172 football games, play in 12 bowls, win national and conference championships, have a Heisman Trophy winner, 20 All-Americans and almost countless all-conference performers.

To be sure, it hasn't been all roses, but it is just as certain there have been far more roses than thorns.

Three years after Jordan became Auburn's coach, he had the Tigers in the Gator Bowl. It was Auburn's first bowl appearance in 15 years and Jacksonville would be a place Auburn people would find themselves often over the next 22 years. Four years later, Auburn had the best football team in the country. They were No. 1, national champions.

Over the years—or "Down Through the Years" as Jordan would say—Auburn has become a national football power. There have been many great moments, and Jordan is hesitant to name any certain team, game, or player as his favorite. Ten years ago, he summed it up saying his greatest thrill was seeing Auburn competitive again.

More recently, however, he has been a bit more specific.

He has, at times, named the 1957 National Championship team and the 1972 team, the Amazin's, as his favorite teams.

He has named Tucker Frederickson, a No. 1 NFL draft choice in 1964, Jimmy Phillips, a 1957 two-way All-American, and Pat Sullivan, the Heisman Trophy winner as his greatest players.

His favorite games? Out of the 172 he has won, he picks the first one, the 1951 win over Vanderbilt, the first one over Georgia Tech, 14-12 in 1955, the 1971 win over Georgia, the 35-20 game that cinched the Sugar Bowl and Sullivan's Heisman and, of course, the 1972 win over Alabama, 17-16.

Still, however, he is careful. These are only examples, he says. His main thrill is now, as always, seeing Auburn football competitive again.

Not only has Ralph Jordan become Auburn's most successful football coach, he has probably added more terms to the Auburn vocabulary than any other man, terms like "Selma, Queen City of the Black Belt," "Light up like a Christmas tree," "Run with reckless abandon," and, of course, "You're so right, Carl!"

His admonitions to the Auburn student body before the Tech and Alabama games have become like family legends, passed down from father to son and mother to daughter.

"Let's go over to Atlanta," Jordan says every year, "and act like the ladies and gentlemen we are, even if they don't act like ladies and gentlemen to us."

Before the Alabama game, for 24 years now, it has been: "We're going to Birmingham with one thought in mind—-BEAT BAMA!"

His retirement announcement was certain to be an emotional affair. And so it was Tuesday at 11 a.m. Standing in the room were seven of the people who had been with him a quarter of a century ago, back there in 1951. Gene Lorendo, Shott Senn and Joe Connally are still on his coaching staff.

Buck Bradberry, one of his first coaches, is now with the alumni association. He was there. So was Kenny Howard, who has cared for Jordan's athletes down through every one of the years. Milton Thurston was there, too. He has equipped Jordan's players, every one of them. Bill Beckwith was there. He had handled the hiring announcement back there in 1951. Now he watched as his protege, Buddy Davidson, handled the retirement announcement. It was an emotional time.

Emily Foster was there, too. She had been his secretary most of the way, more than 20 years. She smiled early, but when Jordan came into the room, there was an unmistakable sadness on her face. It would never be quite the same, not for her, not for anyone at Auburn.

Groups of students gathered in the hallway outside the reception area. It would never be the same for them either. Ralph Jordan was all they had ever known. He was Auburn football. He was Auburn.

At 11:02 a.m., Coach and Mrs. Jordan, Doug Barfield, Lee Hayley and President Harry M. Philpott entered.

At 11:03, Philpott began reading a prepared statement.

At 11:06, he announced that Doug Barfield would be Auburn's next head coach.

Auburn was officially entering the last nine months of The Jordan Era.

The Birmingham News
April 9, 1975

Great Expectations

AUBURN—The little six-foot, 160-pound quarterback who was too small to play at Auburn has finally made it.

That quarterback—Douglas N. "Doug" Barfield—was named Tuesday to succeed Ralph "Shug" Jordan at the close of the 1975 season.

Perhaps it was meant to be, Doug Barfield becoming head football coach at Auburn. There are too many ironies for it to be otherwise.

First, there was Barfield's athletic career. He wanted to come to Auburn when he finished Grove Hill High School in 1952. He wanted to play football at Auburn and did come up to see offensive coach Buck Bradberry. Then, as now, there were no scholarships for 160-pound quarterbacks. Bradberry urged him to be a walk-on, to tryout on his own.

It was during this time that he saw his first Auburn football game. The year was 1951, Ralph Jordan's first year. Barfield was in the stands as Auburn upset Florida and Rick Casares, 14-13. Lee Hayley, who would later hire him, caught the winning touchdown pass. Barfield remembers it well.

There are other ironies, too, like growing up next door to a kid named David Matthews, who in turn would grow up to become president of The University of Alabama, ironies like marrying an Alabama alumnae, a hometown honey who quickly turned into an Auburn fan.

The road to Tuesday's announcement was not easy for Barfield. After an illustrious career at Southern Mississippi—he chose to accept a Southern scholarship rather than walk-on at Auburn—Barfield began a career of high school coaching. "I did everything," he said, laughing, Tuesday. "I learned to scramble and scratch, even line the playing field on Friday afternoons. I've done it all."

He coached at Grove Hill one year, went into the Army for two years, then coached at UMS in Mobile and Andalusia for eight years. His college coaching career began at Southern Mississippi in 1967.

He went to Clemson as offensive coordinator in 1970 and came to Auburn as freshman coach in 1972. Two years later, he became the offensive coordinator, and then, it happened.

It began on a Monday night about 8 p.m. First there were the rumors, the phone calls from Mobile, asking, "Is it true?"

"Is what true?" asked Barfield.

Then, on the third call, he knew something was happening. Auburn President Harry M. Philpott was on the line. It was the first time Philpott had called Barfield.

"Has your phone been ringing?" Philpott asked.

"Yes, it has," Barfield replied.

"Well, you'd better come on over to the house," Philpott said. "I want to talk to you."

That's when Doug Barfield found out that he would be Auburn's 21st head football coach. Waiting at the President's home were Philpott, athletic director Lee Hayley and Jordan. Buddy Davidson, Auburn's sports information director, arrived shortly.

It became official at 11:06 a.m. Tuesday when Philpott, reading from a prepared statement, said "The Board (of Trustees) has decided that Coach Doug Barfield should take over as head football coach, and I am pleased to announce at this time that Coach Barfield has accepted the challenge..."

There would still be many details to be worked out, things such as length of contract, salary, but Barfield was not concerned about such things Tuesday. "I have every confidence in Dr. Philpott and Coach Hayley," he said. "These things will be worked out at the proper time."

Today was low key all the way and that's the way Barfield wanted it. He took pains to see that it was that way. "This is his day," he said, referring to Coach Jordan. "He's the man of the hour."

But there were the inevitable questions, all designed to determine what kind of mark Doug Barfield would put on the Auburn football program. Don't look for any dramatic changes. Not immediately. He plans to retain the entire Jordan staff. "It is one of the finest staffs anywhere," he said. "There is a great harmony between offense and defense because we are all working for the same goal. I'm looking forward to a long association with each member of the staff."

Jordan said he planned no staff changes for the coming season. That means Barfield will assume no new duties in preparation for becoming head coach. Paul Davis will remain the assistant head coach and Barfield will continue to coordinate the Auburn offense.

"There is no need for staff changes," Jordan explained. "We have a very open system here. Everyone is encouraged to make suggestions and comment."

While fielding questions about the future—he likes to play at home, dislikes cowbells and doesn't have anything against artificial grass—Barfield is careful to emphasize the immediate future. That means Tuesday and the start of spring training.

"I'm still Coach Jordan's offensive coordinator," he said. "I ought to be across the hall right now, trying to figure out someway to move the football next year."

If there was a dark spot in Tuesday's activity, it was the premature news leak that forced Jordan to reveal his retirement plans publicly before he could tell his players privately.

After meeting with Jordan and Barfield at 3 p.m., the consensus of player opinion was unanimous. They hated to see Jordan retire, but they believed Barfield was a good choice for the job.

"I hate to see Coach Jordan leave," said quarterback Phil Gargis, "because I was looking forward to playing the rest of my time under him. He has done a great job, and I think Coach Barfield will do a great job, too. Coach Barfield has a way of making players really want to play for him."

"Everybody hates to see Coach Jordan step down," said defensive end Liston Eddins, "because of all the respect we have for him. It is hard to think about Auburn without thinking of Coach Jordan first. I think everybody will get behind Coach Barfield when he takes over. I think Coach Jordan's retirement will make us play much harder."

"I hope we can get it all together for Coach Jordan, " said tailback Mitzi Jackson. "All retiring coaches want to go out a winner and I hope we can do it for him. Coach Barfield can do the job."

Ed Butler, wingback, was somewhat miffed about the circumstances surrounding the announcement. "A lot of us wish we could have heard it first from Coach Jordan," he said. "But we understand how things like this can get out. It is certainly going to be an honor to be a senior on his last team."

Jim McKinney, defensive back on the 1974 team, said he was surprised that the retirement came so soon. "I thought it would come in the next couple of years," he said, "but not now. Coach Jordan is a friend to all of us off the field. He is fair to all of us and would do anything to help us."

While the official activities were going on at Memorial Coliseum, Mrs. Doug Barfield—the former Alabama co-ed who changed her colors—was home answering the phone.

"Yes," she said late Tuesday afternoon, "the phone is still ringing. It's been ringing constantly since last night. Old friends and alumni are calling to congratulate us."

The Barfield children, Gary and Kathy, are, of course, excited about their father's new position, head coach designate, especially 15-year old Gary.

He'll be a sophomore at Auburn High School next fall and, like his Daddy did at Grove Hill 25 years ago, he will play quarterback.

His Daddy won't get to see him play much, however. All of his Friday night time will be spent working for the future of Auburn football. A future, he says, "that lies in that boy from Alabama who puts on that blue jersey, hears the band playing, the crowd yelling when he runs on the field and then does things he usually can't do."

The Birmingham News
April 9, 1975

In situations like this, it is often said that "The Man and The Hour Have Met..." That was not the case with Doug Barfield and Auburn. Saying "I am not one to stay where I am not wanted," Barfield resigned at the conclusion of the 1980 season after five years as Auburn's head football coach. He left behind a record of 29-25-1. That record does not diminish his efforts on Auburn's behalf, nor does it say anything about the lasting qualities of Doug Barfield the man.

After a year as an assistant at Mississippi State, a year in which State beat Auburn 21-17, and several years in private business, Doug Barfield is back in the high school ranks, doing what he loves best—coaching.

Keep Smiling...

When the definitive history of Auburn football is written, this story will not be included.

But it should be—this one or one like it should be—if that definitive history is to accurately indicate the power and influence college football has on the thousands who watch it every Saturday.

It begins on a Friday in 1972. A young Auburn freshman went to see his math teacher. Finals were approaching and, like all young Auburn freshmen, this young man was concerned about the grade he would receive for his quarter's effort. He received little encouragement.

You've got to make 98 on the final, the instructor told him, to get an A in the course. You have to make 28 to keep your B. I wouldn't worry too much about the A, the teacher continued.

It's going to be a pretty hard final and I don't think anyone is going to make 98 on it. I don't know if I could. This is a football weekend. I'd suggest you have some fun and then concentrate on your other courses. You might have a better chance of improving your grade in them.

It was, indeed, a football weekend, and a big one, too. Auburn-Alabama, Dec.2, 1972. Yes—and there's no need to continue—that's the day Auburn blocked two straight punts, ran them both in for touchdowns and upset No. 2 ranked Alabama 17-16.

Auburn was still ecstatically wild that Sunday night when the young freshman returned from Birmingham. Finals began the next day, but he couldn't resist a trip to Toomer's Corner. No true Auburn man could.

He knew he should have been home studying, but the boy in him made him stay. Finally, after one particularly long "War-r-r-r Eagle!" and a thunderous ovation of "Punt-Bama-Punt's," the boy turned from the cheering mob. He was smiling as if some truth had just been revealed to him.

"You know, Housel," he said. "If Auburn can block two punts and beat Alabama, I can make an A on that math test."

I didn't see him much over the next few days. Then late one afternoon—Wednesday I believe it was—he walked into the office. He was smiling. "Remember that math test," he asked, "the one I had to make 98 on? I made 99 on it and got an A in the course."

What, you may ask, does this have to do with football?

Coach Jordan answered that question long ago.

"If we played football only for those who participate," he said, "it wouldn't be worth the time, the effort and the money that goes into it. People who watch football, those who follow it, learn something about themselves and about life. Football often inspires people to do more than they normally could do...."

The young freshman, showing a wisdom far beyond his years, realized that. "Don't lose sight of the necessity to do your best, always," he wrote a friend later, "for if you do your best at all times, success is inevitable....

"Keep smiling, believing in yourself, dreaming up bold ideas and working hard. You'll make it through...."

I've thought of that young freshman often in recent days, especially in Knoxville last week, gazing down at the Tennessee River from Neyland Stadium. We had made the Tennessee trip together two years ago, he and I. It was our last. He was killed in an automobile accident later that year.

I have many fond memories of that young freshman—Jack James of Birmingham —but none is more cherished than the day he discovered something about himself and his own capabilities by watching this strange captivating game that is about to unfold below us.

Auburn Football Illustrated
Auburn vs. Virginia Tech
October 4, 1975

It has been almost 20 years—two decades—since Jack James was killed by a drunk driver. We will never know what contributions Jack James may have made to make this world a better place. Tragedy lies not in death, for death comes to us all. Tragedy lies in lost opportunity and lost contribution. The death of Jack James was, and still is, a tragedy.

From the Sideline ————————————

This is how it was on the Auburn sidelines as the Tigers rallied to jerk victory from the jaws of defeat.

Kentucky led 6-0. Six minutes fifty-six seconds remained in the game. The Cats were on the Auburn 14, fourth and one. They were going for it.

"Come on, defense," shouted Bill Evans, "come on, defense!" His voice sounded like a mournful wail.

Chuck Fletcher, Rob Spivey and the Auburn offense looked on. Jeff Gilligan, who would play a major role in this unfolding drama, paced back and forth like the caged tiger he had been all night.

Ray Powell moistened his lips. The Kentucky band was playing "On, On, U of K."

Kentucky took a long count. When Auburn did not jump off side, quarterback Cliff Hite called time out. Now the Cats would kick.

As he had twice earlier, John Pierce kicked it through. Kentucky led 9-0 with 6:33 left.

Only die-hard Auburns thought the Tigers would win this one. Auburn had made only one first down the second half.

As Kentucky kicked off, Ed Butler pranced, danced and ran in place.

Rick Neel was driven out of bounds by Kentucky kicker John Pierce. "Good tackle, buddy," said Neel. "Yeah," shouted the Kentucky tackler at the top of his voice. He sensed victory.

Then, in came Clyde Baumgartner.

The game was over. Then, suddenly it wasn't. Gilligan, no longer a caged Tiger, caught Baumgartner's pass at midfield and ran for a touchdown. The play covered 72 yards. Auburn was back.

Gilligan, who had missed three of Auburn's first four games, was mobbed to such a degree when he came to the sideline that he could barely smile.

Chris Vacarella, who was also open on the play was the first one to rush him. "Way to go, way to go!" he shouted, slapping Gilligan on the back.

Now, Rob Spivey was there. "Give me a kiss, man, give me a kiss," he shouted, hugging Gilligan. "That's the way to go after that ball."

One player could do no more than walk around saying, "Oh me, oh me, oh me..."

Tommy Hicks smashed Sonny Collins on the kickoff. "I just wanted to knock hell out of him," he would say later. "I knew I got him, but I didn't know he had fumbled."

Kicker Neal O'Donoghue recovered the loose ball. Now it was the defense's turn to wait and shout encouragement to the offense.

"Come on, Big O!" one player shouted. "Come on..."

Rick Telhiard waited on one knee. John Smith, making his first start for Auburn, chewed nervously on his mouth piece.

Auburn was thinking field goal on third down. "Just get in the middle of the field," said Auburn sports information director Buddy Davidson. "Just keep it in the middle of the field."

Kenny Burks broke over left tackle for 17 yards and the touchdown.

Ralph Jordan stood with his hands on his hips, just as he had in three earlier losses and one disappointing tie.

Again, Telhiard watched on one knee. No one would have ever known that Phil Gargis passed to Ed Butler for the two-point conversion by watching Telhiard. His face showed no emotion. Nothing.

Perhaps he, better than anyone else, knew he still had a job to do. Auburn led 15-9, but there was still 4:47 to play. Coach Paul Davis chewed gum incessantly.

Trainer Kenny Howard went up and down the sideline, urging players to step back and not, in their considerable excitement, step on the field, getting an unnecessary penalty. Not now.

Now, O'Donoghue was trying another field goal. Telhiard waited, still on one knee. Tackle Steve Stanaland stood by him. Before the Kentucky crowd cheered, before anyone cheered, they knew the field goal was no good. Telhiard winced and began putting on his helmet. Stanaland's face turned to a grimace.

"Boy, we needed that one," said defensive tackle John Smith, as two desperate Kentucky passes were broken up.

Now defensive secondary coach Dave Beck smiled, maybe for the first time of the long season.

"Don't touch it, don't touch it," the coaching staff shouted to Rick Neel as he dropped back for Kentucky's last punt.

Now the offense was on the field again, for the last time.

"Good job," Smith told Telhiard.

"Way to play," Telhiard told Smith. The seconds were ticking away as Phil Gargis made a determined one-yard for Auburn's last first down, the game clinching first down.

"That Gargis is something," said Smith to no one in particular. "He gets the big ones."

Telhiard looked at a Kentucky manager standing on the Auburn sideline. "Helluva game, isn't it?" he said.

"Yeah," said the Kentucky manager. Both grinned.

"Run it out, run it out," shouted tackle Rodney Bellamy, as the final seconds ticked into eternity. He began to sing "War Eagle."

Then, it was over. A sea of white carried Shug Jordan to the center of the field.

Behind them the Kentucky band was playing "On, On, U of K."

They were cheering at Toomer's Corner in Auburn.

Unofficially, Auburn's 1975 football season had just begun.

The Birmingham News
October 12, 1975

End of the Line

The last hand shaken, the last autograph signed, Ralph Jordan climbed aboard a Greyhound bus for a lonely ride back to Auburn. His 25-year career as Auburn's head football coach was over.

His final record stands at 176-83-7. To equal that record, an Auburn football coach would have to average eight wins a year for 22 years.

Saturday night, however, there were no cheers, no accolades, no merriment. Just a lonely bus ride to Auburn with some of the close ones, his wife Evelyn, Kenny Howard, the trainer who has been with him all the way, Wilbur Hutsell, who was at Auburn when Jordan came as a freshman back in 1928, maybe a few others.

There would be no wine, no champagne, nothing of merriment. Just cold roast beef sandwiches, soft drinks and the satisfaction of sharing these morsels with some of the people who saw the challenge and helped meet it.

Ralph Jordan's final trip home would be like the 24 others before it. No use changing anything now, he has seemed to say since his retirement was announced April 8.

He changed nothing Saturday, the day of his last game.

Always an early riser, he walked into the almost deserted Sheraton Restaurant at 7:42 a.m. Howard was waiting for him as he almost always was.

"Slept like a log," said Jordan. "I woke up thinking about Southern Cal and UCLA. Anytime you can win and fumble 15 times, that's something."

"The Man," as he is affectionately known to his staff and players, was in a good mood.

"Have you noticed the number three on your telephone?" he asked Howard.

"You dial it if you want coffee. I dialed it this morning and nothing happened. I punched it two more times and this voice answered. I said, 'This is Room 128 and I'd like some coffee.' The voice on the other end said, 'This is Room 333 and I'd like some, too.'"

He laughed jovially. If the pressure of the big game, his final one, was crushing in on him, it didn't show, but then Shug Jordan is a master at hiding his emotions.

"He has shown no emotion at practice this week," Howard had confided earlier. "Why, you would think he was going to coach another 100 years. He never lets his emotion hinder him or affect his coaching."

"That was the worst movie you've ever picked," Jordan said, chiding Howard a bit about his selection of "Guerrilla Raid" as the movie the team would see on Friday night. The movie was about Tito and his rise to power in the east European country.

"I thought you'd like that, Coach," Howard said, grinning, "being that you're such a history buff." He knew that if Jordan liked the movie, he would question the selection. That too was ritual.

"I never could tell who Tito was," Jordan retorted. "And I feel like I've walked all over Yugoslavia."

But there was more pressing business. Mrs. Jordan had forgotten her parking pass. Athletic Director Lee Hayley brought another. Auburn President Harry M. Philpott came by. Someone at Midway Plaza had given Mrs. Philpott a gift for Jordan. The AU President was delivering it.

Jordan smiled and unwrapped a decoupage plaque bearing his picture and the caption: "Old coaches never die, they just fade away."

The Auburn coach had an omelet, three link sausages, grits, biscuits, and coffee for breakfast.

Dr. Nick Wheeler, Jordan's longtime friend and personal physician from LaFayette came by bearing a good luck message from a friend in Georgia.

The trio, Jordan, Wheeler, and Howard, adjourned to the Sheraton lobby to continue their pre-game rituals.

Jordan is a member of the old school. He's a mixer, a mingler. He enjoys getting in with those who support his team and his efforts.

He does, that is, until the pre-game meal. That's when the game face goes on.

Saturday's pre-game meal was scheduled for 10:30. A wake up call was left for the players at 10 a.m. They began to drift into their private dining room about 10:15.

Jordan spoke with them individually and in pairs.

Philpott, an ordained minister, asked God's blessing on the group of men assembled "and all they stand for." He concluded by asking that they "always be mindful of the needs of others."

Presumably Alabama, the day's opponent, was not included in the "others."

The scene caused Hayley, a member of Jordan's first team at Auburn in 1951, to reflect back on his last game. Auburn lost 25-7 to Alabama.

"We were pretty beat up going into the game," Hayley recalled. "I got hurt in the game and right before the end, Coach came over and thanked me for what I had done and tried to do.

"I find myself in somewhat of a reverse position today."

For a moment, Auburn's athletic director, a guarded and proud man, showed emotion.

Jordan gathered his players and coaches together for their last ride at 1:00. After a short team meeting, they boarded two buses and left for Legion Field. The buses pulled on to Birmingham's Third Avenue at 1:29, one minute ahead of schedule.

Jordan sat on the first bus, right behind the driver. Dr. Wheeler sat next to him. When he got on the bus, he looked at his regular seat and paused.

"No reason to change anything now," Jordan said, looking at his old friend and smiling.

Only the bleating of the bus flashers and the hum of changing gears could be heard above the wheels grinding on the pavement.

The players walked out on Legion Field's new astro-turf for the first time. Jordan stayed behind in the dressing room as was his custom. The players returned to put on their armor.

At 2:25, Ralph Jordan stepped onto Legion Field for his last great battle.

Hundreds of photographers greeted him with snapping shutters.

Alabama's Paul Bryant was waiting near the goal post when Jordan stepped from under the North Stands. He strolled over to greet his old rival.

Bryant spoke first. "Good to see you," he said. "How you doing?"

"Well, here we are again..." said Jordan. "I'm doing fine. And you?"

All the little pleasantries of two men whose teams will want to beat each other to a pulp in the next two hours.

In a matter of time, 40 minutes to be exact, Jordan and Bryant were battling for the last time. Bryant would win 28-0.

But there was probably little talk of the game on that almost empty bus rushing toward Auburn late Saturday night.

Between the roast beef sandwiches and soft drinks, there was probably talk of Lloyd Nix, Pat Sullivan, Mike Kolen, National Championships, Gator Bowls, Orange and Sugar Bowls, blocked punts, and all of the other little things that have gone into making the last 25 years—the Jordan Era—the most glorious in the long annals of Auburn football.

That sweet wine, born only by the vintage of success down through the years, was being shared by all. Shared bountifully.

The Opelika-Auburn News
November 30, 1975

James Ralph Jordan _____

This is the story of James Ralph Jordan. It is one of the greatest sports stories ever told. Space and time do not permit full disclosure. Indeed, the story is not yet finished. It is still being written.

The story begins in Selma, Alabama, September 25, 1910. Young Ralph Jordan, son of a railroad man, was like other boys of his time. He grew up on sports, but there was no television or radio. Auburn and national acclaim were far away.

His organized athletic career began in 1918. His first coach, Paul Grist, says he will "never forget the day that little tow-headed boy in overalls drug a stalk of sugar cane in the front door of the YMCA and said, 'I want to play basketball.' "

That was the beginning of a life-long friendship between the coach, Grist, and the boy, Jordan. Countless thousands of young men who followed them have been better because of them. Grist's YMCA motto was "Don't wait to be a great man. Be a great boy." Jordan was a great boy, Grist recalls, and together, they have helped other boys become great men.

The young Jordan participated in every sport Selma High School and the YMCA

"Winning the Heisman Trophy was the second highest honor of my life. The first was playing for Coach Jordan." — Pat Sullivan, quarterback, 1969-71.

---

offered. He was not a spectacular athlete, but what he lacked in ability, he made up in determination and desire.

He graduated from Selma High School in 1927, the holder of the state shot-put record and a diploma. The Great Depression was approaching. Money was scarce, so the boy, 16 going on 17, went to work for the state highway department to pay for his first year at college. Determination. Even then his philosophy of success was being formed. Much later, when he was a great man, he would refer to this philosophy as his "Seven D's of Success." They are: Discipline, Desire to excel, Determination, Dedication, Dependability, Desperation and Damn it anyway — do something.

He entered Auburn — then Alabama Polytechnic Institute — in the fall of 1928, a year behind his high school class. He pledged Theta Chi Fraternity, worked at a boarding house and quickly established himself as one of Auburn's most promising young athletes, participating in football, basketball and baseball.

"I have the same deep respect for Coach Jordan that I have for my own father." — Frank D'Agostino, tackle, 1953-55.

He was especially good at basketball. His two-hand set shot and his knowledge of the give-and-go — which Grist said Jordan and a friend invented — would prove deadly to Auburn opponents in the next four years.

As a sophomore in 1929, he led the old Southern Conference in scoring with 112 points. "That's nothing nowadays," he would remark nearly half a century later. "Mike Mitchell scores that many in three games."

"Lefty," as he was called, was elected captain his second year on the team. "He is one of the few that have been elected captain in their junior year," the *Glomerata* recorded. "This alone speaks for itself."

In football, he was a center. In baseball, he was a pitcher-first baseman. Again, what he lacked in ability, he made up in desire and determination. That was becoming a Jordan trademark.

"There wasn't a harder fighter or a more likeable man on the Tiger squad," the 1932 *Glomerata* records. "Although his play could not be called spectacular, he was

---

"He never forgot I was a person first and a football player second." — David Beverly, punter, 1970-72.

---

as dependable a center as any team in the South could boast of. Not one bad pass to the backs is recorded against him in his last year of play."

Jordan's greatest moment as a baseball player came in 1932 when he pitched Auburn to the Southern Conference championship with a 5-3 victory over Florida. "A roundhouse out and an annie-over," is the way he describes his best pitches. He modestly admits, even today, that he hit a three-run homerun to win the game.

Jordan's athletic contributions are one of the reasons the 1932 *Glomerata* proudly, almost jubilantly, proclaimed, "Auburn is back in athletics. 'War Eagle' is once again a national anthem."

James Ralph Jordan was the complete student. He was treasurer of his senior class, a member of Blue Key and Scabbard and Blade. He was tapped for Spades, the highest honor an Auburn man may attain.

The young Jordan learned early, however, that life would not always be kind to

---

"He shows me how a man ought to live." — George Jones, 14-year-old Auburn fan from Selma, Jordan's hometown.

---

him, that it would kick hard and unfairly. Upon graduation from Auburn, he accepted a coaching job at a small Alabama high school — to this day he says the name of the school isn't important — but when school officials noticed that Jordan's religious preference was "Catholic," they quickly withdrew their offer. In later years, that would be called discrimination.

Jordan's coach, Chet Wynne, heard about it. He was not going to let this happen to one of his boys. He offered Jordan a job as an assistant freshman football coach. He would also assist with basketball.

Thus Jordan's stay at Auburn would continue. It would be interrupted only twice in the next 44 years, once voluntarily and once by war.

In 1934, Jordan, now head basketball coach, traveled to South Carolina. While

---

"Coach Jordan is an example of a man who has left his mark on the lives of thousands of individuals forever. We will never know where his influence will end." — Dr. Harry M. Philpott, President, Auburn University.

---

there, he met a Columbia belle named Evelyn. It was an eventful meeting. Three years later, they were married. In the coming years, they would have three children, Susan, Darby, and Ralph, Jr., better known as "Pee Wee."

In a matter of weeks after the Japanese bombed Pearl Harbor, Coach Jordan became Lieutenant Jordan. Over the next four years his life, like that of most

American men, would be risked many times. Only his life would be risked more than most.

He was one of the few soldiers who participated in four of the war's major invasions, North Africa, Sicily, D-Day, and Okinawa. On the 30th anniversary of D-Day in 1974, he recalled loading into those small landing crafts and heading for the smoke enshrouded French shore. "There had been a lot of carrying on the night before," he said, "but it was silent in those landing crafts. I never saw an atheist or an agnostic

---

"Coach Jordan has proven himself a winner not only in the field of athletics but also in the hearts and minds of millions of people who have come to recognize him as 'Mr. Auburn Football.'" — George C. Wallace, Governor of Alabama.

---

when it came time to hit the beach." Jordan hit Utah Beach at H plus two hours. A short time later, he qualified for the Purple Heart.

When the world was once again safe for democracy, Jordan returned to Auburn. He found a strange Auburn, an alien Auburn, the likes of which he had never known before. When he and other coaches had marched off to war, they were assured they would be welcomed back with open arms. They were not. Coaching regimes had changed, and the new head coach was not overjoyed having strangers added to his staff.

These were not happy years for the Jordans. There were doubts, questions and serious decisions to be made regarding the future. Jordan, now 35, turned to an old and trusted friend, Cliff Hare. Hare, who was a quarterback on Auburn's first football team, was dean of the school of chemistry and chairman of the faculty athletic committee. He was also a former president of the Southern Conference. Jordan asked no

---

"I'll remember Shug Jordan for what he is, for the old-fashioned values he always stood for, for the courtly touch of class which has always been his trademark in times of prosperity or of adversity." — John Pruett, The Huntsville Times.

---

favors. He wanted only advice and a friendly ear. Hare sympathized with the young coach, his friend, and gave him valuable advice and counsel.

The two men spent many a Sunday afternoon visiting on the front porch of the Hare home on South Gay Street. Twenty eight years later, in 1973, their names would be side by side on Auburn's Jordan-Hare Stadium.

The Jordans left Auburn with sad but anticipating hearts in 1946. He had coached Auburn basketball to some of its greatest years, but his football future at Auburn

---

"Nearly all successful college football coaches enjoy great popular support, but I can think of no one who is more admired than you. Your appointment to Auburn University's Board of Trustees is a unique vote of confidence in your leadership abilities." — Gerald R. Ford, President of the United States.

---

looked bleak. The Jordans were bound for Miami and professional football. In less than a year, the anticipation was gone and they were moving again. The Seahawks, Miami's first venture into professional football, failed. Georgia had called. Jordan had answered.

At Athens, Jordan was line coach for Wally Butts and head basketball coach. Butts was having some of his best teams, and Jordan became Georgia's winningest basketball coach, a distinction he held until the early 1970's. These were happy days for the Jordans and for Georgia.

Auburn, however, was unhappy. Very unhappy. The Tigers had won only three football games in three years. There was no money in the bank and very little prospect of getting any. Auburn alumni were torn asunder, pulling in several different directions.

Jeff Beard, an old classmate of Jordan's, was hired as athletic director in 1951. His assignment — bring some semblance of order out of the chaos — was simple, but his task was hard. His first act was to hire Ralph Jordan as Auburn's head football coach. The rest of the story is well known. "War Eagle" once again became a national sports anthem.

The next 25 years would be known as the Jordan era. Auburn would win 175 games, appear in 12 bowls, produce 20 All-Americans, 67 all-conference performers, a Heisman Trophy winner (Pat Sullivan, 1971), an Outland Award winner (Zeke

---

"Shug Jordan has always been one of my favorite people in the coaching profession. He has contributed so much with dignity, his handling of his players, his policy of never alibiing in defeat, and his graciousness in victory. All of us at Georgia Tech have the greatest affection and respect for Coach Jordan." — Bobby Dodd, Georgia Tech.

Smith, 1958) and a Jacobs Award winner (Tucker Frederickson, 1964). Auburn would win national and conference championships.

On his way to becoming a legend in his own time, Jordan would surpass coaching greats such as Bobby Dodd and General R.R. Neyland in total victories. A coach would have to win eight games a year for 22 years to surpass his record of 176-83-7.

Jordan's teams were virtually unbeatable at home, posting an 88-15-1 record in Auburn. The Jordan Tigers were especially ferocious on homecomings. The Tigers won 22 times. They lost only two. One ended in a tie.

In addition, he
* was the first SEC coach to win 100 games at his alma mater.
* was the fourth winningest active coach in the country when he retired.
* averaged seven wins a year in his 25-year career.
* was head coach at his alma mater longer than any other coach in the history of the SEC.
* was the first active coach to have a stadium named in his honor (2) — Jordan-Hare Stadium in Auburn and Ralph Jordan Track and Field in Selma.
* is a member of the Alabama Academy of Honor.
* is a charter member of the Alabama Sports Hall of Fame.
* was National Coach of the Year.
* was SEC Coach of the Year (several times).
* is a member of Omicron Delta Kappa, Phi Eta Sigma and numerous other honoraries.
* was appointed to the Auburn University Board of Trustees by Gov. George C. Wallace.

A parkway in Auburn and a meeting room in Selma were named for him. Scholarships were established in his honor. No other athletic figure anywhere has accomplished so much at one school. James Ralph Jordan, the man called "Shug," has done it with quiet, unobtrusive dignity and a gentlemanly demeanor.

On Jordan's retirement after the 1975 season, David Davidson of *The Atlanta Journal* wrote: "Shug Jordan will be missed by many come the fall of 1976. Jordan offered a dignity to Southern football that will be difficult to replace. The Deep South will share Auburn's loss of this gentleman-coach."

Phillip Marshall of *The Birmingham Post-Herald* put it this way: "No matter what level of greatness it may attain, Auburn football will never be the same."

Both were so right.

Appreciation and Commitment
Special A-Day Program
May 8, 1976

Pizza and Patriotism

AUBURN—Patriotism is alive and well on the college campus.

It was late February, time of the annual Step-Sing competition at Auburn University. It was all accomplished in the finest collegiate tradition. Twenty-nine fraternities and sororities competed for giant loving cups and more than 3,000 turned out to hear their fellow students sing selections ranging from a "Four Seasons Medley" to "Songs America Loves to Sing," a collection of advertising jingles.

Not far away from Auburn that night, another tradition was about to unfold. A few people were already drinking beer and eating pizza at the War Eagle Supper Club, Auburn's answer to "the table down at Mory's and the place where Louis dwells." It is the traditional gathering place of all step-sing winners. There, all together, the winners serenade their dates, their friends, each other and anyone else within a mile or so.

About 10:30 this particular evening, the news came. Phi Gamma Delta, Farmhouse, Alpha Delta Pi and Kappa Delta had won. "Well," said Mildred Williams, the proprietor of the War Eagle, "they'll be here soon." She began to make a few last minute preparations.

An hour and half, many songs, beers and pizzas later, it was time to close.

"Reckon you can get word to them that we're closing?" she said with a tired smile.

"I'll try," said a friend who had volunteered to help jerk beers. "Just quit selling beer."

The friend waded back through hundreds of singing students and finally got to the self-appointed song leaders. "Time to close," he shouted, giving the old radio cut-off sign to deliriously happy singers.

"All right, everybody," the song leader shouted, "Sign-off time. Let's sing the National Anthem and adjourn to the house for more partying."

Almost to a student, the young men and women stood at attention, held their beer and soft drinks at their sides, and began to sing, "O, say can you see..."

When the song was over, the students moved quietly toward the door.

Mildred shook her head. So did others. What they had just witnessed was more moving than any Bicentennial event or "Bicentennial Moment" could ever hope to be.

That old Americanism is alive and well at Auburn.

They had just seen proof of it.

The Birmingham News
March 4, 1976

An Auburn Superman ───────────────────

In the old television series, George Reeves played the part of Superman.

At Auburn, Harvey Glance is Superman.

In human terms, he is faster than a speeding bullet, more powerful than a locomotive and able to leap tall buildings in a single bound. About the only thing Harvey Glance can't do is fly, and there are those who will argue that point. Any man who can run 30 miles an hour, they say, isn't running. He's flying.

This is the Harvey Glance who will lead the Auburn track team into the SEC track meet this weekend in Athens, Ga.

He really is almost Superman. At least super human. He runs 100 meters in 9.9 seconds. No one has ever run it faster. He bench presses 305 pounds, more than many professional football players, and he can jump flat-footed from the ground to the top of a Volkswagen. That's where the leaping tall buildings part comes in.

Glance, a freshman from Phenix City, is a track phenomenon. He stands 5-7 and weighs 145 pounds. He has been described as a duffle bag stuffed with bowling balls. It is an apt description. Muscles bulge through his taunt brown skin.

In addition to running, running and running, Glance, who hopes to coach someday, spends several hours a day working out with weights. This, he believes, will help his arms pump faster and his legs move quicker, enabling him to run still faster.

He credits weight work, a faster start from the blocks and a relaxed mental state when he runs for his meteoric rise to world acclaim. "For awhile I was reacting to the start of the other runners instead of the gun," he says, "and I'm always on my form and relaxing while I run."

Harvey's already run himself into the Olympic Trials in the 100 and 200 meters, and if he makes it to Montreal, the childhood dream of every American boy could come true for him.

For Glance, it began in the sixth grade. He had always known he had speed. He found that out by racing friends in the streets of Phenix City. When he was named city champion, something stirred in him. He realized then that he was born to run.

He realized it three years later when, in the ninth grade, he watched the 1972 Olympics on television. He saw American track stars, clad in red, white and blue. That, too, stirred something within him. He's never seen an Olympic medal, but like most Americans, he knows the words to the "Star Spangled Banner" by heart. He's tried to imagine what it would be like, standing there singing, the medal around his neck and the flag rising slowly over him, but he can't visualize it. Not quite. "That's something you have to experience," he says, somewhat modestly.

Fame and world acclaim have not affected Glance. He is still "just ole Harvey Glance" as he puts it, and he is, in the truest sense of the word, a team man. He can be seen moving about the track when a meet is in progress giving encouragement to his teammates as they participate in their individual events.

Unlike many sprinters and distance runners he doesn't try to psyche out his opponents with the silent treatment or threats of what he is going to do to them when the gun sounds. "I just let my running do the talking," he says. It speaks well.

Two times this spring he has equaled the world 100 meter record of 9.9 seconds. He thought he had broken it at LSU. He was clocked at 9.73, at 9.87 and at 9.90.

Instead of averaging the times, however, the middle time had to be taken and rounded off. That made his time a 9.9, only a tie for the world record.

Glance was disappointed, but not despondent. "I think I'll see that 9.8 again," he said, in a rare outward display of confidence.

It could come this weekend in Athens where Auburn figures to battle Tennessee and Florida for the SEC title. Glance gives Tennessee the edge because of the Vols' depth in field events. "We'll have to have some help from other schools to win it all," he said.

Harvey will compete in the 100, the 220, the long jump and the 440 relay.

He expects to run well. He expects to run well in every race he enters. "I run against the clock," he explains, "not against the opposition." That means he is going for the world record every time out. That, he believes, is why some of his best times have come in low prestige events against what would be considered inferior competition. Some of his best times, however, have also come in the big events against some of the best sprinters in the world, such as Ivory Crockett, the world record holder.

Glance's gleaming record and Auburn's chances in the SEC meet have sparked a renewed interest in track on the Plains.

An Auburn student rushed into his fraternity house not long ago. "Guess who's at Burger King?" he shouted.

"Who?" came the reply.

"Harvey Glance."

"Let's go get his autograph," said a third student, rushing toward the door. That's how far track and a young man who wants to be the best in the world have come at Auburn. He could go farther.

The Birmingham News
May 12, 1976

Harvey Glance did set the world record and he also won an Olympic Gold Medal as part of the United States' 4x100 relay team in the 1976 Olympic Games in Montreal. He was named head track coach at Auburn in May of 1991, succeeding his coach, Mel Rosen.

Knute Rockne Christian _____

The two-way football player, the one who played both offense and defense, is a product of a bygone era.

So is another kind of two-way performer, the football player who can claim to have played for both Auburn and Alabama.

Knute Rockne Christian was the last of his breed, the last man to toil on practice fields both on the Plains and at the Capstone.

Christian—whose only tie to Notre Dame is his name—was on the Auburn team briefly in 1951, Ralph Jordan's first year. He transferred to Alabama that same year and started every game for the Crimson Tide in 1954 and 1955.

This is how it happened:

As a senior at Tuscaloosa High in 1950, Christian was sought by both schools. He finally became one of the 140 players signed by Earl Brown, the desperate Auburn coach who, in an effort to save his job, "signed everybody who could read or write," according to Christian.

When Alabama Assistant Coach Hank Crisp—later athletic director—learned of Christian's decision, he sought the young athlete out and gave him some sage Alabama advice. "If you want to be a farmer, son, go live with a farmer," said Crisp. "Don't go down there and try to learn it out of no book."

Not even signing every athlete recommended by an alumnus could save Brown's job. Auburn's 0-10 season in 1950 took its toll. In February of 1951, Ralph Jordan was named Auburn's head football coach.

The fall of 1951 was one of the toughest things Christian ever experienced, before or after.

"Coach Jordan ruled 'em out that fall," Christian recalls. "Players were leaving there on trains, in cars, buses, wagons, anyway they could get out of town. They left in droves."

Christian stayed. He made it through all the tough work, but on the day he was supposed to dress out for the Vanderbilt game, Jordan's first as head coach, Knute Rockne Christian left the Plains.

Looking back, he isn't sure why he left.

"I signed with Auburn because I liked the people. They were the friendliest people I've ever met. I have as much respect and love for Coach Jordan as any man who ever walked. My leaving had nothing to do with him. I guess I just got homesick."

Like a lot of 17-year-old freshmen, Christian went home and found himself "out of the frying pan, into the fire."

"I never unpacked my bags," Christian laughs. "Daddy loaded me up and took me to Columbia Military School. I played the 1951 season at Columbia as a center-linebacker."

Later that year, Christian wanted to come home. The Tide wanted him, but Auburn would have to release him from his scholarship. With an uncle who was in the service with Jordan during World War II, Christian went to see the Auburn coach.

"Coach was very understanding about it," remembers Christian. "He wanted me to do what was best for me. 'If you want to play at Alabama,' he said, 'I hope you get to play all four years.'"

That, however, was up to Southeastern Conference Commissioner Bernie Moore. Auburn gave Christian an outright release, but Moore ruled that he must sit out the customary two years.

"The fact that I waited," says Christian, "shows how much I really wanted to play football. It's tough practicing that long and not getting to play."

He made the best of it. During the 1952 and 1953 seasons, Christian headed a team of scrubs known as "Knute's Brutes." They whipped the Tide into shape for two bowl games, the Orange and Cotton, and often gave the varsity more competition than it wanted.

"We'd laugh when we got to go in early and the varsity stayed out late," Christian laughs. "But they would get even with us in the dressing room."

By 1954 he was eligible to put on his red jersey and hear those "R-o-l-l-l-l Tides!" ringing for him.

Christian was a 60-minute player for Alabama, but these were not good years for the Tide.

The 1954 team, with Christian at center and linebacker, won four of its first five games, then lost four of the last six for a 4-5-2 record. At the end there was a 28-0 loss to Auburn.

The next year was even worse. It was the low point of Alabama football. It was an 0-10 year and Auburn won again, 26-0.

The brightest spot of Christian's career, however, came against Auburn. "I broke through end and blocked two extra points," he says. "Other than my name, I got more publicity out of that than anything else I ever did."

The Auburn game, of course, was special—extra special—to Christian.

"I didn't know too many of the Auburn players by then," he recalls. "Most of the 140 I came with never made it through. The ones I did remember, Dave Middleton, Bobby Freeman, Jack Locklear, and Jack Clark, gave me a hard time.

"We didn't talk that much during the game, but every time we'd hit one another they'd really lay it on me. I made a tackle near the Auburn bench on a kickoff and I thought Clark was going to whip me to death. He just kept slapping me on the shoulder pads and helmet, cheering me on. It was all in fun."

Christian, now a Tuscaloosa businessman, says he doesn't regret a thing. "A lot of people still introduce me as an Alabama football player," he says, "and that has to help business up here."

Where does he stand each November in the Auburn-Alabama game?

"I want Auburn to win 'em all but one," he said, smiling. "Then I've got to go with the Tide."

The Birmingham News
August 29, 1976

Others such as Jimmy Jeffcoat and Merv Romine may have practiced at both schools, but Knute Rockne Christian, as far as can be determined, is the last man to practice at one school and ultimately play at the other. Jeffcoat went from Auburn to Alabama while Romine transferred from Alabama to Auburn.

Phil Gargis—a Competitor

Who said Phil Gargis couldn't pass?

Certainly not his mother, Mrs. Lila Gargis of Ford City, Alabama.

"I've always known he could throw," she said between smiles and tears Saturday afternoon. "I've seen him throw rocks at his brothers all his life. I know he can throw."

And throw young Phil Gargis did Saturday in Legion Field. He threw at almost anyone wearing a blue shirt and, more often than not, he was right on target.

When Tennessee's long afternoon was over, Gargis had completed 10 of 13 passes for 224 yards, three for touchdowns, and Auburn people were talking about a new dynamic duo.

Half of the old duo, Pat Sullivan, the 1971 Heisman Trophy winner, watched from the stands as Gargis hit flanker Chris Vacarella, the other half of the new duo, four times for 141 yards and one touchdown.

Gargis' coach, Doug Barfield, chided members of the press in his post-game interview. "Maybe now," he said, "some of you will write about Phil Gargis' passing. If there's a finer competitor anywhere, I don't know who he is."

No one could question Gargis' competitiveness or his dedication.

He could hardly walk after the game. He needed help from writers, trainers and teammates as he sat down for a second post-game interview. He had been cornered once already, in the shower, now he was cornered again. That was more than Tennessee could do all afternoon.

"Just give all the credit to the offensive line," he said. "Any praise should go to them. They worked their tails off. Anybody can throw when they have the time I had back there. Anybody can."

Gargis ached, obviously, as he talked. He grimaced again and again.

"Where are you hurting?" someone asked.

"Everywhere," he replied, "but it's just the every-game bruises."

He did admit, however, that those every-game bruises were more severe than usual. Never had he been hit harder. Never had he hurt more. But he did not hurt in the heart. And that, late Saturday afternoon, was the only place that mattered.

"We had to have this one," he said. "The whole team worked their tails off this week. It'd been a long time since we'd won one, and it was no trouble getting up for Tennessee. It never is at Auburn."

The Auburn offense, he said, had made up its collective mind to do whatever it took to win this game.

"We'd been going up and down the field," Gargis explained, "and we knew that if we had to do it again, we'd just go out there and do it."

Gargis, of course, led the Auburn charge. In addition to his 224 yards passing, Gargis gained 73 yards rushing and scored one touchdown.

It was his best game as an Auburn quarterback. None other can come close.

He called the Auburn effort a team victory and it was, but it was a personal victory, too. There won't be too much criticism of Phil Gargis' passing, not this week, and maybe not this season.

ABC-television named him the outstanding offensive player of the game, and

Auburn will receive a $1,000 academic scholarship in his honor, but none of it seemed to matter much to Phil Gargis.

He was tired. He was hurting. Auburn had won, and he wanted to see his mother. She was waiting outside.

The Opelika-Auburn News
September 26, 1976

Footnote To History ─────────────

"We weren't thinking about football," the Auburn player said. "All we wanted to do was get the hell out of there."

The place was Havana, Cuba, the year, 1936, the first and only Havana Bowl, also called the Bacardi Bowl and the Rhumba Bowl.

That game, the only bowl game ever played on foreign soil, became the subject of renewed interest in Auburn recently when Carlos Enrique spoke to the Auburn Rotary Club. Enrique was Cuba's minister of sports in 1936, and he was the man who booked Jack Meagher's Tigers for the first and only Havana Bowl.

His story reveals why the Auburn player (Wilton Kilgore) was more interested in getting out of Havana than in playing football.

The idea of a Cuban National Sports Festival originated in the mind of President Machado Gomez. He thought such a sports festival featuring American teams and athletes would increase Yankee confidence in his country's stability, bring tourists there and get his country's youth interested in something other than tearing down the government.

He was not after teams with the best records, Enrique said. He was after good teams with players who represented the best in American youth.

Tram Sessions, an Alabama football player, told Enrique that Auburn might be a good team for his country's sports festival. After watching the Alabama-Tennessee game on Saturday, Enrique came to Auburn on Monday.

He remembers that Auburn had a "cow pasture practice field and no dressing rooms." Players dressed at the school and walked to practice. If they had a good practice, they got to walk back. If not, they had to jog back. That, along with Auburn's 5-2-1 record, impressed Enrique. He signed Auburn for the grand sum of $7,500 and a share of the proceeds.

Meagher and Auburn wanted to play either Pittsburgh or Penn State, both powers of Eastern football. By the time Enrique got to Pennsylvania, the picture had changed.

Villanova had just upset Penn State and risen to the top of the Eastern football establishment. The Villanova coach, Clipper Smith, jumped at the chance to play Auburn.

He had been a teammate of Meagher's at Notre Dame and, he told Enrique, "I want to play him and beat the pants off him."

Such were the events that brought Auburn and Villanova to Cuba the last week in December. Meanwhile, in Havana, the fuse had grown short.

President Gomez had sought to cut the military budget. He was not powerful enough to do it and during the Christmas season, just days before the game, he was impeached. Thrown out might be a more accurate term. Colonel Fulgencio Batista and a group of sergeants overthrew the elite of the army and took command of the country. Auburn and Villanova watched helplessly.

There was some doubt as to whether or not the Havana Bowl would be played. Batista wanted recognition at the game, but Enrique refused. The festival had been Gomez' idea and Gomez would receive credit for it if anyone did.

Such were the volatile conditions in Havana when Auburn and Villanova kicked off at 2 p.m., January 1, 1937. Guns were in evidence everywhere, the Latin sun bore down and when the game was over, there was an average weight loss of 15-18 pounds per nervous man.

Auburn scored in the second quarter on a 40-yard run by Billy Hitchcock. Villanova blocked a punt in the fourth quarter and scored. The game ended in a 7-7 tie.

At the half, Jesse Owens, the United States' Olympic hero, ran against a race horse and won by 12 yards. He had beaten the horse so bad in trial runs that Cuban officials wanted to even up the race a bit, but Owens refused.

Enrique's refusal to recognize Batista was not taken lightly. He was given a police escort for "protection." After a week, he was told to leave Cuba and never return. Twenty years passed before he dared go back.

Prior to the Georgia Tech game, Enrique, now a resident of Birmingham, made his first trip to Auburn in 40 years. On his last trip, he had recruited Auburn for the Havana Bowl.

Now, he's looking for two Georgia tickets.

Auburn Football Illustrated
Auburn vs. Florida State
October 23, 1976

The Bacardi Bowl, as it is commonly called, was the first and, to date, only post-season bowl game played on foreign soil.

Forever More, an Auburn Tiger —————

For Chris Vacarella and Phil Gargis, when the end came, there were thoughts of the beginning.

Four years ago, as David Langner scooted into the end zone with the second blocked punt and a 17-16 Auburn victory, Chris Vacarella leaped a chain link fence and joined the celebration.

It was one of the first public signs that he would, indeed, go to Auburn.

Gargis remembers that day, too. He remembers the Auburn victory and he remembers how impressed he was with Auburn, the Auburn people and their friendliness.

Their football careers ended Saturday in a way far different from the way they began. Alabama won 38-7.

Chris Vacarella and Phil Gargis never knew what it was like to beat Alabama. It was their fondest goal, but one they never reached.

For Gargis, it is his greatest athletic disappointment.

For Vacarella — well, he "wishes it had ended differently." At least once.

They came close in 1974. Auburn lost 17-13 and would have won had Thomas Gossom not stepped out of bounds before catching a touchdown pass from Gargis. That would have made Auburn a winner, 20-17.

Things looked bright in defeat that night. A veteran Auburn team would return for 1975. It could have been one of Auburn's greatest years. It wasn't.

This year was one of Auburn's worst. Not since 1952, twenty-four years ago has an Auburn team lost eight games. In the last two years, Auburn has won only six games. There have been 14 losses and two ties.

Instead of sharing in a great Auburn tradition and building memories to warm the heart for years to come, Gargis, Vacarella and 13 other seniors have been struggling to put Auburn's football program back on track. Auburn football has not been the same since Memphis State took a 24-0 halftime lead in the opening game of 1975.

What will it take to turn Auburn football around?

With the sights and sounds of Alabama's 38-7 victory heavy around them, Gargis and Vacarella offered a few ideas.

Just as he has for 16 of the last 22 football Saturdays, Phil Gargis said, "We'll just have to try harder."

He still used the pronoun "we."

He probably always will.

"It's going to make a lot of hard work and dedication on the part of the younger players," he said. "The older players are going to have to provide some leadership and buy some time for the younger players to mature. We've just got to fill up some shoes."

It can, Gargis said, be done in one year.

"It will take a team-wide effort," he explained. "It's a matter of rebuilding everywhere. It will take a lot of hard work, but it can be done."

Vacarella remembered the two blocked punts when he walked into Legion Field Saturday.

"I was thinking about that today," he said after the game. "I looked at a spot about where I came over the fence. I'll never forget that day. It was a feeling I never experienced again."

What will it take before all Auburn can experience that grand and glorious feeling again?

"We'll just have to get some folks who really want it," Vacarella said. "Folks who want it bad."

There was another thing, too.

"We've got to start winning again," he said. "We've got to get that old feeling back."

Vacarella used the pronoun "we," too.

Neither had any second thoughts about coming to Auburn. If they had it to do over again, they wouldn't do a thing differently — except win more.

"I'd never be happy anywhere but Auburn," Gargis said.

The Opelika-Auburn News
November 28, 1976

Big Zeke

The National Champions...

Oh, how I worshipped them, how I adored them.

Lloyd Nix, Jimmy "Red" Phillips, "Big Red," they called him, Bobby Hoppe, Billy Atkins, Tommy Lorino, Tim Baker, Jackie Burkett, Zeke Smith...

Big Zeke. Number 61. How I did worship him. How I adored him. He alone, above all others, was my favorite football player. He was everything I could ever hope to be, the epitome. I must have written him 15 times that year asking for an autograph. I never got it. He never responded. Not once.

I was only 10 then, and I suppose I should say that I have long since outgrown my adoration for Zeke Smith, but he is like your favorite cowboy. He endures. I finally met Big Zeke a couple of years ago. Even then, I was thrilled, maybe a bit overwhelmed.

There were others, Jerry Wilson, Lamar Rawson, Jim Jeffrey, Bryant Harvard, James Warren, Ben Preston, Frank LaRussa, Dan Presley, Morris Savage, Cleve Wester and many more, three teams of them.

I knew them all and I worshipped them all. An uncle said I could name every player on the Auburn football team, his age, height, weight and hometown but couldn't name the 12 disciples. He was right. He might have been right.

Have you tried to name the 12 disciples lately?

I wish I could say I saw all 10 games, every one of them, but I didn't. I didn't even listen to them all.

I don't remember a thing about the 7-0 victory over Tennessee that started it all, not a single thing. Nor do I remember the 40-7 win over Chattanooga or the 6-0 win over Kentucky.

The 3-0 win over Georgia Tech—I remember that one. I walked into the hardware store just when my father and another uncle—not the one who knew the 12 disciples—turned the radio over to Mr. Jack Wilson, an Alabama fan. They were smiling. "Auburn won," Daddy said, and I smiled, too, because he was smiling.

It should be pointed out, I learned later, that Auburn had won in Atlanta only twice in 17 years.

I missed the Houston game. My family went to a high school game that Friday night, and at the half we got word that Auburn was way ahead. Somebody said Auburn scored on the first play from scrimmage. The *Birmingham Post Herald* confirmed it all the next morning: Auburn 48-Houston 7. Nix to Phillips on the first play, a 71-yard touchdown.

I listened to the Florida game in the back bedroom. Auburn won 13-0.

The next week, Mississippi State scored late in the second quarter and led 7-0 at the half. Normally, I would listen to Tom Hamlin interview people at the half. Not that Saturday. I spent the half pacing the floor or on my knees praying.

God came through. Auburn blocked a punt and Auburn won 15-7.

I didn't listen to much of the Georgia game. It was too close, too hard on me, a mere child.

I walked into the hardware store just as the game was over. Auburn won 6-0, but something else important had happened. Some team called Notre Dame had beaten a team called Oklahoma. It was Oklahoma's first loss in 47 games. Daddy said that would probably make Auburn the Number One team in the nation.

It did.

I don't remember a thing about the Florida State game. I was in Tuscaloosa watching Alabama beat Southern Mississippi 29-2. I was not impressed. I was an Auburn man.

Our family had four tickets to the Auburn-Alabama game that year. All four were on the top row of the South end zone, the bad end zone. It was freezing cold and the wind was blowing straight at us.

I rarely waved my orange "AUBURN" pennant. It was too cold. Big Zeke, my hero, recovered a fumble and Auburn scored on the second or third play from scrimmage. It was 34-0 at the half. I loved it then, and I'd love it even more now.

Five minutes from the end, my father began folding our blanket. "You aren't leaving, are you?" one of my uncles asked. "Yes," my father said, "we're going to beat the crowd. We'll meet you at the car."

"I can't believe we're about to go undefeated and win the national championship," my uncle said, "and you're going to leave."

Auburn led 40-0 and Daddy and I were halfway down the aisle. When the game was over, when Auburn was celebrating one of its greatest moments ever, we were in the john.

Auburn wins the national championship and I'm in the john.

I have long since forgiven my father. My life has taken a dramatic turn for the better since then, thanks in large part to him.

To him and to heroes like Zeke Smith.

You know, I might yet get that autograph.

Auburn Football Illustrated
Auburn vs. Arizona
September 10, 1977

There's no hero like the first hero.

From One Generation to the Next ———

There's an interesting story developing in Auburn's offensive line. It's a story that may have an effect on Auburn football for years to come.

It's not a news story, actually. It began a long time ago, three years to be exact, when Lee Gross was playing his final year of football here.

It continued last week and will continue the remainder of this season. Then, three years from now, another chapter will be written to what by then will be an old, old story. Part of it has been told; there is much more.

Let's begin at the beginning, as Auburn was preparing to play Tennessee in 1974. It was the first conference game of the year and a big, big game to the Tigers, especially to a young sophomore guard named Lynn Johnson. He had always heard of Tennessee, and the prospect of playing the Big Orange the next Saturday was a little more than he was prepared to accept at that particular time.

"Aw, don't worry about them," Gross told Johnson. "They're no different from anybody else we've played. They're people just like we are."

Johnson remembered those words and last week, when the Tigers were preparing to play Tennessee again, they came vividly to mind again.

Young Brad Everett, a freshman guard from Alabaster, had moved to the starting unit. The prospect of playing Tennessee in Neyland Stadium may have been a little more than he was prepared to accept at that particular time.

A year ago, he was preparing to play Calera, Montevallo or somebody like that. Not Tennessee and not in Neyland Stadium.

He wasn't having a very good day in practice, and Johnson eased to him.

"Nervous?" he asked. Everett said he was, something Johnson already knew from experience.

Then, in words of his own, he told young Brad Everett what Lee Gross had told a young Lynn Johnson years before.

This much of the story has been told, but it continues, on to Knoxville and beyond.

Everett and Johnson sat together on the plane to Knoxville. There's always a tenseness, a tightness, that can drive the best man crazy on Friday afternoon before a big game.

Johnson sensed that tenseness in Everett.

"Want to read a magazine?" he asked.

"Sure," said Everett, expecting to be handed the latest copy of *Sports Illustrated, Football News,* or *Kick-off.* Instead, he received a copy of *Sports Afield.*

"Takes your mind off of it some," Johnson said, smiling. "You can think about it too much, you know. It'll get to you."

And so the two guards, the young one and the old one, talked about hunting and fishing. They talked about other things, too, about things unrelated to football. Football and Tennessee were on their minds enough as it was.

They roomed together Friday night, and again they talked of hunting and fishing. They made a date to go dove hunting next Sunday after the North Carolina State game. They passed time watching *Return of the Pink Panther* and assorted cartoons.

Occasionally, they talked of blocking assignments, strategy and what to expect from Tennessee.

Then, it was time to go to the stadium.

The noise, as expected, was tremendous, more than Everett ever heard in Alabaster and more, for that matter, than Johnson had ever heard in Dozier.

But, as Johnson had said, when the game started, the crowd could hardly be heard. All that mattered then was football and beating Tennessee.

Everett doesn't know why Johnson took him under his protective wing, made him one of his "boys," trying to help him out along the way.

"Whatever the reason," Everett says, "I'm thankful, super thankful, he has taken such an interest in me."

"Not just for what he tells me," Brad explains, "but for the way he acts, the kind of person he is. He's been through the good times and the bad. Everybody respects him. I've got a long way to go, and I'm just thankful Lynn is willing to help me."

Johnson is admittedly proud of his "boy," if you please. "He's played in three games," says Lynn, "and he's started one. He's not a freshman anymore."

Lynn was attracted to Everett because of his all-out hustle and the effort he puts forth on every play. "That is what we had in 1974," he says, "and that is what we've got this year."

Brad Everett has never met Lee Gross. Yet, in a way, he has. He met him through Lynn Johnson.

And someday, three years from now, another freshman guard will meet Lee Gross. He'll meet him through Brad Everett, who met him through Lynn Johnson and so on, right on down the line.

That's what tradition...that's what heritage is all about.

Auburn Football Illustrated
Auburn vs. Ole Miss
October 1, 1977

Tradition—every successful athletic program has to have it. Lynn Johnson is now a successful logger and lumberman in Brantley. Brad Everett is a successful Wall Street investor in New York. That Auburn brought them together says a lot for Auburn—and for them.

Farewell to the Kopper Kettle ─────────

AUBURN—The movie *Close Encounters* was supposed to have been shown in Auburn's Village Theater Sunday night.

It wasn't.

It wasn't shown because there wasn't much left of the Village Theater after Auburn's close encounter with tragedy Sunday morning.

No one was killed and only one person was slightly injured when half a city block was turned into a mass of twisted steel at 8:13 a.m.

Had the blast come 20 minutes later, hundreds of worshippers would have been cut by flying glass in the Auburn United Methodist Church.

Had it come three hours later, about 11:13, about a thousand people would have been within a half-block of the blast. Panic might have ensued.

All of these things did not happen. The encounter was close enough, however, for several Auburn residents. To have been closer would have meant almost certain death.

Reverend Charles Britt of the Auburn United Methodist Church was stopped at a traffic light at Toomer's Corner, a block away from the blast site. He wonders what would have happened if the light had been green instead of red. It takes only seconds to drive that Auburn city block.

Merchant Rodney Jones was in the back of his department store across the street from the blast. He wonders what would have happened if he had been in front of the store.

Fireman Tamp McDonnell had been dispatched from the fire department to check out a reported gas leak in the area of the Kopper Kettle, a fast-food restaurant on the corner of Gay and Magnolia. It was supposed to have been a routine check. He parked his car near Auburn National Bank.

He checked the bank first. Then, for some reason unknown even to him, he turned toward the Auburn United Methodist Church rather than the Kopper Kettle.

A few moments later, the Kopper Kettle, long a popular eating place of hurried Auburn residents, was a mass of steel and rubble.

"It just wasn't there anymore," said one Auburn resident.

At least one Auburn University student lives in an apartment above the Kopper Kettle. He had decided to go home this weekend.

Gordon Cone, manager of a fast-food restaurant a block-and-a-half from the Kopper Kettle, wonders what would have happened if the traffic light had caught him instead of the Reverend Britt.

Auburn residents, however, did not have to be near the blast site to know they had been spared.

Attorney Andy Gentry, for example, was at home in bed, reading about Auburn's 81-72 win over Florida Saturday night when the blast took place.

On a normal Sunday—any other Sunday—he would have been in his law office above the Kopper Kettle. Had he been there on this particular Sunday morning, he would have joined his law office as it, his personal books and papers and those of his clients soared 200, 300, maybe 400 or 500 feet above Auburn.

There is an irony to the sparing of Gentry. He is a lifelong Auburn resident. He was a cheerleader for The University of Alabama and yet, on this Sunday, he was saved by a cow, a three-month old calf.

Normally, he would go to the office and read the paper until it was time to go to church. This morning, however, his wife wanted him to stay with the children while she went to their nearby farm to feed her pet calf.

Gentry, now a devoted Auburn basketball fan, went downtown, bought his papers and came home to read them. He heard the explosion, but didn't know what it was.

He knew, however, when a client called him and said he had just found one of Gentry's personal papers in his front yard. He wanted to know if Gentry had thrown it away or if it had come from the blast.

Gentry went downtown, saw how bad the damage was and returned home to get his wife.

She was the first one who realized her husband had been spared. "She said she would never fuss at me or nag at me again," Gentry said late Sunday afternoon, "but I think she will have second thoughts on that."

The Gentrys spent all of Sunday afternoon roving over Auburn picking up pieces of paper that might have once been part of his law practice.

There was one final touch of irony in the Gentry story. Normally Mrs. Gentry would have fed her pet calf on Saturday night.

This Saturday night she failed to do it. "Probably because of the cold," Gentry said later, "or it could have been because we had to go to a party."

Whatever the reason, it saved her husband's life. It would have been certain death to have been in his office on that particular Sunday morning.

As Gentry spoke, department store manikins littered the sidewalks and streets of Auburn, almost as grim reminders to Auburn residents of how close they had come to an encounter with tragedy.

The Birmingham News
January 16, 1978

For those who have eaten at the Kopper Kettle, there is no doubt that it was destroyed by a "natural gas" explosion. The Kopper Kettle was Auburn's first all-night eatery. It is still missed. Each January, a group of Kopper Kettle devotees still gather to have coffee and bemoan the loss of one of Auburn's most colorful meeting places.

——News Correspondent Boone Aiken of Auburn contributed to this story.

A Positive Response

This is the story of one man, Charles R. Britt, and his positive response to Jesus Christ.

It is the story of how, through this one man's positive response, Jesus Christ has touched and continues to touch the lives of thousands.

We are fortunate to be among those whom this man has touched. We are fortunate to have him among us.

Charles Robert Britt was born 55 years ago today, January 19, 1923, in Lockhart, South Carolina.

He was the youngest of four children born to Edward Johnson Britt and Lillie Henderson Britt. There was nothing about him to suggest that he would, one day, be a man of God, an effective man of God, leading, guiding and influencing the lives of thousands.

He has always been that kind of man, like us, an average person trying to do what is right and seeking to know God's will for his life.

His father was a construction worker. He built dams, and wherever there was a dam to be built, that's where the Britts called home. That's what Edward and Lillie Britt were doing in Lockhart, South Carolina, the day Charles was born.

They returned to Alabama to stay in 1928. They set up permanent residence in Tallapoosa County, East Tallassee to be exact. Not Tallassee. East Tallassee. There is a difference.

His father farmed between construction jobs, and Charles Britt worked in the summers in the cotton mill and went to school. He graduated from Tallassee High School in 1939 and went to Tuscaloosa and The University of Alabama for two years.

It was about this time that he made a conscious decision to become a man of God. He had been God's man for quite some time.

Charles Britt's love affair with the Master began when he was about seven. It was not a "flash, bam, boom, washed in the blood" experience. Not solely.

It began when he came to what he would later call "an awareness of some need to respond positively to the message of Christ." He emphasizes that word "positively."

At about 15, he had an old-fashioned salvation experience, a crisis conversion in modern terms, at a revival meeting.

This was the basic turning point.

It happened, he says, because of the warmth of his church. It was a church where you felt you belonged and where you felt very much a part of it all.

It happened because he was old enough to think very seriously about the quality of his life. Not necessarily what he would do with it, but what the quality of it would be.

And it happened, he says, because it was supposed to happen. Such revival experiences were "expected" to happen to a young man his age in 1938.

This "crisis" salvation was not an immediate call to preach. In fact, a "call" as we commonly associate the term, never came to Charles Britt. At least he remembers no "call" or obsession to enter the ministry or to go to the mission field. He has never been a man of special calls or commissions. He is just a common, ordinary Christian—like us.

As he was preparing to go to college, his parents told him he should go with a goal in mind, he should have a "reason" for going.

Well, he said, I'll be a Methodist preacher.

Again, no bells, no angels, no flashes of light, just a simple, "I'll be a Methodist preacher." Long journeys, it is said, often begin with the first step. That was Charles Britt's first step toward Africa, toward Auburn and toward this night.

He went to Alabama two years before transferring to Birmingham-Southern College, a "good Methodist school." He earned a degree from Southern in 1943. In 1945, he received a B.D. degree, bachelor of divinity, from Vanderbilt University in Nashville.

But, he received far more than that from his stay in Nashville.

While at Vanderbilt, he met an attractive young lady from Hazelton, Pennsylvania, Blanche Lucille Beck.

They dated while he was at Vanderbilt and she was studying at Scarritt College, also in Nashville. When he went to the African mission field in 1947, they continued their courtship by mail. They planned their wedding by correspondence. As soon as she was eligible, Blanche joined him in Africa. They were married in Ganta, Liberia, in June of 1949.

The story of one man and his positive response to Jesus Christ now becomes the story of two people and their positive response to Christ.

The Britts were educational-evangelistic missionaries. Their time was spent preaching and teaching the Gospel, often traveling many miles to teach and preach. They also worked in the leprosy control program.

With the exception of one year, 1951, when he was in Nashville earning a master's degree at Scarritt, the Britts were in Africa from 1947 through 1954.

They left the mission field for two reasons, again, neither of which had anything to do with a great call by God or a sense that their mission was complete.

They left for health and career reasons. Both Charles and Edward, their son, had malaria and intestinal parasites.

Also, the Britts had been assigned to full-time school work, rather than "people" work. Both were—and still are—vitally important tasks, but the Britts believed they were meant for people work, preaching and ministering.

They returned to the Alabama-West Florida Conference, and he was appointed to the Slocomb church in the Dothan District. He pastored churches in Theodore, Prattville and Brewton.

Then, in 1968, when he was District Superintendent of the Pensacola District, word came that there would be an opening at Auburn. The Britts "wanted very much to come."

Several of the other District Superintendents were in general agreement that Charles R. Britt was the man for Auburn and, in June of 1968, Bishop Kenneth Goodson made the appointment. It may be the best appointment he ever made.

That appointment has made all the difference for Charles Britt and for the Auburn United Methodist Church.

He wanted to come to Auburn for three reasons. The Auburn church, he believed, was a great place for preaching. He liked the idea of living in a college community, and the opportunity to influence so many young lives with so much to offer appealed to him.

Britt, like any other Methodist preacher, thought he and his family, Blanche, Edward, Mary Claire and Martha, would have a short stay in Auburn—"for about five years and then something else would come along."

Nothing has, thank God, and the Britts, now minus their grown children, are completing their 10th year in Auburn. John Saidla, chairman of the Pastor-Parish Relations Committee, prefers to call it their "first 10 years," and District Superintendent Paul Duffey, a college friend of Charles, has been asked to see that the appointment continues.

No records are kept of such things, but Charles' 10-year stay at Auburn ranks as one of the longest tenures in the Alabama-West Florida Conference and may be one of the longest in modern Methodism.

When he came in 1968, Charles saw three great opportunities at the Auburn church. There was the opportunity to enlarge the worship attendance. There was the opportunity to tap the resources of the church for community service, and finally, there was the opportunity to indirectly affect the quality of life at Auburn University by affecting the lives of responsible people within the University.

He planned to make the most of the opportunities by doing three things. First, he wanted to do the best job of preaching he was capable of doing. He believed preaching ought to be exciting. Also, he wanted to identify people who already had a vision of what their church could be and help those people tie into the life of the church. He wanted to make them leaders of men. And, as such, they would be fishers of men. Finally, he wanted to become the connecting link between the church, the community and its needs.

How successful has he been?

"Well, I don't know," he says. "Numerically, I've been very successful, but I worry sometimes whether that numerical response is to me or to Christ. If it's to me, it's not enough. If it's to Him, then that's exactly where we want to go."

As for community service, he says the church serves the community well, citing the Auburn City Schools Dental Clinic, the Auburn Social Concerns Council, the Mother's Day Out program, plans for a retirement home and various other programs.

"The initial push for all of these," he says, "came from members of the Auburn United Methodist Church."

It is, he says, impossible to measure the influence he has had on his people and, in turn, their influence on others.

Yet, it is in this area, in the spiritual lives of his congregation, that Charles Britt has had, perhaps, his greatest success.

Thousands of Auburn University students have come through the doors of Auburn United Methodist Church for four years, then departed to serve throughout the world.

Auburn University met their educational needs, and the Auburn United Methodist Church, through the person of Charles Britt, took care of their spiritual needs. His influence has been multiplied a hundredfold, maybe more.

Auburn is indeed a better place to live and learn because he, a man who responded positively to God, has been here.

Still, however, there is much to do. Our journey—and his—is not yet complete.

"We have to discover ways to attract as many people to the first service as we now have at the second service," he says. "We have to double attendance and we can do it.

"We have to move toward a broadened and deepened understanding of the Christian faith on the part of adults in this church," he says.

"And, as Wayne McLaughlin, chairman of our Administrative Board, so appropriately put it, "We must enter into new forms of ministry that do not necessarily cost dollars, but involve people."

With God's help, we, as Auburn United Methodists, can do it.
With Charles Britt's guidance, we will do it.
Charles was once asked how he would like to be remembered.

He said, "As a person who intends to be a Christian, as a man who worked at being a preacher and a pastor and as a man who loved trying to help people be all they could be."

If those were his ultimate goals, then Charles R. Britt has been eminently success-ful.

Charles R. Britt
The First Decade
1968-1978
Auburn United Methodist Church
January 19, 1978

Charles Britt left the Auburn United Methodist Church in 1979 to accept a full-time teaching position in Family and Child Development at Auburn University. He retired from Auburn University in 1989 and continues to serve rural Methodist Churches in the Auburn area. He was made Pastor Emeritus of the Auburn United Methodist Church February 10, 1991.

A Loyal Son of Auburn

AUBURN—Joe Beckwith is a good kid.

An All-American kind of boy who says "yes sir" and "no sir"—all those kinds of things.

And his story, thus far, is a carbon copy of what an All-American success story should be.

Joe is a product of Auburn High School and Auburn University, athletically and academically, and in two weeks he gets his big chance. He reports to big league training camp with the Los Angeles Dodgers, defending National League champions.

Joe is realistic. He doesn't expect to be with the Dodgers in Atlanta April 7 when they open defense of their title, but he does hope to be in Albuquerque in Class AAA. That's only a short stop away from Dodger Stadium and the big leagues.

Like any All-American boy, that's where Joe wants to go, and he's got a good start.

Last year, after being selected in the second round of the free agent draft, Joe played for San Antonio in the Texas League where he had a 5-5 record and a 3.33 earned run average.

That ERA is the thing that is impressing the big Dodgers.

"That doesn't sound too good around here," Joe explained, "but the Texas League is considered a hitter's league and anything under a 4.00 is considered a great ERA. It's like a 1.50 or 2.00 around here."

Ben Wade, director of scouting for the Dodgers, rated Joe as the best college pitcher available in last year's draft, mainly because of his fast ball.

"If a pitcher has a good fast ball," Wade said, "he's got the one thing most outstanding pitchers have—a good arm. We feel we can always work with a kid enough to give him a breaking ball and the other tools he will need to make it."

Apparently Wade and the Dodgers believe the son of Auburn athletic business manager Bill Beckwith has what he needs to make it. Joe was one of five minor league pitchers invited to participate in a Kid's Clinic in Baton Rouge two weeks ago. The other 35-40 instructors were all big league players or former big league players.

Joe admits to "feeling like a little kid" when the big league stars came up and introduced themselves and treated him as their equal.

"They were so nice and friendly," he recalled. "It proved that professional athletes can get away from the pressure and take time out to help people."

Joe was one of six Dodgers in Baton Rouge. Others were Doug Rae, Bert Hooten, Bill Russell, Joe Simpson and Joe Ferguson.

Also, there was Jack Baker, a former Auburn first baseman who had just been traded from Boston to Cleveland, and Doyle Alexander, a Birmingham product who pitches for the Texas Rangers.

If he had it to do over again, Beckwith would handle his career in the same way, especially his education. That's not so much a word for Auburn as it is for education.

Joe had a chance to sign before he completed his college eligibility, but he chose not to, and he has never regretted it. And, he says, he never will.

"Just associating with professional baseball players has shown me how important it is to go to college," he said.

"So many players think they can go right in and play. Most can't do it and they play five or six years and then don't have anything to do." Baseball, he said, has given him a job. Education has given him security.

Joe is a full-fledged professional athlete now, working out all day, every day. Much of his time is spent strengthening a knee that was operated on in October. He says it's doing fine, thanks in a large part to the care of Herb Waldrop, Auburn's trainer.

In addition to working on the knee, he runs more than a mile a day and throws quite a bit. He is working out presently with the Auburn baseball team which opens its season Feb. 23.

No matter what happens in spring training, Joe considers himself a fortunate young man. First, he is a professional baseball player on the verge of getting a chance in the major leagues. That alone is a dream come true.

He got married in December, and he and his wife, Jeanne Ann, have been living in Auburn. He is especially glad that he and Jeanne Ann are able to start their lives together in Auburn, his hometown.

"Everything I am or ever will be, I owe to Auburn, to Auburn University and my family," Joe said, "especially my Dad. He's always been there when I needed him.

"My baseball career has meant a lot to him. He has enjoyed it," said Joe, "but he's never pushed, never got in the way. He's always been there for me and with me.

"Whatever success I have, I am glad he will be able to enjoy it with me," Joe said, "and the same goes for the people of Auburn.

"I may be a Los Angeles Dodger, but I will always be an Auburn man at heart."

There was never any doubt about that. Never.

The Birmingham News
February 12, 1978

Joe Beckwith's dream came true. He played for the Los Angeles Dodgers and the Kansas City Royals. He played on two World Championship teams in his eight-year major-league career, the '81 Dodgers and the '85 Royals.

Joe is back home, in Auburn, Ala., where he is putting his Auburn degree to good use as Vice President of Sales and Operations for Blue Circle-Williams Brothers Concrete Company. As vice president, Joe oversees the company's operations in LaGrange and Columbus, Ga., Phenix City, Eufaula and Auburn.

He still loves Auburn, he still follows major league baseball and he has grown even closer to his father.

A Change of Plans _____

AUBURN—The shock that swept this university town following Coach Paul Lambert's tragic death was best exemplified by Bill Busby, manager of the Heart of Auburn Motel.

Lambert was staying at Busby's motel until his family moved here from Carbondale, Illinois where Lambert had coached at Southern Illinois University for eight years. When Busby heard that the Auburn basketball coach of two months had been killed in a Columbus, Georgia motel fire, he couldn't believe it.

He grabbed a pass key and ran to Lambert's room, fully expecting that it had all been a tragic mistake. He had seen Lambert late Monday afternoon, and he expected to find Lambert in bed or at least find signs that he had slept there that night, that the terrible story coming out of Columbus was, somehow, in error.

He opened the door to room 147 and the terrible reality of it all came through to him.

Lambert was, indeed, dead, exactly two months from the day he was hired to coach Auburn's basketball team.

Busby's shock was multiplied many times over in the Loveliest Village Tuesday, and nowhere was it more evident than in the athletic offices in Memorial Coliseum where Lambert worked and was to have coached.

Auburn football coach Doug Barfield was among the most shocked...if there can be a category of "most shocked." Barfield was a frequent golfing buddy of Lambert and they, along with business manager Bill Beckwith, had a golf game scheduled today. The two Auburn head coaches frequently watched baseball games together, too.

"There are some people," Barfield said, "who it takes you a long time to get to know. There are others who you get to know immediately and know you don't like, and then there are the people you get to know immediately and know you will like. Coach Lambert was that kind of man."

Lambert was in Columbus, along with his assistant coaches, to conduct a coaching clinic for all Muscogee County high schools. He was on the job when he died, and that prompted Barfield and every person who had ever accompanied an Auburn team—be it coach, player, reporter or fan—to think how many motel and hotel rooms he had stayed in.

The news first reached Auburn when Herbert Greene, one of Lambert's assistants who had been staying at the same motel, called sports information director Buddy Davidson. The call came at 10 minutes after six, just as Davidson was plugging in the morning coffee.

Greene told Davidson that there had been a fire at the motel where they (the coaches) were staying. There was a body in room 244, Greene said, and Coach Lambert had been registered in that room. At that time no one knew for sure that it was Lambert's body.

Immediately Davidson, representing the university and the Lambert family, drove to Columbus, 30 miles away. A short time later, athletic director Lee Hayley and assistant athletic director Kenny Howard arrived there.

In Auburn, it was Graduation Day, and the Loveliest Village was awakening to a beautiful day. News of the tragedy in Columbus came slowly, in bits and pieces at first. There were rumors that both Greene and Herman Williams, who came to Auburn from Southern Illinois with Lambert, had both been injured in the blaze. Later the Village learned that was not the case. Both had escaped without injury after using a chair to break out the sliding glass door in their rooms.

All the telephone lines to the athletic department were busy. Members of the media and fans alike had questions to ask.

Three Auburn ministers, the Reverends Charles Britt, Dick Cobb and John Jeffers, came quickly to the offices to see if they could be of assistance. The Reverend Mr. Cobb later accompanied Davidson back to Columbus to pick up Lambert's belongings.

Fulton Jones, proprietor of the Auburn Grille, a popular uptown eatery, was serving a group of early morning coffee drinkers when the news came over the radio.

"Did they say Coach Lambert?" someone asked. Jones said he wasn't sure, then the bulletin was repeated.

"It's been a shock to the whole community," Jones said late Tuesday night. "Not that we knew him that well, but all of us had been mighty impressed by him. We liked him as a person and expected great things out of him as a coach."

By early afternoon, the facts were in.

Lambert had not planned on staying in Columbus Monday night. He had originally planned to return here, thinking that he was scheduled to speak to the Lee County Medical Society at noon today. He double checked his schedule, discovered the speech was not until tonight and decided to stay in Columbus. He conferred with Greene and Williams about their plans for the coaching clinic and went to bed early.

Columbus fire officials say the fire broke out from undetermined origin about 4:15 a.m.

Lambert had planned to go to Carbondale, Ill., where his family was awaiting its move to Auburn, later this week. The move was scheduled for June 16.

Funeral arrangements were expected to be completed later today.

The Birmingham News
June 7, 1978

Because of the warmth of Auburn people and the Auburn community, the Lambert family went ahead with their plans to move to Auburn. Auburn is now their home.

Sonny Smith became Auburn's head coach and led Auburn to some of its greatest years in basketball.

Paying the Price ──────────────────

Most of you probably think sports writers have it easy. That's not true.

Allow me to share with you what surely must rank as one of the worst college football trips ever taken.

It was the Kansas State game two weeks ago, and if you've ever had a worse trip, I would like to know about it.

It all began in Birmingham on Friday afternoon at the Southern Airways ticket counter. I was the next person in line when the ticket agent said, "I'm sorry ladies and gentlemen, but this flight has been overbooked..."

That meant that I and about five others would not get aboard, that all of my connecting reservations would have to be re-made.

I was traveling with Alf Van Hoose, sports editor of *The Birmingham News*. Alf was one of the lucky ones. He got on the Southern flight.

Eight hours later—and four hours late—I got to Kansas City and the hotel where Alf and I were staying. Muhammad Ali, my main man, was putting the finishing touches on Leon Spinks, and I wanted very much to see him win the fight, but the desk clerk didn't find any Alf Van Hoose registered. Nor did they have a David Housel. Nor did they have any reservations for *The Birmingham News*. And they had no vacancies.

By now Ali had already become the first man in history to win the heavyweight championship three times. After an hour, the desk clerk found Alf's credit voucher. He was in room 206. "Great fight," said Alf. "Sorry you missed it."

The next morning, Alf went to the rental car desk while I went to the Delta ticket counter to change our return reservations. We were leaving Saturday night so I could get back to Auburn in time to hear Charles Britt's Sunday sermon at Auburn United Methodist Church. Like Ali, he, too, is one of my main men.

I had just finished exchanging the tickets when a disgusted Van Hoose walked up. "I need help," he said. "My driver's license expired three days ago. They won't let me have a car." Down went my name, right on the dotted line.

The game went fine—Auburn won—but it was an hour longer than any game in the history of college football. That put us in a time bind for writing our stories, transmitting them back to Birmingham and getting back to Kansas City for a 9 o'clock flight.

We used a Teleram to send our stories back to Birmingham. A Teleram is a complex computer terminal that transmits stories in computer talk over a telephone line. Sometimes they don't work.

My player-quote story got lost "somewhere in the air" as computer people say. My best player-quote story ever turned into four quick 'graphs dictated over the telephone and a "hit-the-road" command from Alf.

It was now 6:15. We had two hours and 45 minutes to make the two and one half hour drive to the airport.

Alf picked up the Teleram while I went after the car. Heeding his request to get as close to the press box as I could, I got in, cranked up and headed straight for the press box door and trouble.

In the Kansas sunset it was impossible to see the cable-like wires that cut across the gravel parking lot. I ran straight into one. It was like walking through a glass door. The wire stretched like a rubberband, then snapped back, breaking the windshield, the radio aerial and ripping off the windshield wiper.

I had demolished a rental car and hadn't even gotten out of the parking lot. Now we didn't have but two and a half hours to make Kansas City.

"We're dead," said Alf. "We're dead."

I didn't know if he was talking about me and the rental car or us and the airport, but I didn't wait to find out. We skimmed across the Kansas plains at 75-80 miles an hour, making the two and one half hour trip in two hours and 20 minutes. We stopped for gas, too. Alf made the flight. I didn't. I still had to settle up with Hertz.

There was a nice lady—thank God—Shirley Smoot, at the Hertz counter and as soon as I had filled out the accident report and gotten the last available room around the airport, I began trying to get home. My shaving kit, travel bag and change of clothes were, by that time, already in Birmingham with Alf.

I asked the Delta agent how soon she could get me to Atlanta and Birmingham. "We have a flight out of Kansas City Monday morning at 8:30," she said. "You gotta be kidding," I replied. She assured me she wasn't. All Kansas City-Atlanta service was booked until Monday. The best Delta or anyone else could do was K.C-Memphis Sunday morning. Then hope. Southern—good ole bump'em off Southern—is the only airline that services Memphis-Birmingham, and they were booked too.

At Memphis, Southern said there was no way to get to Birmingham until 9:30 Sunday night. That meant an 11-hour layover in the Memphis airport. Greyhound could beat that. They had a bus leaving Memphis at 11:30 a.m. and arriving in Birmingham at 6:30 p.m.

In desperation, I went to Delta and asked if there was any way —any way at all— they could get me to Birmingham before 6:30. The agent—who soon became one of the most beautiful people I have ever seen—looked me over.

"By yourself," he asked.

"Yes sir," I said.

"Got anything to check?" he asked.

"No sir," I said.

"Got a ticket?" he asked.

"Yes sir," I said.

He took my ticket, looked over his shoulder as if he was expecting someone to pounce on him and began to type at a computer terminal.

I had enough of computer terminals in Manhattan, Kansas.

"How fast can you run?" he asked.

"Faster than I look," I said.

With that, he handed me a piece of paper and off I went, ala O.J. Simpson. Maybe not faster than a speeding bullet, but certainly more powerful than a locomotive.

I got to the plane just as the door was closing. "Whoa," I yelled. "I got to get on that plane."

I got on and plopped down in the last available seat. It was first class. My luck was changing.

A stewardess asked, "Can I get something for you, sir?"

It was Sunday. I would still miss Charles Britt's first football sermon of the season at Auburn United Methodist, but my three-day ordeal seemed to be nearing an end.

"Yes," I said, trying to smile. "Bring me a Bible and a Bloody Mary..."

Auburn Football Illustrated
Auburn vs. Tennessee
September 30, 1978

I have been back to Kansas many times over the years, but never back to Manhattan, Kansas.

Here Am I, Send Me...

This is a story about Bob Fleming. It is not necessarily a happy story or a jubilant story, but it is a heartwarming story, and those, in the final analysis, are the best kind. They endure.

Bob Fleming came to Auburn four long years ago. That was Auburn's last good year, a 9-2 season, a Gator Bowl win over Texas and all of that. Bob Fleming, an eager freshman from Mobile, was going to be a part of all that. He was going to make that kind of thing happen again and again. His uncle, Ed Dyas, had come to Auburn before him. He had been a football hero. Now, it was Bob's turn.

He had completed a good senior season at Murphy in Mobile. He wasn't the greatest prospect in the world, a blue chipper as they are called, but he was good enough to play, and he was good enough to help.

Auburn had a good complement of running backs in 1974: Rick Neel, Mitzi Jackson, Secdrick McIntyre, Kenny Burks. You remember them. Bob Fleming played on the freshman team that year and patiently awaited his turn to share in the varsity glory.

Three years went by and Bob never shared in the varsity glory. He came close once, in 1976, when he started the FSU, Florida and Mississippi State games. His best game came against FSU when he gained 40 or so yards on seven or eight carries. He didn't start the Georgia game, however, and Bob Fleming's star began to sink slowly in the West.

There were reasons for that: a knee injury and the advent of such running backs as Joe Cribbs, Williams Andrews and later, James "Bye-Bye" Brooks. Bob Fleming was a steady back with average speed. Compared to Andrews, Cribbs and Brooks, Fleming was a steady back with slow speed and there wasn't much room in the backfield for slow steady backs.

This is not so much a comment on Andrews, Cribbs, Brooks and Fleming as it is on God-given ability. All any of us are asked to do is do the best we can with what we have. To be all that we can be. Bob Fleming had done that, and maybe more.

In January of this year, Bob Fleming had a decision to make. He had been at Auburn four years, one of them a redshirt year. He had not shared in the glory, and the handwriting, so to speak, was on the wall. He would not share in the glory at all. Andrews, Cribbs and Brooks were back, and they were joined by others. 1978 for Bob Fleming would be just like 1975, 1976 and 1977.

No one could have blamed him if he had followed the course set by Bob Bradley, another fine football player and an even finer person, who had given up his fifth year, put football behind him, graduated and got on about the business of living the rest of his life. Bradley and Fleming were in similar situations. Both were steady backs with average speed. No one would have blamed Bob if he, too, had passed up his fifth year. That would have been the sensible thing to do.

But Bob Fleming didn't want to do the sensible thing. He would be in school anyway, and if he was here and was going to be on athletic scholarship, he wanted to do something to help.

He and Coach Doug Barfield sat down and talked frankly and openly about Fleming's situation. Barfield is that kind of man. So is Bob Fleming. They agreed that Bob would pass up on the field participation. He would work in the weight room helping younger, healthier, faster, quicker Tigers get ready for the '78 campaign.

Fleming did that and he stayed in shape, not because he thought he would be some kind of Horatio Alger hero, getting the call to come in and win the Alabama game at the last possible moment. Nothing like that. He stayed in shape because he had always been in shape and always wanted to be in shape.

He went to practice and worked with the walk-on backs on the junior varsity. He seldom watched the varsity practice. It hurt on occasion. Bob Fleming is human, too. We all are.

He was at practice the day Andrews was injured. He was there the day Cribbs went down, too. Auburn's stable of running backs, rated the best in the SEC, was depleted and in bad need of some help, some depth.

Bob Fleming was at home the Sunday afternoon he got the message that Barfield wanted to see him. Fleming went to Barfield's office immediately and again the two men sat down and talked frankly and openly.

Auburn needed help, part time temporary help, and Barfield wanted to know if Fleming would provide that help. No one would have blamed Bob if he had said no. Six days later, he was lining up to receive a Kansas State kickoff. He returned two kickoffs that day and carried the ball once from scrimmage. He also played against VPI.

Bob told me his story last week at Legion Field, on a Friday while the team worked out in preparation for Tennessee. He was not one of those who worked out. He was dressed in street clothes and he sat on the bench. He had made the trip, but he would not dress out for the game because of an NCAA rule that limits a team to 60 players for a conference game. And, there were 60 players who, in the opinion of the coaches, would help Auburn more than Bob Fleming.

"Yes," he said. "It's hard to take at times."

"But," he added quickly, "I understand. Somebody has to make decisions like this and I understand."

"The team," he said, "the team. That's the most important thing."

It always will be to people like Bob Fleming.

What does the future — the next eight games — hold for Bob Fleming? He will dress for the Miami game today since it is not a conference game, and he hopes to make the dress out squad on down the way. That is not a sure thing.

The important thing to remember about Bob Fleming, however, isn't whether or not he dresses. The important thing to remember about Bob Fleming is Bob Fleming. When he was called, he answered.

He was prepared and did the best he could do. That is all that can be asked of any man. That is all that any man can expect to do.

Bob Fleming, in the words of the ancient prophet Isaiah, said, "Here am I. Send me..."

Auburn Football Illustrated
Auburn vs. Miami
October 7, 1978

Bob Fleming is back home in Mobile with his wife Leigh Anne and their two children, both boys. Bob, administrator of a sports medicine and rehabilitation center, considers the 1978 season, the season in which he was able to make a contribution, the highlight of his athletic career. He has no regrets, only fond memories. Would that we could all be so fortunate...

Earning His Way

This column had its beginnings a long time ago, in a place far away. Jackson, Mississippi, 1976.

Auburn played Mississippi State that day and a young tight end—a sophomore—had a good day. His name was Dick Hayley.

He had come to Auburn without a scholarship, earned one and was now realizing a dream. He was playing big-time college football, and he was making a significant contribution to his team.

I was sitting next to his father that day, Lee Hayley. Oh, he was a proud man. You could see it in his eyes and in the way he tried to hide his smile when Dick made a good play.

"I know you're proud of Dick," I said, more in comment than in question.

"Yes," his father said, "I am. He did all of it on his own. We didn't want to push him. He made the decision."

"Yes," I said, "I know. This will make a good story..."

The mental notetaking had already begun.

Lee Hayley looked somewhat embarrassed.

"I would appreciate it," he said, "if you wouldn't mention that he's my son. This is Dick's moment. He did it all on his own and he deserves all the credit. If you want to write a story about the fact that he's my son...well, you know how some people are..."

Yes, I knew.

People—some people—would say that Dick Hayley got his scholarship because he was the athletic director's son. They would say he was playing for the same reason. Favoritism. Nepotism. They might not say it in those exact words, but the intent, the feeling would be there.

They would not accept—in some cases not even consider—the fact that Dick Hayley, in his own right, might be a pretty good football player.

This is strange and, perhaps, a bit tragic. It is a comment on the times in which we live. The people who won't accept the Dick Hayley story are the same ones who so readily accept, even hunger and thirst after, a genuine success story, one of those rags to riches kind of stories that warm the heart, cleanse the soul and make you feel good all over. An "all-is-right-with-the-world" story.

The Dick Hayley story is that kind of story.

He played high school football at Auburn High School. He was not good enough to play college football. No scouts looked at him. He hadn't planned on playing college football. Then, one day in the fall of his freshman year, he went out to watch Auburn High practice. He knew then that football was not out of his blood, that there was some strange yearning within to play football again, to see if he could make it on the college level.

He talked to his father about it. "Do what you want to," his father advised. "It's your decision."

His father did one thing. He reminded him of the family rule. "If you start something, you aren't going to quit. Not until the season is over." That would apply in this case too.

Dick agreed and he went to see Claude Saia, then the coach of the Auburn junior varsity team. Saia put him on a weight program, and he has grown from 185 pounds to 212. He has also become one of Auburn's better football players.

"He's the best tight end we've got," says Paul Davis, who coaches Auburn's tight ends. "I've never seen a kid with more determination. He's playing with a bad back, but you would never know it from the effort he gives."

Hayley has graded consistently well this season and has been chosen game captain twice. He is an adequate pass receiver and a ferocious blocker. That's what tight ends are supposed to do best. Auburn has had eight scoring drives of eighty yards or more. On each of those drives, Dick Hayley's blocking has been perfect.

All of this under the watchful eyes of coaches who know their every move will be interpreted by some as favoritism toward the athletic director's son.

"If I had somebody else as good," Davis said, "I'd start him. I'd do it just to take some of the pressure off Dick..."

Lee Hayley wanted it made clear that he did not have this story written. He wanted it made clear that it was done without his encouragement or discouragement.

That is done.

Even so, there are those who will read these words and say, "Look at this..." and the old innuendoes will surface again.

So be it. This is more of a comment on the people making the charge than on the people in the story. There are always those who seek to detract, to defame and to tear down. Then, thank God, there are those who build.

This story is about one of those who chose to build.

Auburn Football Illustrated
Auburn vs. Wake Forest
October 28, 1978

Dick Hayley is in the construction business in Auburn. He and his wife Kathy have five children. Lee Hayley left Auburn in 1981 to become associate athletic director at the University of Georgia, a position he still holds. He and his wife, Floyd, proud grandparents that they are, visit Auburn often.

Snow White _____

AUBURN—Auburn honored an old friend turned enemy over the weekend.

Auburn honored Joel Eaves, athletic director at the University of Georgia. Eaves was an athlete at Auburn, a four-sport star in the late 30's. Later, he was an assistant football coach and head basketball coach.

He is best known at Auburn for his basketball teams. Auburn had only one winning season between 1941 and 1949. Eaves took over the basketball coaching duties part-time in 1950 and led Auburn to 14 straight winning seasons.

He had a 214-99 overall record and at one time his teams won 30 straight games, still an Auburn record in all sports. His 1959-60 team won the Southeastern Conference championship. It was and still is the only Auburn team to win that championship.

Eaves' championship team was known as "Snow White and the Seven Dwarfs" because of Eaves' snow white hair and the lack of height on the team.

Most of Eaves' success came with the "shuffle," an offense he developed and perfected at Auburn. It was based on one premise: every player moving all the time. It enabled him to use his short players to maximum efficiency.

John Logue, a former Eaves' player, now executive editor of *Southern Living* magazine, told the "real" story of how the shuffle developed to a crowd of 200 former players and friends who gathered in Auburn for "Joel Eaves Weekend."

"Coach Eaves was so tight with money," Logue said, "that he made all of his Auburn teams wear the same uniforms. For 14 years we had to wear the same uniforms, jock straps and all. As the uniforms were washed through the years, those jock straps shrunk and it became physically impossible for an Auburn basketball player to stand still. We *had* to move around and that's how Coach Eaves developed the shuffle..."

Eaves' fiscal policies came up again during the dinner. When he was coaching, he would give each player a dime to tip the waitresses. That prompted a former player to write a little loose verse:

> Our coach was in line
> With a dime each time
> A dime for a tip
> On each road trip.

Of all the "roasts," that one seemed to embarrass Eaves most of all. His players gave him a plaque bearing a dime and the verse. They also gave him and Mrs. Eaves a trip to Scotland.

When the roast was over, when everyone had had his say, Eaves took the microphone and said, "I've never heard so many lies at one time in my life..."

Then, he proceeded to tell some of his own.

It was that kind of weekend for Eaves and the players who organized it to honor him. It was not an official athletic department function, but all of the Auburn athletic officials were here.

The weekend began with a reception Friday night. A golf tournament, "The Great White Father Open," was held Saturday afternoon, and the great white father's team won.

"They won," said host and organizer Rex Frederick, "not because they had the lowest golf score, but because they made the most noise on the greens. That made everybody *think* they had the lowest golf score."

Along with the fun and merriment, there were serious times, too. The word "love" was used often. It was surpassed only by words such as character, respect, admiration and integrity.

All were used to describe Eaves.

"Coach Eaves brought not only innovation but also character to the game," said Logue. "He believed that the game was built on a fair premise and if you played the game, you played it fairly. He never cheated the rules with anybody. He never looked for an unfair advantage."

Eaves said coming back to Auburn, being with his players again, was like coming back home.

"The place has changed," he said, "but the people haven't, and the people are what make the world go around. What you have done for me tonight is the nicest thing a player, a manager or friend can do for a man who coached."

"And," Eaves added, "you did a lot more for me than I ever did for you."

It sounded natural to hear Georgia's athletic director rolling off such Auburn names as "Miss Cora Hardy's rooming house" and "Toomer's Corner."

As athletic director Lee Hayley said when he gave Eaves a lifetime pass to Auburn's home basketball games, "Underneath all that Red and Black, there's still a whole lot of Orange and Blue."

That was the real reason Auburn honored Joel Eaves. Not because he was Georgia's athletic director, and certainly not because he is an enemy, but because he was one of their own, one of their own made good.

As the events of the weekend ended, Eaves paused Sunday and looked back over his long and varied athletic career, a career that ends, officially at least, June 30 with his retirement.

"If I had it to do over again," he said, "I wouldn't do anything differently. I'd play better and I'd want to win more, but I wouldn't do anything differently."

Eaves said he would change only one thing, and that one thing has nothing to do with college athletics. It is a personal matter.

"If I could change anything," he said, "it would be the loss of our son, but I can't talk about that. I get choked up..."

Eaves' only son died of kidney disease in 1974.

Eaves said he had been fortunate along the way, all the way from the parents he had to the people he worked with, coached with and with whom he played.

"All I ever wanted to do," he said, "was play, and my parents understood that. They were very supportive. They gave me every opportunity. They weren't rich people, but they were loving people. We never ate steak, but we never went hungry. I guess some people would say they were average people, but I could never say they were average. They were never average to me."

Of the Auburn-Georgia rivalry and his role in it, Eaves said he never had any special desire to beat Auburn more than any other school.

There was never, he said, any divided loyalty, not after he took the job as Georgia's athletic director on Nov. 22, 1963, an hour before President John F. Kennedy was shot.

"When someone is paying you to work for them," he said, "you have to give them the best you can and that includes your loyalty, too."

Auburn, Eaves said, was the only place where he had stayed over after a game. "In all these years," he said, "no matter who won, there has never been an unpleasant incident. Nothing close to it. Auburn people are still my friends, but when the game starts, we're enemies. After the game's over, we are friends again. That is the way it has to be."

And that's the way it was at Auburn Saturday night and Sunday. There were no games to be played, only a man to be honored.

Joel Eaves was that man.

The Huntsville Times
May 21, 1979

Toomer's Corner, the cornerstone of Auburn Spirit, as it was in the 1890s when football came to Auburn and as it is now in the Golden Era of Auburn Football.

Dick Schmalz, Terry Beasley and Pat Sullivan combined to form one of College Football's most effective passing games. Records set during their era of Auburn Football still stand more than 20 years after they played.

Rufus Dorsey of Auburn scored the first touchdown of the Auburn-Alabama series in 1893 and James Joseph celebrates scoring the first touchdown in Auburn's 30-20 win over Alabama in 1989, the Crimson Tide's first trip to Auburn.

Auburn is the only school where John Heisman coached to have produced a Heisman Trophy winner. Shown here with the Heisman Trophy are Coach Pat Dye, Bo Jackson, winner of the 1985 Heisman Trophy and Pat Sullivan, winner of the 1971 Heisman Trophy. (The Heisman Trophy is pictured with permission of the Downtown Athletic Club of New York.)

Press parties have changed over the years. Coach Jeff Beard is shown hosting what appears to be a fish fry for the media in the late forties or early fifties while Coach Pat Dye is pictured with the media at a reception hosted by Auburn at the 1982 Tangerine Bowl.

Trey Gainous and Coach Pat Dye share a happy moment on the Auburn sideline.

Toomer's Corner, the intersection of College Street and Magnolia Avenue, has always been a gathering spot for Auburn students, whether it be in the 1930s or after a big football victory in the 1980s.

Coach Pat Dye hugs his wife, Sue, after Auburn beat Alabama 10-0 and won the 1987 SEC championship. Wanda Dye (left), their youngest daughter, awaits her championship hug. It was the second of four SEC championships won by Dye's teams in the Decade of the Eighties.

Coach Ralph "Shug" Jordan, one of the men for whom Auburn's Jordan-Hare Stadium is named, made his final entrance as head coach on Nov. 8, 1975 prior to the Auburn-Mississippi State game.

Five years later, on July 18, 1980, six of his former players, Rusty Deen, Mike Neel, Pat Sullivan, Terry Beasley, Terry Henley and Phil Gargis, laid him to rest. (*Huntsville Times* Photo by Tony Triolo.)

Randy Campbell led Auburn to 20 wins in 24 games in 1982-83, including an 11-1 season, an SEC championship and a Sugar Bowl championship in 1983.

This cup was presented to Auburn in honor of its 32-22 win over Alabama in 1893 in the first game of the Auburn-Alabama series.

John Heisman, for whom the Heisman Trophy is named, coached at Auburn from 1895-99, compiling a record of 12-4-2. He was one of the first people to buy a lemonade at Toomer's Drug Store on Toomer's Corner.

Kevin Porter, Coach Pat Dye and Benji Roland in a reflective moment after Auburn's win over Georgia at Athens in 1988.

Publicity Director Bill Beckwith and the assembled media look down the driveway of the President's Home in 1951 to see if an approaching automobile might be bringing Auburn's new head football coach, Ralph "Shug" Jordan, to meet President Ralph B. Draughon.

Coach Pat Dye meets the media for the first time as Auburn's head football coach on January 3, 1981.

Two seasons later, on Nov. 27, 1982, Auburn beat Alabama for the first time in 10 years. Auburn would go on to win the Decade of the Eighties six games to four.

Bo Jackson, winner of the 1985 Heisman Trophy, did not start his first game at Auburn, but he was the game's leading rusher and leading scorer with 123 yards and two touchdowns as Auburn defeated Wake Forest 28-10.

Ralph "Shug" Jordan and Paul "Bear" Bryant of Alabama met for the final time on Nov. 29, 1975.

Coach Pat Dye and David Housel share a lighter moment at Fan Day, prior to the start of an Auburn football season.

The Price of Fame

Joe Cribbs sat alone on the bench in front of his locker.

The press had not yet discovered he was out of the shower.

"What can you tell me about the game?" I asked.

"Well," he said, "We won. There's not much else I can say. We won. That's what really counts..."

Joseph Stainer Cribbs was obviously a very tired young man, beat up, battered and perhaps bruised.

A kid came up. He was nine, maybe 10. No more. This was the second time he had approached Cribbs. The first time he said, "*James*, can I have your jersey...."

Now he had another question, the one that should have been his first question. "Which one are you?" he asked.

Fame can be a very impersonal thing.

"I'm Cribbs," Joe said.

"Can I have your chin strap?" The kid was aggressive. He wasted no time.

Cribbs shook his head. He didn't smile and probably couldn't laugh. "I haven't got a chin strap," he said. "I don't have a jersey either. Somebody has already got them. I'm sorry..."

He smiled as he looked at the clutter around his feet. "I don't have anything. I don't even know where all my equipment is."

The souvenir hunters who always managed to get into a dressing room had long since scavenged his locker and equipment, taking anything they thought they could get by the guard at the door.

It is a wonder Joe Cribbs had a towel to dry off with. He must have gotten it as he got out of the shower. That, or taken it with him.

The price of fame is high, and Joe Cribbs was paying the price.

He has been paying the price for some time.

A young sports writer for *The Tuscaloosa News* and the *Opelika-Auburn News*, Donnie Anthony, noted that a week before at the Kansas State game.

"He must get tired of all that," Donnie said, showing a wisdom and understanding beyond his years. "Every day it's the same thing all over again. Somebody different is asking the questions, but the questions are always the same, over and over. I don't know how he takes it..."

Joe Cribbs takes it because Joe Cribbs is an exceptional athlete. Learning to deal with the pressure is part of being an exceptional athlete. It can be what separates the great from the near-great.

I mentioned the price of fame to Cribbs as we sat on the bench. "It must," I said, "be a high price to pay."

He smiled a smile of understanding and agreement.

"I like to be alone at times," he said. "I like to be off to myself..."

He shook his head again. He knew that privacy and solitude would be a long time in coming, at least 11 more weeks.

By now the press had discovered his presence in the dressing room. They descended on him in droves. It might seem unfair to Cribbs, but they were only doing their job.

He wrapped a towel around his naked body and began answering their questions. He smiled freely as he spoke. This was the public Joe Cribbs. He was no longer tired. He was no longer battered and bruised.

Joe Cribbs was taking his place among the great.

Auburn Football Illustrated
Auburn vs. Southern Mississippi
September 22, 1979

Joe Cribbs was one of the greatest running backs in Auburn history. After the 1979 season in which he gained 1,120 yards rushing, Cribbs held virtually every rushing record at Auburn. He went on to an outstanding pro career and entered private business in Birmingham after retirement. He was inducted into the Alabama Sports Hall of Fame in 1991.

Mistaken Identity

In a sense, Jerry Beasley came back from the dead to play football Saturday.

For about two hours early Friday morning, his family and some of his coaches thought he was dead.

This is not a happy story. It is one of relief for the Beasley family, and one of supreme sadness for the family of Donnie Givens, the defensive captain of last year's Auburn football team.

Givens died in a one-car accident near Tuskegee early Friday morning.

Givens borrowed Beasley's car late Thursday. He was driving it when it went out of control on I-85 west of Auburn, hit a bridge abutment and exploded. Identification was impossible.

Authorities found a golf course receipt in the trunk. It had Beasley's name on it and the Beasley family was notified about 2 a.m. that their son was dead.

Only when Coach Doug Barfield checked Beasley's room about 3:45 a.m. did the truth become known that it was Givens rather than Beasley who was dead.

"Coach Barfield looked scared to death when he came in my room," Beasley said, "and that scared me, too. I didn't know what was happening."

Beasley and Barfield called his home in Montgomery immediately. Beasley's mother came to Auburn Friday morning to see her son.

Auburn didn't practice Friday afternoon. "We just went out and walked around the field a bit," Beasley said.

Nothing was said to the team officially about Givens' death. There was no dedication of the game — nothing like that — but the Auburn football players, according to Beasley, had Givens on their mind.

Beasley especially.

"He was a hustler," Beasley said. "He would hustle from the word go. He never slacked up. I knew that's what he would of wanted me to do today, and that's what I tried to do."

The Birmingham News
September 23, 1979

Jordan, the Trustee

Four years ago today, Ralph (Shug) Jordan was busy preparing his Auburn football team to play Tennessee. He hardly even noticed when his birthday passed.

Early this week, he asked a caller if he could change an appointment. "It's my birthday," he said, "and I don't want to be all tied up on my birthday."

Such is the life of Auburn's retired football coach, James Ralph Jordan. He turned 69 last Tuesday. In many ways, life began at 65.

For Jordan, a normal day begins about 5:45. That's when he and his wife Evelyn "bounce out of bed and greet the morning." Then it's off for their daily exercise. Jordan compares their exercise routine to that of a B-52 bomber and a jet plane.

"I walk exactly a half-mile out and a half-mile back. I've got it staked out. I plod along like a big bomber, but Evelyn is like a jet fighter. She takes off. I bet she walks two miles or more a morning down the road and across the field in front of the house."

After breakfast, it's off to work. Mrs. Jordan works with foreign students at Auburn University and Jordan, as football coach emeritus, reports to his office in Memorial Coliseum.

He gets there about nine every day and spends most of the morning on the telephone or answering letters.

In the old days, he would worry about scouting reports and recruiting. Now, he is worried about budgets and academic programs. As an Auburn University trustee, he is concerned with the overall operation of the university.

He is a member of the search committee to find a replacement for retiring Auburn President Harry M. Philpott. That will take up most of his time in the immediate future, but he will say little about it.

"We met Saturday morning," he said, "and agreed that none of us on the committee will make any statements about the committee or its work. All statements will come from Senator Bob Harris of Decatur. He is chairman of the committee. I was among those making the agreement and I intend to abide by it."

Jordan has received numerous calls from alumni and friends of Auburn wanting to make recommendations and suggestions for the presidency. He has referred them all to "Search Committee, Room Seven, Samford Hall, Auburn University." That is headquarters for the group.

Being an active Auburn trustee is not new for Jordan. He has been one of Auburn's most active trustees since being appointed to the Board in 1976 by then Governor George C. Wallace.

He has an open-door policy to Auburn students, faculty, staff and Auburn alumni. His visitors have been impressed with his overall knowledge of and concern for the total university program.

"He has been one of the biggest assets I've had," said Ron Taylor, student government president. "His door is always open and he is always available to me. I have found him to be very open and responsive to reasonable requests. His knowledge of the university is amazing."

When he is not in his office, the man who led Auburn to its greatest football heights is at home, piddling around in the yard. Of late, he has had to do more than piddle.

"That yard has taken most of my spare time lately," he said. "With all this wet weather and wind, it has been a full-time job keeping it in shape. I spent all yesterday afternoon working on it. It was hard work, but it sure did look pretty this morning. I was proud of it when I looked at it."

Jordan chuckled when asked about those two pecan trees he and Mrs. Jordan planted in their back yard 26 years ago. Their good years at Auburn were just beginning, and those two trees were symbols that the Jordans planned to stay in the Loveliest Village for a long time.

"You know," he said, "we've never gotten a single pecan off those trees. They are beautiful trees and should be at the height of their production years, but Evelyn won't let me do anything about the neighborhood squirrels. They get all the pecans. We get all the shells."

Mrs. Jordan is an avid traveler. Coach Jordan is not. They just returned from a trip through the Black Sea countries, and Coach Jordan was less than enthusiastic about it. He didn't like eggs and sardines for breakfast, and he was afraid the PLO would be waiting in every port.

"That is one of their big training areas," he said without apology, "and you can never tell what the PLO will do."

Jordan would prefer to stay around home. If he is going to go visiting, he wants to go visiting with his children and four grandchildren. He's trying to make up for lost time.

"I feel like my children were orphans," he said. "Evelyn raised them. I was always off at an alumni meeting, on a recruiting trip or tied up with football some way. I should have found more time for my children.

"I'm trying to make up for lost time, but I will never be able to retrieve some of those days when young Ralph and I should have been out there fishing or skiing."

Asked if he ever thought he retired too early, Jordan responded with a quick and firm, "No."

"I waiver a bit at times," he said, "but Evelyn convinces me I did the right thing. I'm convinced, too, but it's normal to second guess yourself."

If anything, Jordan says, he may have retired too late.

"It might have been best for Auburn and for me if I had retired right after the Gator Bowl (a 27-3 win over Texas), but I had a coaching staff to think of. By prolonging it a year, we did get a man from our staff (Doug Barfield, now Auburn's head coach) and that's what I was after.

"As for the decision to retire, I've never seriously regretted that the timing might have been a bit off, but that was all."

The Birmingham News
September 25, 1979

(Part Two)

Ralph Jordan, Auburn University head football coach emeritus, won't be at Neyland Stadium Saturday when Auburn plays Tennessee. He will be home, listening to it on the radio.

He will be listening closely and he expects to hear an Auburn victory.

Jordan has made a conscientious effort to remove himself from the Auburn football scene since his retirement four years ago. He estimates that he has seen a total of 30 minutes of practice since 1975 and not more than five or 10 minutes of that at any one time.

Yet he remains vitally interested in the program he headed for 25 years, and he considers himself one of its biggest supporters.

"It's not out of lack of interest that I don't go to practice," he said. "I don't go out of deference to Doug (Barfield, head coach). I tried to be as invisible as I could at the start, and I don't know what an old retired football coach could do out there anyway.

"That doesn't mean," he emphasizes, "that I don't support Doug Barfield and the program 100 percent. I try to help Doug and Lee (Hayley, athletic director) whenever they call on me. I do whatever I can and whatever I'm asked to do. Both Lee and Doug would have to say 'Amen' to that."

Jordan, who had a 176-83-7 record at Auburn, attends all of Auburn's home games. Usually, he and his wife, Evelyn, sit in the press box. But this year, with a new press facility under construction, they sit in the President's Box with retiring President Harry M. Philpott.

Jordan rarely goes to out-of-town games.

"I made that a policy when I got out," he explained. "The Alabama game is the only exception I make. That game means so much to the players at Auburn. I have to go to that one."

Jordan says Auburn has a fine football team this year and freely predicts a victory over Tennessee.

Jordan won't predict the score of Saturday's game other than to say it will be a tough game between two fast-jelling football teams. He is much freer about his Predictions about 1980.

He makes two predictions about that 1980 game, one that Auburn will win 21-6 and the other that 72,500 fans will be in Jordan-Hare Stadium to see it.

Auburn will win 21-6, he says, "because Tennessee doesn't kick extra points very well."

He is much more concerned about the 72,500 fans in the stadium.

"Despite all the criticism and second-guessing," he said, "we are going to be real proud of the stand we took when we voted 4-3 to enlarge the stadium. It is going to be one of the great things we did in the athletic history of Auburn."

Jordan was one of four trustees voting for the stadium enlargement. Three voted against it and five did not come to the meeting.

The stadium controversy — if it can accurately be called a "controversy" — is not the first furor Jordan has been involved with since he became a university trustee in 1976.

There is a segment of Auburn alumni and faculty who say he was instrumental in bringing about the retirement of Philpott. Jordan denies it.

"It was strictly his decision," Jordan said, "and his alone. I had nothing to do with it. In my opinion, he has done a splendid job for Auburn."

Last spring Jordan called the Auburn Board of Trustees a "rubber stamp" for the administration and said that the board was not carrying out its constitutional duty to set policy for the university.

"A lot of people thought I just drew that out of a hat," Jordan said, "but I didn't. I've been on the board three years and I've been around Auburn 50 years. It's always been this way. I merely told the public how it really was."

Jordan said the board is supposed to set policy, and the administration is supposed to run the university on a day-to-day basis.

"The word 'policy' was a misnomer," said Jordan. "The board has met to legalize what the administration wanted to do. We rubber stamped whatever they wanted."

Jordan's remarks may have changed that.

"My words were not directed at any one individual or at any of the people on the board," he said. "I just wanted to be honest about how the university was being run.

"Sometimes you have to hit a mule between the eyes with a two-by-four to get his attention. I guess I got some attention. I can already see a difference. This board is already different from any board Auburn has had in 50 years.

"I have to believe Auburn will benefit from that."

The Birmingham News
September 26, 1979

They Also Serve

Ray Benson came to Auburn in 1975, a year before Joe Cribbs, two years before James Brooks. There was little about his 5-10, 145-pound frame to suggest that he was an athlete.

He came from Mountain Brook near Birmingham, and he wanted to be a veterinarian. There was really no other school for Ray Benson. Scholarship or no scholarship, he was coming to Auburn.

Things didn't go exactly according to Ray's plan at Auburn. His course of study was not as rewarding as he had anticipated. There were other things to do, too. Whole new worlds opened to him.

A new era was beginning in Auburn football. Ralph Jordan was hanging up the whistle. Doug Barfield was moving in behind the big desk in Memorial Coliseum. Barfield recruiting efforts brought much young talent to the Plains, Brooks and Cribbs among that talent.

There was no mention of Ray Benson.

Neither was there mention of Jimmy Youngblood, Mike Lee, Rudy Goldschmidt or Robbie Bouchillon and others like them. They were among Auburn's forgotten people.

Still, however, they kept their appointed rounds. They did what was asked of them and sometimes more.

They spent hours and hours in preparation and practice. They learned their assignments well. They knew their part and the role it played in the total effort. They knew what they were supposed to do and they had a great desire—a great, great desire—to do it well. Like Cribbs, Brooks, Harris Rabren, James McKinney and others, they, too, wanted to excel.

These young men never played a down for Auburn. They never made a block, never caught a pass and never made a tackle, but they have made a significant contribution to Auburn nonetheless.

Don't look for their names on today's roster. They are not there. Benson, Youngblood, Lee, Goldschmidt and Bouchillon are in the stands today, cheering the Tigers on to what they hope will be another victory.

They want Trotman to complete every pass. They want Brooks, Cribbs and other Auburn runners to score every time they get the ball. They want the Auburn defense, Rabren, McKinney, Freddie Smith and friends to stop every play for a yard loss. More if possible.

If it were their duty, these young men would do all they could to help. Football, however, is not their game. They perform on stage, not on a field.

They are actors, Auburn actors, and they are very good at what they do. They are as good in their chosen field as Brooks, Cribbs, Frank Warren or Edmund Nelson are in their field. That is no small compliment.

All five have put in all-star performances. If they gave All-America or All-Conference honors in drama, these five would surely qualify.

The point to this piece is quite simple.

As they cheer for the football players on the field today, let those of us who are football fans cheer for them when they come to their great hour on the stage. For they, in their own way, in their own field, have made just as great a contribution to Auburn as those we cheer today.

Auburn Football Illustrated
Auburn vs. Vanderbilt
October 13, 1979

After starring on Broadway, Ray Benson and his wife Jodi are living in Los Angeles. Youngblood, Goldschmidt and Bouchillon are still in the entertainment business or allied fields. Mike Lee is dead.

A Touch of Class _____

TO WHOM IT MAY CONCERN:

Mark Robbins has not asked me to write this letter of recommendation. I do so of my own volition and I do so gladly.

Mark is a senior in the school of business. He has always maintained a high scholastic average. Last spring, for example, he made the Dean's List with a perfect 3.0 average. He may be on it again this fall, even though football has taken up much of his time.

Mark is a kind, considerate, salt-of-the-earth person, very unpretentious and thoughtful. Letters of appreciation from a third grade class mean as much to him as awards for athletic achievement. That says something about his values.

Mark is a Christian. He attends Trinity United Methodist in Homewood. His witness is not that of the Bible-Beater, "Are-You-Saved?" variety that turns people away. He witnesses by living rather than speaking.

The week of the Kansas State game Mark spent the better part of a Tuesday evening with a 10-year-old Opelika girl. There had been a death in her family, and Mark, knowing that the girl was a big Auburn football fan, thought she might like to take her mind off things for awhile. He went over to visit her. He didn't make a big deal out of it. He just went about doing good in the quiet Mark Robbins kind of way.

Mark has dreamed of playing football for Auburn since he was in the third grade. Pat Sullivan, Auburn's Heisman Trophy winner, was his boyhood hero. He met Sullivan once and what transpired had a profound impact on Mark Robbins' life. It helped make him what he is today.

He asked Sullivan what it would take to earn a scholarship to Auburn. His hero told him it would take hard work, effort and total dedication. Sullivan probably doesn't remember the meeting, but young Mark never forgot it. Sullivan's words became commandments to him. By putting them into practice, he earned the football scholarship for which he yearned.

Those words—work, effort and dedication—still describe Mark Robbins. Coaches and teammates alike use them and with good reason.

He is a pass receiver in a run-oriented offense, but he doesn't spend his time wishing Auburn would throw more. He does something constructive, something to help the team. Backs, no matter how fast they run, need downfield blockers. Mark Robbins was not always a good downfield blocker. Now he is. Hard work, effort and total dedication made him good.

As a reporter, I have observed Mark Robbins in victory and in defeat. I cannot say that he is the same in victory as in defeat—the good ones never are—but I can say that he has always been available and that he has always been genuine. There has always been a touch of class about him. Always, in every situation, there has been that touch of class. I appreciate that and respect him for it.

I respect him, too, for the deep regard he has for his parents and the way he expresses it. They are waiting for him outside the dressing room after each game. He always embraces them. He does so unabashedly.

Living in Auburn has many great pleasures. One of them is getting to know the

Auburn athletes on a personal basis. Getting to know Mark Robbins has been especially meaningful. He is a good man.

If you are looking for someone who is all a student-athlete should be, you would do well to look in Mark Robbins' direction.

Auburn Football Illustrated
Auburn vs. Florida
November 3, 1979

Mark Robbins and his wife Laura live in Birmingham with their two children. They come to Auburn as often as they can. Mark is still proud to have been an Auburn Tiger, and always will be.

Marty

Take a minute today and look at the Auburn cheerleaders.

Look at the head cheerleader in particular. His name is Marty Yates and he is quite a guy.

Make that quite a man. Because that's what Marty Yates is—a man.

The road has not been easy for Marty. It seldom is for children of broken homes. In Marty's case, there were complicating factors. His mother died when he was 13. For personal reasons, he could not live with his father. Marty lived with his aunt for a year and with his grandparents for awhile. But to Marty and to his older brother Don, there was only one place for Marty to be.

Marty and Don had always been close. Marty saw his first Auburn football game when Don, an Auburn student, drove home and brought him back to the 1969 Florida game. As soon as Don graduated from Auburn, Marty moved in with him. Don was 22. Marty was 15.

They shared a one bedroom apartment in LaGrange. Don got the bed and Marty got the couch. It was an uncomfortable situation, but a lot of love made it bearable. Marty used his social security check to help with the rent. He worked, too, to help buy groceries.

These were lonely times for a boy of 15. His brother traveled for LaGrange College. Marty was alone from Sunday night through Thursday night. Suppers were the worst times. The alone-ness of his situation settled in on him then. He would heat up a TV dinner or a can of spaghetti and eat alone. There was loneliness and there were tears.

Dinner invitations were a welcome thing, and the good people of LaGrange responded the way good people always respond. A number of LaGrange families still consider Marty one of their own and tell him so.

Marty tried to be a normal high school student at LaGrange, but his home situation made that difficult.

The harsh realities of his situation came home to Marty as never before as graduation approached. His friends were planning their college careers. Marty wanted to go to college, but there was no money. The unsettled past made the future even more clouded.

Then came graduation. Marty cried that night, but they were tears of joy. An anonymous benefactor gave him $1,000 toward his college education. He also won a partial scholarship.

There was, at last, a ray of hope.

You can look on the field today and see what Marty Yates has done with that ray of hope. He will graduate in June with a degree in marketing.

He has worked throughout his career at Auburn. He is working in the High School Relations office now and Auburn could not have a better goodwill ambassador.

It is altogether fitting and proper that we consider Marty Yates on this Homecoming Day, for he is living, visible proof that there is still truth in that old Auburn motto, "Where There's a Will, There's a Way..."

Marty Yates had the will.
Auburn, the good people of LaGrange, and a brother who loved him provided the way.

Auburn Football Illustrated
Auburn vs. Mississippi State
November 10, 1979

Marty Yates is now a successful Atlanta banker. He is, and forever shall be, an Auburn man.

A Certain Goodness

Every football team needs to have a Charlie Trotman.

"Those athletes who contribute to the team just by being the kind of people they are." That's the way Coach Bryant puts it.

"The people who add depth to a program." That's the way Coach Ralph Jordan put it. "Those people who put bottom in your program."

They are talking about people like Charlie Trotman.

Charlie Trotman plays his last football game today. In a matter of hours now, his football career which began in the second grade will be over.

The moment will not pass without notice.

It would serve no purpose to list Charlie Trotman's statistics here, the yards gained, passes completed, touchdowns scored, that kind of thing.

It should suffice to say that he has quarterbacked Auburn to two straight winning seasons. The Trotman-directed Auburn offense has equalled the efficiency of the Pat Sullivan years in yards gained and points scored. The record speaks for itself.

Yet, Charlie Trotman has never captured the fancy or affection of Auburn football fans. They always seem to ask, "Couldn't Barfield play somebody better than Trotman?" As Alf Van Hoose, sports editor of *The Birmingham News* observed, "War Eagle alumni don't respect their man nearly as highly as their enemies..."

If that's ever bothered Charlie Trotman, he's never shown it. He just kept right on doing the best he could with the talent and ability God gave him. That is all that could be asked of any man.

To limit a discussion of Charlie Trotman to the football field would be to limit the discussion to only a piece of the man. In this case, a small piece.

His contributions to his university cannot be measured by the lines and boundaries of a football field. A football field, though an oft-used instrument, can be a poor standard of measure.

Charlie Trotman has contributed to the life-blood of what will soon become his alma mater. He was selected for membership in Spades, said to be the highest honor an Auburn man may attain. Spades are selected not for what they have done, but for what they have the ability to do. After their selection, they must prove themselves worthy.

Previous Spades have included Ralph Jordan, Jeff Beard, Walter Gilbert, Pat Sullivan, Lloyd Nix, Morris Savage and Fob James. That is putting Charlie Trotman in some pretty select company.

He has proven himself worthy in every respect. Every respect.

He is worthy, not because he has played football, but because he has given of himself to others and to Auburn. Because he has been a student here, Auburn is a better place to live and to learn.

That can not be said of many people.

It can be said of Charlie Trotman.

Coach Jordan had a way of describing football players and football teams: "They have talent. They have size. And they have a certain goodness about them which will enable them to accomplish great things."

A certain goodness.
That is what I have admired most about Charlie Trotman. That certain goodness...
That is what I shall miss most of all.

Auburn Football Illustrated
Auburn vs. Alabama
December 1, 1979

Charlie Trotman has a law degree and is now a Montgomery real estate developer. Though he no longer wears the Orange and Blue, he continues to follow and support the Tigers as the color analyst on the Auburn Football radio network.

Kenny Howard—Friend, Confidant ———

One of the most significant careers in Auburn athletic history will end June 1.

Milford K. Howard never won a medal, never scored a touchdown, never made a free throw. He never tried to do any of those things, but no one has had more influence on those who did than the man affectionately known as "Kenny."

The record will show that Kenny Howard has been an Auburn trainer and assistant athletic director for 35 years.

But he was always more than that—much more. He was a friend and confidant to Auburn coaches. To Auburn athletes in all sports, he was a father, a friend, a big brother, a favorite uncle, whatever was needed.

Kenny Howard's love affair with Auburn and Auburn people began long ago, so long ago that not even Kenny remembers how it really started. He surmises it must have begun back in Crossville, up on Sand Mountain.

He remembers hearing the folks up at the Ag Experiment Station talk about Auburn. He never heard of another place, and so as far as he was concerned, Auburn was the only place to go.

He came to Auburn in 1945 as a freshman in civil engineering. But it took Professor Herbert Martin only two weeks to teach him that he was no engineer.

Somewhere along the way, he made friends with a man named George O'Neil. It was to be a fateful friendship, for it was O'Neil who first introduced Howard to Wilbur Hutsell. Hutsell was head trainer then, and he needed a student assistant.

Howard, then an ag student, needed a job. The two got together and the rest is history.

Down through these 35 years, Howard has become one of the best in his chosen field. He has been an Olympic trainer twice and head trainer of the World University Games twice. He is in constant demand as a lecturer and a consultant.

It says something about Kenny Howard that when he decided to retire, Wilbur Hutsell was the first man he sought out. "He gave me my first job."

Hutsell, now in his nineties, shares an office with Howard in Auburn's Memorial Coliseum.

Through the years, Kenny has seen a lot of great individual efforts. Some of them come quickly to mind. Some involve Auburn, some do not.

The 1949 Auburn-Alabama game is one of those moments that comes quickest to mind.

"They had beaten us 55-0 the year before," Howard recalls. "Their fans were yelling '56...56...56' but we beat 'em 14-13. Any time the underdog wins, any time you win a game you weren't supposed to, it's a great moment."

There was Joe Childress with his 35 carries against Miami in 1954. Auburn was a winner, again 14-13. And again Auburn wasn't supposed to win. There was the National Championship team of 1957 and the Sullivan-to-Beasley passing era.

Even so, Kenny says Connie Frederick is the most exceptional player he has ever seen. He is referring to Frederick's entire kicking game, but especially to two plays in the 1968 season.

Against Clemson and again against Arizona in the Sun Bowl, Frederick, the punter, had the ball snapped over his head—far over his head. Both times he ran the ball down and got off outstanding punts. Both plays turned the game in Auburn's favor.

Still, however, Howard's greatest personal thrills have come in the Olympics. Helsinki, 1952, will always be special. It was his first.

"There's nothing in the world quite like the Olympics," he says. "There's an air about it. It is above the minds of men. It is a special feeling, seeing people from all over the world trying so hard to win the gold medal.

"Winning should be everybody's goal in every sport. Don't settle for anything but first place, but when the event is over, be proud of where you finished. There is a feeling that transcends international and cultural boundaries."

Kenny's great love for Auburn may be surpassed only by his greater love for his country.

"I've never been around an emotional experience like the opening ceremonies of the Olympic Games," he says. "When you walk into the stadium representing your country and hear those cheers, it does something to you. You'll never forget it."

It goes without saying that he hopes other young Americans will get to experience the same feeling this summer.

Kenny Howard is not leaving athletics. If anything, he may be getting more involved. He will join Dr. Jack Hughston's Sports Medicine Foundation in Columbus, Georgia, promoting care-of-the-athlete educational symposiums nationwide.

The Birmingham News
April 19, 1980

Kenny Howard and his wife Jean live in Auburn. Kenny Howard continues to conduct himself with class and dignity, both hallmarks of his 35 years' service to his alma mater.

July 17, 1980

AUBURN, July 17—Ralph "Shug" Jordan died peacefully at his home in Auburn today.

His family was with him when he died early this morning according to Dr. Jim Mathews, the family physician. Jordan, 69, had been battling acute leukemia for four months.

Funeral arrangements are incomplete, but the family requests no flowers.

Jordan coached Auburn football for 25 years and led the Tigers to their greatest heights. His teams won 175 games from 1951 through 1975, an average of seven games a year.

His 1957 team won the National Championship, and Jordan-coached players won every major award in college football. He produced 20 All-Americans and 70 all-conference players. His Auburn teams appeared in 12 bowls.

In many ways, Jordan was Auburn football. His association with the game and its players went back to the beginning of the game at Auburn. He was a close friend of Cliff Hare, Auburn's first quarterback who later became dean of the school of chemistry.

When Jordan was an assistant coach at Auburn, the two men visited often, and they spent many a Sunday afternoon talking, visiting and reminiscing about Auburn football.

Auburn's 72,000 seat stadium is named Jordan-Hare in honor of the two men.

Jordan was born Sept. 25, 1910. His athletic career began in his beloved Selma. His first coach, Paul Grist, remembers that day in 1918 "when that little tow-headed boy in overalls drug a stalk of sugar cane in the front door of the YMCA and said 'I want to play ball.'"

He graduated from Selma High School in 1927. The Great Depression was approaching and money was scarce, so Jordan went to work for the state highway department to pay for his first year at college. It was then that he began to form the philosophy that would lead to his success on the football field, his "Seven D's of Success" as he called it. They were: Discipline, Desire to excel, Determination, Dedication, Dependability, Desperation and Damn it anyway—do something."

He entered Auburn in the fall of 1928, a year behind his high school class. He pledged Theta Chi, worked at a boarding house and quickly established himself as one of Auburn's most promising young athletes in football, basketball and baseball.

He would be an Auburn resident for all but four of the next 51 years.

"There wasn't a harder fighter or a more likeable man on the Tiger squad," the 1932 *Glomerata* recorded. "Although his play could not be called spectacular, he was as dependable a center as any team in the South could boast of. Not one bad pass to the backs is recorded against him in his last year of play."

Jordan was a complete student. He was treasurer of his senior class, a member of Blue Key and Scabbard and Blade. He was tapped for membership in Spades, the highest honor an Auburn man may attain.

Jordan graduated from Auburn in 1932 and became an assistant football coach and head basketball coach. Coach Jordan became Lieutenant Jordan shortly after Pearl Harbor. Over the next four years his life would be risked many times. He participated in four major invasions, North Africa, Sicily, D-Day and Okinawa.

On the 30th anniversary of D-Day in 1974, he recalled loading into those small landing crafts and heading for the smoke enshrouded French coast. "I never saw an atheist or an agnostic when it came time to hit the beach," he said.

Jordan returned to Auburn after the war, but a new coaching staff had replaced the old one and his future did not look promising. He went to the Miami Seahawks, a short-lived professional venture, in 1946, then on to Georgia in 1947 to coach the line for Wallace Butts.

Jeff Beard, an old classmate of Jordan's, was hired as Auburn's athletic director in 1951. Auburn had won only three football games in three years and Beard's assignment was simple—he had to rebuild Auburn football. His first act was to hire Jordan as Auburn's football coach. The next 25 years were known as "The Jordan Era" and no period of Auburn football can compare to it.

Jordan would surpass such coaching greats as Bobby Dodd and General R.R. Neyland in total victories. His overall record was 176-83-7. A coach would have to win eight games a year for 22 years to surpass it.

When Jordan became head football coach, Auburn's stadium—then known as Cliff Hare Stadium—had 21,500 seats. When he retired in 1975, it had 62,000 seats. Three years later, as a member of the Board of Trustees, Jordan voted to enlarge the stadium to seat 72,000. It was renamed Jordan-Hare Stadium in his honor in 1973.

Winning games was never the most important thing to Jordan. "It is not enough to make them football players," he often said. "We have to help them become men, too."

Jordan was often referred to as a "gentleman-coach." When he retired after the 1975 season, sportswriter Phillip Marshall wrote: "No matter what level of greatness it may attain, Auburn football will never be the same."

Jordan is survived by his wife, Evelyn, three children, Darby Jordan of Atlanta, Georgia, Susan Pilgreen of Memphis, Tennessee and Ralph Jordan Jr. of Morristown, Tennessee and four grandchildren.

* * * * * * *

STATEMENT FROM RALPH JORDAN'S FAMILY PHYSICIAN, DR. JIM MATHEWS:

"Coach Jordan died early Thursday morning, July 17, of acute leukemia. His family was at his bedside. At the end stages of the disease Coach Jordan experienced no painful suffering.

"Coach Jordan's leukemia was diagnosed four months ago. The leukemia arose from myelofibrosis, an abnormal condition of the bone marrow. His treatment consisted of chemotherapy and blood transfusions to which he failed to satisfactorily respond.

"Coach Jordan had previously been treated at Baptist Brookwood Medical Center in Birmingham for heart rhythm difficulties which required a pacemaker."

* * * * * * *

FUNERAL SERVICES

Services for Coach Ralph Jordan will be at 2 p.m. Friday at Holy Trinity Episcopal Church in Auburn. Burial will be in Memorial Park in Auburn.

The body will lie in state at Frederick's Funeral Home in Opelika Thursday night and Friday until 1 p.m.

The family requests that donations be made to the Auburn University Foundation Shug Jordan Fund in lieu of flowers. Donations may be sent to the Auburn University Foundation Shug Jordan Fund, Auburn University, AL 36849.

Auburn University Press Release
July 17, 1980

Losing a Friend

AUBURN—It was my great pleasure to know and love Coach Jordan. And to know that he knew and loved me. "Pleasure" is not the right word, but I'm not sure what the right word is. Maybe "privilege." Certainly "honor."

Most people knew him as a football coach. I knew him as a man, a totally wonderful, beautiful man.

It was written when he retired in 1975 that Auburn had lost a patriot. The same could be said today. Auburn has indeed lost a patriot. And many of us have lost a friend.

I went to see him often through the final weeks. He was always the same. That was one of the beautiful things about Coach Jordan. He was always so sincere, so genuine, so open, so honest, so thoughtful, so kind.

Never a day went by that he did not ask about my mother who is recovering from a stroke, and he always asked about the little boy from Gordo, the boy he had called once, just to encourage him to fight the good fight in his personal battle against cancer. The boy won his battle. Coach Jordan lost his.

Coach Jordan a loser?

How can it ever be said that he lost in the things that really mattered, things like love, loyalty, integrity and courage. Courage. We must not leave that one out. Above all Coach Jordan was a courageous man.

He was a people-person. He cared deeply about his fellow man and he believed in Auburn because the Auburn he knew and loved—the Auburn he sought to preserve—cared about people, too.

Ralph Jordan was not without his faults and shortcomings. He was, after all, human. He was said to be stubborn, and he was not afraid to use his power within the bounds of honor. People might disagree with his position, but they could not question his dedication and commitment. I know of no man who had more trust and faith, more love for a school and its people, than he had for Auburn and Auburn people.

The betterment of Auburn—that was the hallmark of Coach Jordan's life. It was the thing he worked for and lived for. Everything he did was, in some way, directed toward that ultimate goal—the betterment of Auburn. His deeds can't be numbered. Many were never mentioned, but I think he would like to be remembered in that way, in that short, simple way: "Shug Jordan—he worked for the betterment of Auburn."

It would be a fitting remembrance.

Coach Jordan....

So many memories, so many images come vividly to mind:

—the 1977 pep rally when he quietly and effectively admonished Auburn students for leaving a game early by saying simply, "Auburn people don't do that..."

—the jaw set and tilted upward toward the moonlight as the final seconds ticked off the clock in his last game against Alabama.

—the way he said, "Good God a-mighty" when something went wrong on the field.

—the sheer utter joy he showed in the dressing room after Auburn beat Georgia 35-20 in 1971 and earned a Sugar Bowl bid. He stuck his tongue out, rolled his eyes back and shook his head back and forth like a little kid. A piece of hedge was tucked behind his ear.

—his glistening eyes as he embraced Wade Whatley at midfield after the Gator Bowl in 1972. Whatley—the substitute quarterback who had come out of nowhere to lead Auburn to one of its sweetest victories ever. Colorado was the opponent.

—planting the pecan trees in 1953, a sign that he and Mrs. Jordan planned to be in Auburn a long time. Those trees are still there, like his influence, growing large, strong.

—the faded old beige athletic department jacket he wore for good luck throughout the 1971 season. It worked every game but one.

—the bright orange sweater that became a Jordan trademark.

—the quiet voice, the Selma accent, that always marked his gentlemanness.

—his dedication to Auburn, his commitment and great love that expressed itself every day in every way.

—that faraway look that would come to his eyes and the smile that would creep gently across his lips when he talked about the old days in Selma and Auburn.

—the deep chuckle that came so freely and so often.

—the way he said, "You're so right, Carl," "Down through the years," and "Selma, Queen City of the Blackbelt." There was always a slight pause between Selma and the rest of the phrase, "Queen City of the Blackbelt."

—the way he said, "We're going to Atlanta with only one thought in mind...Beat hell out of Georgia Tech."

—his Seven D's of Success: Discipline, Desire to excel, Determination, Dedication, Dependability, Desperation and the final one, when all else failed, "Damn it anyway, do something..."

The record will show that he won 175 football games—176 if a forfeit with Mississippi State is counted—but that is an incomplete record. A record, no matter how great that record may be, is incapable of measuring and remembering a man. It is a poor substitute.

At this moment I see his life as I have known it flash before my eyes—a man at the height of his power, a man entering retirement and a man facing old age. A strong and faithful man facing death.

I will remember his love, his loyalty, his compassion. In a word, his kindness. That and his sternness.

An Atlanta writer once said talking to Coach Jordan was like talking to your father. How true.

A father—that is what I and countless others have lost today.

We loved him.

And it will mean so much—Down Through the Years—to know that he returned that love.

The Birmingham News
July 18, 1980

146

Remembering Coach Jordan —————

Two stories come to mind when I think about Coach Jordan. I believe they indicate what kind of man he was.

The first took place at the Gator Bowl in 1974. Auburn had just beaten Texas 27-3. The game was not that close. It was one of Coach Jordan's greatest victories, certainly one of his most satisfying.

Texas had not wanted to play Auburn. They did not have much respect for Jordan's team and had bothered to practice only a few times.

There were other reasons this win was sweet too. Texas Coach Darrell Royal was one of three or four coaches who enjoyed great national fame and acclaim. Everywhere he went he drew attention.

Coach Jordan on the other hand was low key. He was modest to an extreme. He was hardly known by the general public outside the South, but that didn't bother him. He was happy doing what he loved best—coaching Auburn football and living the quiet life in Auburn, Alabama.

Coach Jordan never said anything about it—not to the public at least—but he was irritated at the way Texas regarded him and his players. As Rodney Dangerfield would put it, Jordan and Auburn weren't getting any respect—at least not the respect they deserved.

That had its good side, too, however. It allowed Coach Jordan to play the role he loved best, the one he was most successful at utilizing, that of being the underdog. Jordan and his Tigers had something to prove in the Gator Bowl that night and there was no doubt that they proved it.

Amid the shouting, the hugging and the wild jubilation in the Auburn dressing room, Wayne Hester, a sports writer for *The Anniston Star*, thought about a question.

"Wouldn't this," he thought, "be a good time for Coach Jordan to bow out?"

Jordan was 63 years old. His 24th Auburn football team had just won 10 games including the rout of Texas and that got the whole nation's attention. It could have been 50-3 instead of 27-3.

Hester started to ask the question, but he didn't. "What the heck," he thought, "Coach Jordan's not going to retire. He's going to coach as long as he can."

Little did Wayne Hester know that retirement had already been discussed in the Auburn dressing room that night. Auburn President Dr. Harry Philpott had called Jordan aside just as the celebration got underway. He wanted to know if Jordan would reconsider his decision to retire.

The answer was "No." Coach Jordan had not reconsidered and he would not reconsider. The next year would be his last.

Some three months later, on April 8, 1975, the word leaked out. Ralph Jordan, Auburn's head football coach for 25 years would retire after the 1975 season.

A few days after the announcement, Hester told Buddy Davidson, Auburn sports information director, about his thoughts in the Gator Bowl that night. He speculated about what would have happened if he had asked Coach Jordan about retirement?

Davidson grinned. "Wayne," he said. "You could have had the scoop of your life."

Hester smiled. He knew Jordan would not have lied. He might not have answered the question, but he would not have misled him.

Coach Jordan was an honest and truthful man. He was an honorable man.

The other story that comes to mind involves Mark Winne, now a reporter for *The Birmingham News*.

As a student reporter for *The Auburn Plainsman*, Auburn's student newspaper, Winne was somewhat of a maverick. Some people would say that was putting it mildly.

Winne lambasted Jordan when he voted for the enlargement of Jordan-Hare Stadium. Winne said Jordan was guilty of a conflict of interest and accused him of using his position on the Board for personal gain. Winne never said how Jordan would gain personally from the stadium enlargement, but he threatened to report him to the attorney general. He may have done it.

Few men of Jordan's dignity and esteem have had to face such an attack.

A few weeks later, Winne had to interview Jordan on another story. He had never met Coach Jordan and he had seldom spoken to him. He did not look forward to a face to face confrontation. He was in for a surprise.

Never, he said later, had he been treated kinder. Coach Jordan gave him all the time he needed. They talked about a variety of subjects forthright and candidly. The subject of Mark's editorial never came up. When the meeting ended, Jordan invited Winne to go to a football game with him.

Winne was flabbergasted.

He just didn't know Coach Jordan.

When I told Coach about Mark's reaction to their meeting, Coach Jordan threw his head back in his familiar fashion and laughed.

"You tell Mark," he said, "that I believe in the first amendment as much as anyone."

Coach Jordan—the gentleman-coach. It was my great pleasure to know and love him.

He won 176 football games at Auburn, but as the reaction to his death poured in, that was seldom mentioned. Words like "love," "compassion," "kindness," "strength," "fortitude," "concern," "gentleness," "class," were far more evident.

That was fitting and proper.

Paul Grist, Coach Jordan's first coach, had a saying that Jordan often repeated: "Don't wait to be a great man, be a great boy."

Coach Jordan helped many a boy to become a man.

I was one of them.

Personal Reflections in
Several Alabama Newspapers
July 18, 1980

Last Rites

Funeral services for Coach Ralph Jordan were conducted by Rev. Bill McLemore of Holy Trinity Episcopal Church. Reverend John Blow, priest associate, assisted with the ceremony.

In keeping with the Episcopalian tradition and belief, there were no lengthy eulogies. The church believes that death is common to all men and at the point of death all men are equal. For that reason, flowers and lengthy eulogies are kept to a minimum.

McLemore said, "The people gathered here are the sermon for Coach."

No crowd estimates were made, but the 250-seat church was filled to overflowing long before the services began at 2 p.m. Representatives of Southeastern Conference schools and many of Coach Jordan's former players were among the hundreds of people at the services.

The church yard was filled with people unable to get inside the church.

The service began with the singing of "Holy, Holy, Holy."

That was followed by a reading of Lamentations 3:22-26 and 31-33.

The Twenty-third Psalm was recited. It was followed by a reading of John 14:1-6. The passage begins, "Let not your heart be troubled. Neither let it be afraid..."

After three brief Episcopalian prayers, the service closed with the singing of "A Mighty Fortress Is Our God."

The entire service lasted about 15 minutes.

Brief interment rituals were held at Memorial Park Cemetery in Auburn.

Active pallbearers were Terry Beasley, Rusty Deen, Phil Gargis, Terry Henley, Mike Neel and Pat Sullivan.

Auburn University Press Release
July 18, 1980

Spirit(s) of Auburn _____

Since we last visited, Auburn has endured two great losses.
Coach Jordan and Dean Cater are no longer with us.

For our visitors from Duke, I am talking about Coach Ralph "Shug" Jordan, our football coach for 25 years, and Dean Katharine Cater, our Dean of Women for 34 years.

I cannot tell you, I cannot begin to describe to you, what these two people mean to Auburn and to those of us who consider ourselves sons and daughters of Auburn.

We know what they meant to us individually and collectively. We know that they were, for so many years, the heart, soul and moral fiber of that which is Auburn.

But let us not look back. Let us look forward. The torch has been passed, and it is up to us, the living, to carry on.

If that which is Auburn is to endure, if it is to prevail, we must pass it on, from generation to generation. We may not be ready. We may not be prepared, but it is our task, it is our duty, to carry on. We must pass *Auburn* on to others as Coach Jordan and Dean Cater passed it on to us.

What is *Auburn*?

Far be it from me to try to answer that question. There are as many definitions of *Auburn* as there are Auburn men and women.

It would be safe to say, however, that *Auburn* is much more than a football game. It is much more than winning and losing.

It is a spirit. It is an attitude. It is a way of looking at life and at one another. It is, almost, a way of living. Unless you have experienced it, you will never know what it is; you will never understand it. Once you have experienced it, you will never be the same. A part of you will, forevermore, be an Auburn man or an Auburn woman.

This is the heritage that Coach Jordan, Dean Cater and others before them passed down to us. It is the heritage we must pass on to those who follow in our footsteps. It is the moral fiber that binds us together as Auburn men and Auburn women.

So let us carry the torch in our hand and let us carry it high for all the world to see. But more importantly, let us keep the glow within our hearts and the fire in our determination.

It would, I believe, be fitting to close this discussion with *The Auburn Creed*. It, better than anything else I know, describes what it is like to be a part of Auburn.

I believe that this is a practical world and that I can count only on what I earn. Therefore, I believe in work, hard work.

I believe in education which gives me the knowledge to work wisely and trains my hands to work skillfully.

I believe in honesty and truthfulness, without which I cannot win the respect and confidence of my fellowmen.

I believe in a sound mind in a sound body and a spirit that is not afraid, and in clean sports that develop these qualities.

I believe in obedience to law because it protects the rights of all.

I believe in my Country, because it is a land of freedom and because it is my own home, and that I can best serve that country by "doing justly, loving mercy, and walking humbly with my God."

And because Auburn men and women believe in these things, I believe in Auburn and love it.

Auburn Football Illustrated
Auburn vs. Duke
September 20, 1980

Fear and the Chinstrap

We are honoring the Team of the Decade today, and what better way is there to honor that team than to recall some of the memories they left behind—especially the memories they left in the hearts and minds of the young people who watched them play and worshipped them.

George Stephenson was one of those young people. He was 13 years old in 1970, and he still remembers the long ride to Auburn from Hartselle when coming to see his brother Jim was an excuse to go to the football game.

He remembers sitting in the north end zone with his parents. He remembers going down on the field when the game was over, hoping for a chin strap, a shred of jersey, a knee pad, a thigh pad, anything to commemorate his close encounter with his beloved Tigers.

In his upstairs room at home in Hartselle, he still has mementos of those early days: programs, pennants, a few ticket stubs, a "Pat Who" sticker. There is, however, no chin strap.

"I guess I wasn't aggressive enough," he says, smiling in his warm downhome way as he speaks. "Some of the other kids would run up to the players and almost demand their chin straps. I'd always hang back a little. I guess I was a little shy."

George was downright scared the first time he saw an Auburn football player up close in street clothes. He doesn't remember the year or the game, but he does remember seeing "a big ole Auburn football player with two girls."

His father tried to get him to go up and ask for an autograph, but George wouldn't go. "I was scared," he says. "He was too big."

That is George Stephenson's first memory of Auburn football.

It is significant that he now stands 6-4, weighs 246 pounds and is known as "Big George." He wonders if children might be scared of him.

George always dreamed of being an Auburn football player. He wanted to be the next Pat Sullivan. He was one of the first kids in Hartselle to get a blue Auburn jersey with the number 7 on it, and the first day he went out for midget football, he went out for quarterback. The next day, however, he was moved to center and he's been an offensive lineman ever since.

Now, he's one of the best in the country. At Auburn he is being compared to Ken Rice, Forrest Blue, Dave Hill and Chuck Hurston.

Big George doesn't make a big deal of it, but he often thinks about where he was, where he is, and how far he has come.

He's always careful about who gets his chin strap. He doesn't give it to the first boy who asks. He waits awhile. He waits until he sees a boy standing off to the side. "One watching like I used to do." That is the boy who gets his chin strap.

And who is to say, 10 years from now, when they're honoring the Team of the 80's, some Auburn football player, a back or lineman perhaps—one of those kids straining to get over that fence today—might smile and say, "I remember the day George Stephenson..."

Auburn Football Illustrated
Auburn vs. Tennessee
September 27, 1980

George Stephenson made All-SEC in 1980, and his college dream of going back home and being a successful dairy farmer has come true. Big George is, and always will be, an Auburn man.

Booing

This is not a pretty story. If you want a pretty story or a happy story, turn elsewhere.

If you're an Auburn fan, and if you're serious about your love and loyalty to your school, you'd better stay here. We're doing some things we ought not to be doing.

Charlie Trotman was at the football game last week. It was the first time he had seen a football game since he graduated. Giving up football has been hard on Charlie. Getting up the courage to come back and not be an intimate part of it had not been easy.

He was sitting with his parents when the booing started. It hit him hard, like a knife to his stomach. He was heartsick. Tears came to his eyes. Tears of anger. Of all the people in Jordan-Hare Stadium, only he knew how Charles Thomas felt when you started booing him.

It was a year ago, you will remember, that many of you booed him, Trotman, and cheered Charles Thomas. Funny, isn't it, how times change.

"It really made me mad," Trotman said late Sunday night. "It took a lot for me not to jerk some people's heads around and ask them if they knew what they were doing...

"I could just feel for Charles. It really does hurt. Nothing you can do to an athlete would hurt him more. You could stab him, clip him, kick him in the face or jerk his face mask. Nothing hurts like being booed. It hurts you mentally and emotionally.

"It makes you want to sit in your room alone and think about a lot of things. It makes you wonder why you are going through all of the pain and agony. I remember waking up on Sunday morning wanting to cry like a baby."

Charlie Trotman has learned about the fickleness of fate. He learned the hard way. He doesn't smile when people make jokes about the "What-Have-You-Done-For-Me-Lately" syndrome.

Charlie Trotman went down to the Auburn dressing room after the game last week. He hoped to see Charles Thomas, but he missed him.

He planned to write Charles this week and offer him a word of encouragement. What he said to him is a matter between the two young men, but you should know this much.

He told him that it doesn't matter what others think. The only thing that matters is that you do the best you can do. The ones who boo you today will cheer you tomorrow. He told him to keep his head up, that he, Trotman, knows he can get through this. He knows from personal experience. But the hurt, it stays with you.

Our friends from Richmond will have to excuse me for airing our dirty laundry in public. It was not my choice. It was aired last week before 75,000 people here and hundreds of thousands listening on radio throughout the nation.

We at Auburn have always prided ourselves on being something special. Alabama booed Richard Todd in 1975. Tennessee booed Jimmy Streater last year and we booed Charles Thomas, one of our own, last week.

The question is obvious.

Are we really special anymore?

Auburn Football Illustrated
October 4, 1980
Auburn vs. Richmond

A Deep South Tradition _____

AUBURN—The Auburn-Georgia game is one of the South's oldest and most colorful traditions. Auburn-Georgia transcends the bounds of sport.

The first Auburn-Georgia game was played at Atlanta's Piedmont Park on February 20, 1892, when Dr. Charles Herty of Georgia, the man who would perfect the process for making paper out of southern pine, accepted a challenge from his friend Dr. George Petrie of Auburn.

Both men had "discovered" American football while in graduate school at Johns Hopkins. Until they brought the game to Auburn and Athens, American football, as it was called, had never been played south of Raleigh, N.C.

Auburn won that first game 10-0, but what happened at the game is more important and more interesting than the score. Clyde Bolton, in his book, *War Eagle, A Story of Auburn Football*, (Strode, $8.95) noted a few of the things that happened that day in Atlanta.

Georgia Tech did not have a football team so 150 Tech students walked to Piedmont Park to see the first football game in the Deep South. They arrived an hour before kickoff and, though it would be unbelievable in this day and time, they wore red and black and cheered for Georgia.

The Tech students quickly took over the Piedmont Park grandstand and began to make their presence known with "cowbells, horns and lusty lungs," according to Bolton.

Their favorite yell was, "Techety tech, who wrecks, who wrecks, boom rah, boom rah, Geor-gia."

The Tech students liked to do another yell too: "I love codfish—I love codfish—I love codfish balls...."

All of this went on before the game even started. It is little wonder that Georgia Tech students soon became and to this day remain the arch-enemy of both Georgia and Auburn.

Bolton points out that though the Tech students cheered for Georgia in the first game, they had switched to Auburn by the time the two teams played again in 1894. They switched because the Georgia students rocked the Tech players at the first Georgia-Georgia Tech game in 1893.

Both Auburn and Georgia had unusual mascots for that history making first game. Georgia had a white goat named Sir William. Auburn's team was accompanied by a black man dressed in orange and blue.

Although there is no historical fact to prove it, legend says Auburn's world-famous battle cry "War Eagle" was born that February Saturday in Atlanta.

According to the legend, an Auburn student fighting with Robert E. Lee in Virginia during the War Between the States—that's what true Southerners called it—was wounded in the wilderness battles and left for dead. When he regained consciousness, he was one of two living things on the battlefield. The other was an eaglet, a baby eagle.

Showing the veterinary spirit that would later make Auburn famous, the student took the eagle with him and nursed him back to health. When he returned to Auburn after the war, the eagle came with him. He called the bird "War Eagle" because of the circumstances under which he was found. Auburn was a small village and everyone was familiar with War Eagle.

The student later became an Auburn professor and accompanied the team to Atlanta for that very first Auburn football game. War Eagle, of course, went with him.

According to the legend, when the crowd began to cheer as the game began, the old eagle, now 28 years old, broke away from the professor and began to circle high above the playing field at Piedmont Park. Auburn people looked up and, seeing the eagle, pointed skyward and shouted "War Eagle!"

On the field below, the men clad in Orange and Blue, hearing that familiar phrase, rolled toward the victory in the first football game ever played in the Deep South.

Although there is little historical basis for the legend, it is generally accepted as the "true" origin of Auburn's "War Eagle" cry, probably because of the colorful romanticism that surrounds it.

Those early Auburn-Georgia games rotated between Atlanta, Montgomery and Savannah until 1916 when the game found a "permanent" home in the quaint little Memorial Stadium in Columbus, Ga.

While in Columbus, the Auburn-Georgia game rivaled the Georgia-Florida game of today as the world's largest cocktail party.

Columbus businesses, eager to be good hosts, would give cocktail parties that would last well past kickoff. It was not unusual for the Auburn-Georgia game to start with very few people in the stands, only to have thousands storm in midway of the second quarter.

Some of college football's greatest fights took place at the Georgia-Auburn game under those conditions. The most serious one was in 1953. The fight started on the field, but quickly spread into the stands. In a matter of minutes, thousands of fans were fighting for the honor of the Orange and Blue or the Red and Black.

The fight stopped only when both bands began playing the national anthem. Since it was 1953, not very long after World War II and right at the end of the Korean War, patriotism was still very much alive and the crowd, good Southerners that they were, stopped fighting, stood at attention, and the game proceeded.

The Auburn-Georgia game moved from Columbus to a home-and-home basis in 1959. Georgia won the first game in Athens, 14-13, to clinch a conference championship. Auburn won the next year in Auburn, 9-6, when Ed Dyas kicked three field goals to Durwood Pennington's two. Fran Tarkenton was the Georgia quarterback in both games.

The series has taken on an unusual twist since moving to a home-and-home basis. Georgia has won only four of 11 games played in Athens and Auburn has won only four of the 10 played in Auburn. Both teams seem to play better on the other team's home field.

Overall, the series is tied, 38 games for Auburn, 38 games for Georgia and there have been seven ties.

Only 3,000 people attended that first Auburn-Georgia game. Tickets were fifty cents for an adult and a quarter for children. A carriage space sold for $1.00.

Those 3,000 people had no way of knowing what they started.

More than 76,000 people and the eyes of the nation will be in Auburn Saturday at

Jordan-Hare Stadium. Tickets sell for $10.00 and game programs sell for $1.50. There will not be enough of either.

It is, after all, Auburn-Georgia.

Auburn University Press Release
November 11, 1980

The 40-Year Break ─────────────────────

Auburn and Alabama did not play football for 41 years because of a disagreement over $34.00.

It was this, rather than a fight or a killing, that caused the two state rivals to stop playing football between 1907 and 1948.

For many years, many reasons were given for the break in the series after a 6-6 tie in 1907. Most prevalent was the implication that a fight had broken out at the end of the tie game and several people had been cut and injured. One rumor even had the governor's son being killed in the melee.

None of these reasons are true. There was a fight at the end of the 6-6 tie— a game in which Alabama used trick plays such as the "German Play," "the Military Formation" and the "Dance-Trick" to come from behind to tie— but there was nothing more than a flurry of fists between players at the end of the game.

The real story of Auburn's break with Alabama, or Alabama's break with Auburn depending on which side you are on, came to light when Bill Cromartie was researching his book, *Braggin' Rights*, (Gridiron Publishers $9.95) which is a complete, detailed history of the Auburn-Alabama rivalry.

Cromartie's extensive research revealed that the real trouble between Auburn and Alabama began in the winter of 1908 when the two schools began to make plans for their game that year.

Auburn wanted to increase the travel squad and up the per diem. In 1907, the two schools had been allowed 17 players at a per diem of $2.00 per day for two days. Auburn wanted 22 players at $3.50 per day.

Auburn's reasoning was simple. Birmingham hotels would not negotiate suitable lodging and meal rates in 1907, and the Auburn team wound up losing $1.50 to $1.75 per man for the two day stay.

Alabama offered a counter proposal—20 players $3.00 a day. Auburn refused Alabama's offer saying that any reduction in the number of players or the per diem rate was unacceptable.

The difference in what Auburn proposed and what Alabama offered was $17.00 a day, a total of $34.00 for the entire weekend.

The stalemate lingered on and early that spring a new point of contention arose. This one was a more football-like disagreement. The two schools could not agree on an umpire to officiate the game. Alabama said Auburn insisted on having a non-Southerner because Auburn didn't think there was a man in the South capable of calling the game.

Auburn said that was not true. Thomas Bragg, the team manager, apparently the athletic director of his day, said Auburn suggested an Eastern official only after no agreement could be reached on a Southern man to call the game.

That could have been a veiled reference to Alabama's use of trick plays in the 1907 game.

The Auburn-Alabama rift then spread to the newspapers. Representatives of both schools did a lot of name calling, some of which sounds familiar. Alabama said Auburn did not have any class. Auburn said Alabama didn't know anything about class. If they had class, Auburn contended, they wouldn't play such an easy schedule every year.

Each school claimed the other would play only on its terms and both refused to compromise.

One last minute effort almost broke the stalemate. In late September, Auburn agreed to accept an official suggested by Alabama, and Alabama agreed to meet Auburn's demands on players and per diem. All that remained was the selection of a date.

Auburn offered four possible dates, but Alabama waited four weeks to reply. By that time two of the dates had passed and it was too late to change dates of other games.

Two chances remained, November 21—when Alabama had a game scheduled with Haskell Institute, an Indian school—and November 28, the Saturday after Thanksgiving.

Alabama would not cancel the Haskell Institute game. In an honorable stand, Hill Ferguson, one of the men assigned to work out details with Auburn, refused to be swayed by the pressures of his day. "Even though they are Indians," he said "we feel their contract should be protected unless they are willing to release us, which is not the case."

That ruled out November 21, and the Auburn Board of Trustees refused to change its long standing rule prohibiting football games after Thanksgiving.

The Auburn-Alabama series had stopped, and the hard feeling that accompanied the break ran so deep that many were concerned about what could happen if the two schools ever played again.

Auburn rejected a resumption of the series in 1911 saying it was acting in "the interest of true sport."

In 1923, Auburn president Dr. Spright Dowell rejected another Alabama overture saying an Auburn-Alabama series in football saying that such a game would make "other games, contests and events subservient to the one supreme event of the year."

By 1944, Alabama had come around to Auburn's way of thinking. When Auburn wanted to renew the series, Alabama's Board of Trustees refused, saying that an Auburn-Alabama rivalry would lead to an over-emphasis of football in Alabama and an unhealthy increase in rumor and rancor between the two schools.

The Board also said an intra-state rivalry would make it impossible for either school to hire coaches of high character and proven ability because they would be afraid of beating the cross-state rival every year.

Several legislative attempts were made to force the two schools to play again, but all such attempts failed. The Legislature did, however, pass several resolutions calling on the two schools to play another. Each of those was rejected by both schools.

Finally, in 1948, the series was renewed.

Jeff Beard, Auburn's athletic director from 1951-72, was business manager at the time. He remembers the renewal this way:

"Dr. Draughon (Auburn President Ralph B. Draughon) and Dr. Gallalee (Alabama President John M. Gallalee) were attending a meeting in Birmingham.

"They were good friends and on the way to their cars, Dr. Gallalee said, 'Ralph, there's no reason in the world why Alabama and Auburn can't play one another.'

"Dr. Draughon agreed and a meeting was set up at the Ann Jordan Farm near Kellyton, just off U.S. 280 near Alexander City."

This was in April of 1948, and the two schools agreed to resume athletic relations immediately. The first football game was played December 4, 1948.

Alabama won that first game 55-0. Auburn won the next year, 14-13, and the series has continued without interruption ever since.

Although many of the fears expressed by Dr. Dowell in 1923 and by the Alabama Board of Trustees in 1944 have come to pass, the Auburn-Alabama series, one of the bitterest rivalries in the nation, remains strong.

Alabama leads the overall series 26-17-1.

Auburn University Press Release
November 18, 1980

The Pat Dye Era Begins ─────────────

**OPENING STATEMENT BY AUBURN PRESIDENT DR. HANLY FUNDER-
BURK AT THE PRESS CONFERENCE ANNOUNCING THAT PAT DYE HAD
BEEN NAMED AUBURN'S 22ND HEAD FOOTBALL COACH...JAN. 3, 1981:**

"We are here today to present our head football coach. We have been very busy
during the past month trying to find the right person for Auburn University. We have
found that person. We have found a man who has been successful in this business.
He is going to build a championship football team for Auburn during the eighties. I
want to call on all Auburn people to unite behind this gentleman. Even though he is
good—we know he is the man for the job—he can't do it alone. I'm calling on all
Auburn people, wherever they are, to come together behind Pat Dye so that he can
get on with the business at hand. That business is building a championship football
team. I present to you now head coach Pat Dye."

**PAT DYE WAS NAMED AUBURN'S 22ND HEAD FOOTBALL COACH ON
FRIDAY, JAN. 2, 1981. HE MET WITH THE MEDIA FOR THE FIRST TIME AT
A PRESS CONFERENCE SATURDAY, JAN. 3. HERE ARE EXCERPTS FROM
THAT PRESS CONFERENCE:**

"I am extremely happy to be back in Alabama—Auburn, Alabama that is—and see
so many friendly faces and be in an area where football means so much to the people.
I am also grateful to the press for being here, for being so patient and for not writing
any speculative stories about the new head football coach at the University of
Auburn. You've been very tolerant with the committee, and I really appreciate having the ability to talk to you candidly and not having you put into the paper some of
the things that might have been said.

"I am very excited about being at the University of Auburn. It is what I consider
one of the top jobs in the south. It is a school that has tremendous football tradition.
It is a school that I remember playing against and watching my older brothers play
against back in the fifties. I remember coaching against the University of Auburn at
times when it was certainly a feared football power in the South.

"I am confident that with the support of Auburn people, the alumni, the former
players, the student body, the faculty and the administration, we will be able to bring
this great football tradition back to what it once was.

"We look forward to this challenge with great anticipation and a lot of enthusiasm.
We realize fully that it will take a lot of hard work and probably a lot of patience on
your part and our part, but we will get the job done in the end.

"I know very little about the Auburn football team or the football program at this
time. I've been away from the state of Alabama for seven years now, but I am confident that, given time, we will bring it (Auburn's football tradition) back to what it
once was."

QUESTION/ANSWER SESSION

On contract and terms: "I've got a four-year contract that I'm very pleased with. I did not come to Auburn for money. I came for the opportunity. To me that's a lot more important right now than the financial gains."

On assistants that will be coming with him: "I would anticipate four or five coaches coming depending on whether Al (Kincaid) gets the head coaching job at Wyoming. I feel confident that Neil Callaway, Wayne Hall, Bobby Wallace, Oval Jaynes as administrative assistant, will come, and I'm sure that Al will come if he does not get the Wyoming job. Frank Orgel will probably come from Clemson."

Have you assembled a staff in anticipation of getting the Auburn job?: "I felt like I was the best choice for the job. I also knew that I'd never been unemployed and if we didn't get this job something else would become available. I discussed it with my wife, Sue, and we felt like that this opportunity may come along once in a lifetime and I was not in a position where I would let the administration at Wyoming force me into making a decision that would affect my coaching career the rest of my life. I understand the position they were in..."

Did you know that you were Auburn's No. 1 choice?: "No. I called Dr. Funderburk, and he said that no decision had been made. You're still a top candidate, but that's as much as I can tell you. As long as I'm a top candidate I'm not going to take my name out of the picture."

Were you discouraged by the pace of the search?: "I was born and raised on a farm and when you watch those crops grow, you learn to be patient."

Any present Auburn coaches to remain?: "I don't know. I know some of the coaches on the staff, but I'm not sure how many of them want to stay."

Recruiting plans: "I've got a meeting with Coach (Frank) Young (AU recruiting coordinator) this afternoon to find out where we are. I've got to find out what we've got coming back to find out where we need to put the most emphasis on the remaining 16 players we can sign."

Wishbone—will you run it at AU?: "I really don't know. If we have the personnel to run it, I'd like to run it, but we're like most wishbone teams—maybe a little more so than most—we run eight or nine formations out of the wishbone. Our offense is a little different from what Alabama and Oklahoma are doing."

What are the "fine" points of your contract: "The committee was concerned about my connections with the University of Georgia and The University of Alabama. I don't have any plans to go to the University of Georgia. It's kind of an unwritten law (that you don't go from one school to another within the same conference). Even though he's a native son, I'm kind of surprised that Dooley would consider coming back to Auburn after having been at Georgia for 17 years. I hope that down the road somebody will want Coach Dye. If they do, that will mean we've been winning at Auburn and will have the kind of situation we want, and we'll all be having a good time. It's in the contract that I will not go to any other Southeastern Conference school in the next four years. That's no problem with me."

Did you talk to Coach Bryant before taking the Auburn job?: "I talked with Coach Bryant a day or two before I met with the selection committee the first time. I've called Coach Bryant in the past and discussed with him any move I was considering. He's always discouraged me from making a move regardless of where it was, and I think that's his nature. Then, if you go ahead and do it, it was something he wasn't going to change your mind on anyway."

Did he try to discourage you from coming to Auburn?: "Naturally he didn't want me to come to Auburn. I don't think that would be unusual in a case like this. Coach Bryant and I are very, very close friends and have a warm relationship that I hope will certainly continue. I owe a great deal to the man for being able to be right here."

Can you out-recruit him?: He's been pretty good at it over the years. I imagine I'll work a little harder at it than he will right now. Coach Bryant will be difficult to compete against. The University of Alabama has great tradition, but so does Auburn. We've got to go about rebuilding this program in the same manner that it was rebuilt back in the early fifties—just hard work, dedication, loyalty and the things that will win for you. In the game of football you can still win with intangibles, and if you couldn't, then I wouldn't be standing here."

With your Alabama ties, will it be hard for Auburn people to accept you?: "Not really. I think we've got to focus on Auburn. Anytime there is a coaching change, anytime there is a new personality coming in, there is always some reservation, some anxiety and some frustration, but as long as Auburn is a focal point, then we can all rally together and go in the same direction—putting Auburn number one. We're all working for the same thing. My relationship with Alabama is in the past. I have great Alabama friends that I hope I'll have a lifetime, but when we start competing in recruiting, selling Auburn against The University of Alabama, and playing on Saturday afternoon, that's a different thing. There won't be any question in Coach Bryant's mind about us getting ready to play against Alabama, and I hope there won't be any question in the mind of Auburn people either."

Did the fact that Coach Bryant is nearing the end of his career at Alabama influence you to come to Auburn?: "Not really. This has been a great job for years. It has been a great opportunity for years. I don't want to speculate on what's gone on in the last four or five years. There could have been some things there that were very difficult for Coach Barfield and maybe no coach could have come in and done a better job than he's done. But now we have a new era. There will be enthusiasm, and the fact that Coach Bryant is in his last years should not hold Auburn back a bit in the world."

On returning to the SEC: "It's like coming home. This is the number one football state in America. It's a way of life here. We've carried the same excitement and enthusiasm wherever we've been, but it just hasn't been the same. The people in Wyoming are talking about rodeoing in July. The people in Alabama are talking about the Auburn-Alabama football game. The people in North Carolina are talking about the four-corners offense. In Alabama, they'd be talking about why you didn't run the ball on third and one instead of throwing it. That's the difference."

How close did you come to coming to Auburn? Were you recruited by Auburn?: "Coach Jordan was a personal friend of my family. Coach Jordan and my father were very close. Mrs. Jordan was born and raised 15 miles from where I was born and raised. Coach Jordan knew our family and he knew I had two older brothers who went to Georgia. He was the type gentleman who, when I came along as a highly recruited player, said that he wanted me at Auburn, but he understood my family ties and understood that I might want to go to Georgia. He said he wanted me at Auburn, but would not put any pressure on me. That's the kind of gentleman he was."

Is there a timetable to bring Auburn back?: "Not really, because I don't know what type players we have in the program right now. I know Auburn people want a winner, and we will have a winner, but the timetable will be determined by the type people we have in the program. I'll measure our success by the improvement we show from day to day, from week to week, from month to month and from year to year. If we have continuous improvement we'll be looking at a long range thing rather than a spur of the moment thing. I want to build the Auburn football program on a good, solid foundation with solid people whom we can tie to and rally around 10 years from now."

Does the "mover" reputation bother you?: "I am not a mover. This is my fourth coaching job. I stayed at Alabama nine years and I was offered a job every year I was on the staff. I was at East Carolina six years and was offered a job five of those years. I went to Wyoming with the anticipation of staying there and getting that job done, but at the same time, we were working for an opportunity like Auburn. I'm just really, really excited about this opportunity to be back at home with home people."

Will the fact that you were not a clear choice from the beginning hurt your support?: "I was the third son and my mother and daddy wanted a little girl, so I've been living with that all my life. I was supposed to be named Patricia. That (the search process) doesn't bother me at all. What is important is that they ended up with the best coach."

Auburn University Press Release
January 3, 1981

Rowdy

Rowdy Gaines didn't take the conventional way to the top of the swimming world. He took the unconventional way and it has made all the difference since.

To truly understand the human phenomenon that is Rowdy Gaines, one must go back to his birth—before actually.

That's when he acquired the nickname "Rowdy"—before he was born. Clint Eastwood had a lot to do with it.

There was a popular television show back in the late fifties. *Rawhide* was its name and Clint Eastwood was the star. He played a character named "Rowdy Yates," and Rowdy Yates was Buddy Gaines' favorite cowboy.

It followed then that when his unborn son began to do a lot of kicking, his mother and father nicknamed him "Rowdy." Nobody thought the name would last, but it has, for 21 years now.

Rowdy laughs about it now. "Beats Ambrose," he says, smiling. "And it certainly beats Ambrose Gaines IV" which is his legal name.

As might be expected, the boy who would become the greatest swimmer in the world learned to swim—at least float—before he could walk.

"We lived on a lake," he explains. "Everybody in Winter Haven lives on a lake, and you have to learn how to swim to survive."

There was no indication, however, that Gaines would one day achieve fame and worldwide acclaim in the water. Like other boys, he played the sports as the seasons came around, Little League baseball, football and basketball. He soon realized, however, that he was "too little for football, too short for basketball and too slow for baseball," and wrestling didn't exist in central Florida.

He began swimming competitively when he was 8 or 9 years old. He was "pretty much of a winner" then, but he doesn't know to what degree or to what extent.

It was about this time that Gaines began his unconventional climb to the top of the swimming world.

After a promising start in competitive swimming, he decided that swimming was not for him. One day he quit—"Just up and quit" is the way he describes it. "One day I was at workout, the next day I wasn't."

Rowdy believes that was one of the wisest decisions he ever made. That decision, he says, has enabled him to accomplish what he has in swimming.

"My coach wanted me to get serious about the sport," he explains. "He wanted me to go into year-round training. There was no way I was going to do that. I would have burned out by the time I was 12.

"It is important to note," he says, "that my parents were behind me 100 percent. They did not pressure me one bit even though I know they enjoyed seeing me swim and seeing me win."

Gaines began to swim again his junior year in high school. He started back, he says, "because I was 17 years old and I needed to do something with my life. I had no idea what I would do with my life. I'd never thought about college."

He thought about playing tennis, but he didn't like his chances there. "There were too many good players," he recalls, "and I hate to lose."

That "I-hate-to-lose" feeling is an important part of the Gaines psyche.

His parents never pushed him. Occasionally they would call his attention to other swimmers and say, "Look at those guys. You can beat them...," but they never pushed him. Just that. Nothing more.

Somewhere between his junior and senior years, Ambrose Gaines IV—Rowdy—made the decision to "be the best swimmer I can be."

The rest is history.

The little boy who once gave up swimming because he didn't want to take it seriously is now the finest sprint freestyler in the world. He holds the world record in the 200-meter, the American record in the 100- and 200-yard freestyles and he was "World Swimmer of the Year for 1980."

His coach, Auburn's Richard Quick, says he does things in practice that nobody else in the world can do.

It did not come easy.

He swims twice a day for 11 and a half months out of the year. He has two weeks off in September. That's all.

A typical day finds Gaines getting up at 6 a.m. and at the pool by 6:30 for a two hour workout. He's in school from 9 until 1, at home from 1 to 2 and in the weight room from 2:30 until 3:30.

He swims from 3:30 until 5:30, eats, goes home and studies from 7 until 9. Big tests might force more study, but he is usually in bed by 9:30.

Gaines is a mass communications major, and even though he swims an average of 10 miles a day, he is still a good student. He was one of Auburn's Top 20 scholar-athletes fall quarter and he has an overall B average.

The sacrifices have been many, yet Gaines really wonders about only one—social life.

"I've missed a lot of things," he says, "but others have made those same sacrifices." Occasionally, Gaines finds himself thinking about his Russian counterparts, wondering what they are doing, how they train, how they handle their social life.

He knows they think about him, too, and that makes it all worthwhile.

Rowdy and other Americans missed the chance to compete against his Russian adversaries head-to-head when the United States decided to boycott the Olympic Games.

"It was," he admits, "one of the biggest disappointments of my life. For a year and a half, my one goal in life was to go to the Olympics."

His obsession with the Olympics—that's what he calls it—ended a relationship with a girl he planned to marry. He is, however, philosophic about it all. "Life goes on," he says, flashing a smile and a slight shrug.

In a matter of weeks now, Gaines faces his greatest decision. At 21, he is an old man in his chosen sport. Unlike football, basketball and baseball, there is no professional future in swimming. When it ends, it ends, and for Rowdy Gaines, the end could be near. The NCAA championships and the AAU championships are his last scheduled events.

His coach says he is good enough to lay off a couple of years and come back as good—maybe better—than ever. Gaines is considering that option, but he is making no commitments.

"It has to end sometime," he says, "and this might be a good time. I don't know. It's kind of scary."

Ultimately Gaines wants to go into the film industry like his father, directing and producing TV shows, movies and sports productions.

One thing is for certain. If Ambrose Gaines IV went back to competitive swimming to find direction for his life, he has found that and much, much more.

Auburn Press Release
March 19, 1980

Rowdy Gaines retired after the 1982 NCAA and AAU championships. He retired as the greatest swimmer the world had ever known. At his prime, he could swim faster than any man who had ever lived on earth. He came out of retirement in 1984 and achieved his ultimate goal, winning three Gold Medals in the 1984 Olympic Games. He narrowly missed making the 1988 Olympic team when he was 29 years old. Rowdy Gaines was, and is, truly a remarkable man.

No Limits

AUBURN—Auburn swim coach Richard Quick toyed with his dinner salad as he pondered the question. His would not be a simple or casual answer.

An hour earlier one of his swimmers, Rowdy Gaines, had been named SEC Swimmer of the Year. Gaines, a senior from Winter Haven, Florida, had dominated the SEC swim meet, winning three individual titles and swimming anchor on each of Auburn's three winning relay teams.

Gaines won the 50, the 100 and the 200 freestyles. He set American records in the 100 and 200 and he already held the world record in the 200-meter freestyle (1:49.16). He was World Swimmer of the Year in 1980.

The question then was simple. Simple, yet penetrating...

"What makes Rowdy Gaines great?"

"To begin with," Quick said, putting down his salad fork, "Rowdy has the freedom to win.

"Most people have psychological limitations as to what they can do. Rowdy is free of those psychological barriers. His only goal is to win. He would have done whatever it took to win those races without thinking it couldn't be done."

Quick is hesitant to talk about goals Gaines may have set for himself. "We seldom talk about that kind of thing," he said. "Goals themselves can be limiting. That's what I mean by Rowdy's freedom to win. He doesn't place any limitations on himself. He is free to do whatever has to be done."

Quick compared his star swimmer to other athletes in comparable tight situations.

"There are some people," he said, "who rise up and make the winning shot in basketball or who make the first down you have to have in football.

"Rowdy is one of those people," Quick said. "He doesn't care what it takes, he is willing to do it as long as he touches the wall first. When you are talking about races that are won by one one-thousandth of a second, it's no longer physical. It's mental."

Physically Gaines is not lacking either.

To say that he has all of the physical tools would be an understatement, according to Quick.

"He's a good-looking, well-built athlete to start with," Quick said, "but it goes far beyond that. He has big hands and feet that enable him to move through the water easily. He's very flexible in his shoulders and ankles, and his upper body allows for a lot of strength development.

"He has no hips, no waist and no buttocks. His legs are small and slender, but they are strong," Quick said, "deceivingly strong.

"On top of that, he has an iron will and a determination that enables him to be free—free to win.

"Frankly," Quick said, "I don't know how good Rowdy can be, and I don't believe he knows. To say how good he can be is to put limits on him and Rowdy Gaines knows no limits."

With that Quick returns to his salad.

Not far away, Rowdy Gaines, the greatest sprint swimmer in the world, munched on his salad as he visited with his mother and his teammates.

Auburn Press Release
March 23, 1981

Richard Quick left Auburn after the 1982 season to go to the University of Texas. When Rowdy Gaines came out of retirement in 1984 to try for the U.S. Olympic team, he went to the Texas Aquatic Center and worked with Quick. Gaines won three Gold Medals in the 1984 Olympic Games, the most Gold Medals ever won by an Auburn athlete.

Patrick Fain Dye

Patrick Fain Dye was named head football coach at Auburn University January 2, 1981. His goal, stated that day, was simple and direct. He wants—he intends—to restore Auburn football to the heights of glory it knew in the mid-fifties, the late sixties and the early seventies. "I remember," he said, "when Auburn used to put on those blue jerseys and put the fear of God in people..."

That is his goal as Auburn's head football coach, a return to yesteryear.

And as far as Auburn fans are concerned, the dye has already been cast. It's just a matter of time.

Dye's appointment was met with a wave of enthusiasm and contagious optimism.

Auburn people saw a man who doesn't hope to win. They saw a man who intends to win.

They saw a man who understands discipline and the need for it. They saw a man who exacts discipline from himself and demands it from others.

They saw a disciplined man with dedication and a desire to excel.

Auburn people liked what they saw and four months later, on May 9, Dye was named athletic director. He would be in charge of not only football, but also the entire Auburn athletic program.

As athletic director, his goals are the same, only broader. He intends for Auburn to have a championship program in all sports, and he intends for Auburn people to have an athletic program with the class and integrity they deserve.

Pat Dye is a winner. Make no mistake about that.

When he made All-American as a guard for the University of Georgia in 1959, the headlines of his hometown newspaper screamed, "Born to be an All-American." He was born to be a winner, too.

He has been associated with only two losing teams since he began playing football 28 years ago. The first was in ninth grade. The only other loser was at Georgia in 1958. It was that team, he said, that taught him the value of discipline.

"We had a lot more talent on our 1958 team," he said, "but we didn't have much discipline. We had less talent and more discipline on our 1959 team and won the conference championship. I learned the value of discipline right there."

What is discipline?

To Dye, the answer is simple: "I like to coach kids I enjoy being around. I want my wife and children to enjoy being around them. We don't ask our players to do anything that won't make them better people and better citizens."

Discipline and a desire to excel has paid off for Pat Dye. He was a two-time All-American at Georgia, on the playing field and in the classroom. He graduated from Georgia in 1962 with a degree in education.

He married Sue Ward in 1961. Four children, Patrick, Missy, Brett and Wanda, would be added to the family in years to come.

Dye got his first coaching job in 1965 and he got it with the best, Paul "Bear" Bryant at Alabama. Alabama would win 80 games and play in nine straight bowls while Dye was on the Crimson Tide staff. One of the reasons was good linebacking—Dye-coached linebacking.

He left Alabama after the 1973 season to become head coach at East Carolina University. Over the next six years, "that little school in Carolina" knocked off ACC powers like North Carolina, North Carolina State and others. East Carolina, thanks to Pat Dye, wasn't so little anymore.

When Dye left for Wyoming in 1980, East Carolina had won 48 games, lost only 18 and tied one. It had become one of the nation's offensive and defensive leaders.

In one year at Wyoming, Dye turned the Cowboy program around. Wyoming went 6-5 in its only season under Dye. It was Wyoming's first winning season in eight years and only its second in 12 years.

Dye succeeded at Wyoming as he had at East Carolina—with discipline, dedication, determination, a desire to excel and a willingness to work—to work hard.

Then, on January 2, 1981, Auburn called.

The rest of the Pat Dye story is yet to be written.

Auburn Football Illustrated
1981 Season

This was one of the first sketches of Coach Dye to appear in an Auburn Football program. The rest of the Pat Dye Story—that part written so far—has proven to be exceptional. And more is yet to come.

A New Beginning

Save your ticket stub.

Save your program.

You will want them one day as proof, proof that you were here when the Pat Dye era of Auburn Football began.

There have been four great eras of Auburn Football. From all indications, today marks the beginning of the fifth great era.

The first great era was the John Heisman Era. The second was the Mike Donahue Era. The third great era belonged to Jack Meagher, and the greatest era of all belonged to Ralph "Shug" Jordan.

Auburn football history began on February 20, 1892, when Dr. George Petrie, a professor of history, took a group of Auburn students and faculty members to Atlanta to meet a team from Georgia "coached" by Dr. Charles Herty, a professor of forestry. It was the beginning of college football in the Deep South, and the Auburn-Georgia game has become the South's oldest continuous rivalry.

College football in those early days was not limited to student-athletes. Professors could play, too, and the biggest, most feared man on that very first Auburn team was a professor, Floyd McKissick, from the electrical engineering department.

McKissick formed the center—or "centre"—of Auburn's flying wedge.

Dr. C.B. Glenn, Class of '91, remembered that first game. He said it was a fearful and awe-inspiring sight to see the flying wedge come down with McKissick at its point—as irresistible as an atomic bomb.

Auburn won 10-0 and life in the Deep South, in the fall at least, has never been the same.

That was the only game played in the 1892 "spring season." Football resumed that fall, but on a less glamorous note. Auburn lost to Trinity (now Duke) 34-6 and North Carolina 64-0 before beating Georgia Tech 26-0.

The first game with Georgia Tech is significant in that it inaugurated the second oldest continuous rivalry in the Deep South, Auburn-Georgia Tech.

Ironically, Georgia leads the oldest series in the Deep South 39-38-7 while Auburn leads the second oldest series in the Deep South 40-39-4. Things do, as they say, even out over the long haul.

John Heisman, the man for whom the Heisman Trophy is named, became Auburn's head football coach in 1895, and the first great era of Auburn football was born. Heisman posted a 12-4-2 record in five years as Auburn's head coach.

Heisman left after the 1899 season to go to Clemson, and that may account for the similarity between Auburn's football traditions and Clemson's football traditions. Both schools are called Tigers. Auburn's colors are blue and orange and Clemson's colors are purple and orange.

Heisman later went to Georgia Tech as head coach and, while he was very successful at Tech, posting a 102-29-2 record, he always had trouble beating Auburn. He lost nine of his first 10 games against Auburn and his overall record was 5-10 against the Tigers.

The second great era of Auburn football began in 1904 with the advent of Mike

Donahue. Donahue coached at Auburn from 1904 to 1906 before inexplicably taking the 1907 season off to be athletic director. He returned as head coach in 1908 and led Auburn to some of its greatest years.

Donahue's 1913 and 1914 teams were two of the best in the country. Auburn went 8-0-0 in 1913 and 8-0-1 in 1914. The great Kirk Newell was quarterback of the 1913 team which may have been the best in the country that year.

Donahue left Auburn for LSU in 1923. LSU, of course, made Donahue a fine offer, but there may have been other reasons he left Auburn. Donahue was a devout Catholic and reportedly never felt at home in the Bible-belt predominantly Baptist state of Alabama. Thus the offer to return to a more Catholic-oriented society in Louisiana was attractive in many ways.

Whatever his reasons, Donahue left Auburn as the winningest coach in Auburn history. He compiled a record of 89-26-4. His record for the most wins by an Auburn coach would stand for almost 50 years.

Chet Wynne became Auburn's head coach in 1930. His 22-15-2 record does not qualify him to be listed among Auburn's all-time great coaches, but his era was not without its moments to remember.

Perhaps the greatest moment came in 1932 when Auburn went 9-0-1 and halfback Jimmy Hitchcock became Auburn's first All-American.

Jack Meagher became Auburn's head coach in 1934 and gave stability to what had been an up and down football program. Meagher's teams never lost fewer than two games a season, but there was never any doubt that a Jack Meagher-coached team would hit you. Meagher's teams served the nickname "Tigers" well.

Auburn went to its first bowl game while Meagher was head coach. It was the 1936 Bacardi or Rumba Bowl in Havana, Cuba, and it remains, to this day, the first and only post-season bowl game played on foreign soil.

The game, a 7-7 tie with Villanova, was of little historical significance, but the circumstances under which it was played are worthy of note.

The game was played in strife-torn Havana just days after dictator Fugelialmo Batista had overthrown the Cuban government. Batista threatened to cancel the game unless his picture was in the game program. An ad was quickly dropped and Batista's picture was added in its place so the game could be played. This is the same Batista who was overthrown by Fidel Castro in 1959.

The Meagher-coached Tigers also went to the 1938 Orange Bowl and defeated Michigan State 6-0 in one of the greatest defensive games ever played.

There is no way of knowing what kind of record Meagher may have had at Auburn had it not been for Adolph Hitler and his National Socialist Party.

War was more important than football, so Auburn, like most other Southern schools, disbanded its football program after the 1942 season and sent the players and coaches off to fight for right, truth, justice and the American way.

The Auburn team of 1942 did, however, leave Auburn fans something to savor during the war years. In the next to last game of the 1942 season, Auburn, behind the great Monk Gafford, beat undefeated Rose Bowl-bound Georgia 27-13 in a game that was not as close as the score indicated.

Football resumed at Auburn in 1944. The late forties were lean years for Auburn football, lean years and dry years.

There was only one highlight. The Alabama series was renewed in 1948. It was the first time the two intra-state rivals had played since 1906 when the series was broken off over a dispute on per diem allowances, the number of players to receive per diem and the date of the game.

The 1948 renewal was a much ballyhooed affair. Long before it was over, Alabama was doing the ballyhooing, Auburn fans the moaning. Alabama won 55-0. It was a great day for Alabama, but it only set the stage for an even greater day for Auburn the next year.

Auburn won the next year, 14-13, in one of the greatest upsets of all time. Overjoyed Auburn fans ripped seat cushions apart and made the west stands of Legion Field a sea of cotton and confetti. Auburn 14-Alabama 13.

Little did they know it would be two years before they tasted the fruits of victory again.

Earl Brown was the coach of Auburn then and, after an 0-10-0 season in 1950, it was clear a change had to be made.

Ralph "Shug" Jordan, Class of '32, was called home from Georgia in 1951 and Auburn football has never been the same.

Over the next 25 years, Jordan became Auburn's all-time winningest coach. He surpassed Mike Donahue in October of 1965 when Auburn beat Kentucky 23-18.

When he retired after the 1975 season, he had compiled a record of 176-83-7. A coach would have to average eight wins a year for 22 years just to equal Jordan's record.

Auburn won the national championship under Jordan's tutelage in 1957, and while he was coach, Auburn players won every major award in college football at the time. Zeke Smith won the Outland Award as the nation's outstanding lineman in 1958. Tucker Frederickson won the Jacob's blocking trophy in 1964 and Pat Sullivan won the Heisman Trophy in 1971.

Overall, Auburn has won 446 games, lost 296 and tied 41. The Tigers have been champions of the Southern Conference and the Southeastern Conference, and there have been nine undefeated seasons. Auburn has played in 14 bowls and has had 27 players to make All-America teams.

And today, a new link is being added to the golden chain. A new era, The Pat Dye Era, is beginning.

Welcome ladies and gentlemen, welcome to history.

Auburn Football Illustrated
Auburn vs. TCU
September 5, 1981

In Coach Pat Dye's first game as head coach at Auburn, the Tigers, struggling at times, defeated TCU 24-16. It was not an epic victory, but it proved to be the beginning of an epic era of Auburn Football.

Bo and Randy _____

Freshman running back Bo Jackson and junior quarterback Randy Campbell were the stars of Auburn's first game-type scrimmage of the fall.

Jackson, the heralded freshman from McAdory High School near Bessemer, gained 111 yards in seven carries in the first half. He had touchdown runs of 38 and 36 yards and caught a 27-yard touchdown pass from Campbell.

He was easily the game's leading rusher. Quarterback Clayton Beauford was next with 69 yards on four carries. The ever-consistent, ever-steady Lionel James gained 43 yards on four carries.

It may have been Campbell's best day at Auburn. He completed 12 of 13 passes for 161 yards and three touchdowns. The other pass was complete, but the receiver was out of bounds when he caught the ball. Campbell directed the offense six times in the first half of the game-type scrimmage and scored five touchdowns. A Ron O'Neal fumble kept the offense from getting started on its second possession.

Split end Mike Edwards caught three passes for 57 yards, Jackson, two for 36 yards and one touchdown, Ed West, three for 29 yards and one touchdown and Chris Woods, three for 28 yards. Campbell's third touchdown pass was a 15-yard strike to tight end Carver Reeves.

Campbell won the starting quarterback job in spring training and he gave no indication in the first game-type scrimmage that he was ready to give it up.

Jackson, 6-1, 218, was in the starting backfield along with Campbell, fullback Ron O'Neal and running back Lionel James. Auburn head coach Pat Dye said that did not mean, however, that he would start against Wake Forest next week.

"Willie Howell, Mike Cowart and Terry Walker were hurt," Dye said, "so the fact that he started tonight doesn't necessarily mean he will start against Wake Forest. It's obvious, though, that he will play a lot."

Jackson broke tackles on each of his touchdown runs and showed moves that reminded practice watchers of a scat-back rather than the power runner he is. The first offense and defense scrimmaged reserves, but it was obvious Jackson has talent and that Campbell has reached a new plateau as a quarterback.

As for the scrimmage overall, Dye seemed pretty well pleased.

"I thought at first there was not going to be a lick passed," he said. "Everybody appeared dead-legged, but the contact picked up as it went along."

The first half of the scrimmage was a regular game-type situation with the first unit going against the reserves. The second half was designed to take a look at younger people trying to make their mark on Auburn football.

"We got to look at a lot of people," said Dye. "The Blue team (first unit) ran a lot of offense. The defense looked pretty salty at times, but I don't know about the competition they were facing.

"You've got to be impressed with the quarterbacks," he said, "especially Randy Campbell. Clayton Beauford, Mike Mann and Pat Washington did some good things, too. There's no question that we're further along at quarterback than we were in the spring. Offensively, we're looking a lot better."

When asked about the defensive standouts, Dye cited freshman Gerald Williams at noseguard. "We know all the old ones," he said. "We're looking for some young ones who want to run in that briar patch and knock somebody on the ground.

"When they decide that it is better to hit than be hit, they'll all be better football players."

Dye said punter Lewis Colbert was kicking the ball better this fall than in the spring. He also pointed out that placekicker Al Del Greco was eight for eight in extra points with two field goals to his credit.

"We should be getting better," Dye said. "This was our 15th practice session and that is nearly a whole spring's worth of work."

Auburn will continue to work twice a day this week in preparation for a late-week dress rehearsal scrimmage. The scrimmage, like all Auburn practices, will be closed to the public.

Auburn opens the season Sept. 11 hosting Wake Forest in a night game. Kickoff is scheduled for 6 p.m. Tickets are available.

Auburn University Press Release
August 28, 1982

This is the first mention of Bo Jackson in an Auburn Football regular season press release. That freshman, first mentioned here, went on to become the greatest running back in Auburn history, winning the Heisman Trophy in 1985. At the end of his career, Bo held virtually every Auburn career and single season rushing record. He is the standard by which to measure all future Auburn running backs.

But Bo Jackson did not start his first game at Auburn. Willie Howell started in front of him. Bo was in on the second series of the game, however, and gained 123 yards on 10 carries and scored two touchdowns in Auburn's 28-10 win over Wake Forest. Howell, a senior, gained one-yard on one carry. Jackson was not officially listed as Auburn's starter until the third game of his freshman season when Tennessee came to town. Auburn defeated the Vols 24-14 with Bo gaining 110 yards and scoring one touchdown.

Randy Campbell embodied what the Auburn Spirit and Auburn Football have come to mean to Auburn people down through the years. A year earlier, he had been a down-the-line junior varsity quarterback with little chance of ever playing. On the day Auburn played Tennessee a year earlier, Randy Campbell pondered his future as he rode in the back of a bus to Gainesville, Florida for a junior varsity game. A year later, at the start of 1982, he was about to lead Auburn to 20 victories in its next 24 games. He succeeded through hard work, discipline, desire, dedication and confidence—confidence in himself, in his abilities and in his coaches and teammates.

To those who know him and to those who saw him play, one word will forever symbolize Randy Campbell—"heart." And he, Randy Campbell, will forever symbolize the best of Auburn and Auburn Football.

Lewis Colbert, All-American _____

The walk-on success story is alive and well at Auburn.

Lewis Colbert is writing the latest chapter.

Colbert, the punter for this year's Auburn team, was awarded a scholarship by Auburn Coach Pat Dye this week. He now joins a long list of walk-ons made good at Auburn, a list that includes some of the greatest names in Auburn Football.

Colbert is from Phenix City, Ala. He attended Glenwood School but he didn't start punting until his senior year in high school. A physical deformity — a clubbed foot — prevented any athletic dreams Colbert had of coming true.

Colbert was a manager for Glenwood through most of his high school career, but several operations corrected his foot problem and when football came around in his senior year Colbert was ready to go.

He averaged 42.6 yards per punt in his first and only year of high school punting. At the urging of his coach, El Edmonds, he decided to give college football a try.

"He said I averaged as many yards per kick as a lot of college kickers," Colbert recalls, "and told me I ought to give it a try."

Colbert picked Auburn because it was the four year college closest to Phenix City where his widowed mother lives. He also knew of Auburn's reputation of giving walk-ons a chance to prove themselves.

Allan Bollinger was the Tigers' punter when Colbert came to Auburn a year ago. Bollinger graduated last year and the job was wide open. When Scott Selman, Bollinger's back-up in 1981 was injured in the spring, Colbert moved to the first unit and he has held the job ever since. He has shown no inclination to give it up.

Going into the final game-type scrimmage of the spring, he had averaged 44.0 yards per measured punts. In the scrimmage, his average was 45.0 on two punts.

After practice on Tuesday of last week Dye walked by the punters and called Colbert aside. "Come up to my office after practice," he said, "and sign your scholarship."

It was the first Colbert knew of a scholarship. It was a dream come true and it was a relief. He knew his mother would not have to work so hard to help put him through school. Helping Lewis get a college education was her main goal in life.

His mother, Mrs. Mary Colbert, came to Dye's office the next day to sign her part of the scholarship. "They were a happy couple when they left," Dye said. "More than anything else she was pleased that Lewis had worked hard to make his own dream come true. He showed everybody he had the stuff down inside she always knew he had. Seeing a player and a parent like that is one of the greatest thrills in coaching."

Colbert will be one of seven walk-ons playing key roles for Auburn when the Tigers host Wake Forest Saturday. Others will be offensive tackle Jay Jacobs, cornerback Tim Drinkard, defensive end Scott Riley, safety Dennis Collier, snapper Mike Hicks and center Casey King. All are on the first or second units or on the specialty team.

All are proof once again that dreams do come true at Auburn.

Auburn University Press Release
September 18, 1982

Lewis Colbert went on to become an All-America punter for Auburn. He punted for four years averaging more than 40 yards per punt for his career. He holds the Auburn record for career punts and the most yards punting. Most importantly, he is an All-American person, too.

Out of This World _____

A few words to the men we honor here today, Ken Mattingly and Hank Hartsfield...
We are proud of you. Oh, how we are proud of you. How you made us proud of Auburn and of being Auburn men and women.

There was a special warmth, a special glow, when the NBC commentator mentioned the "Good Luck, War Eagles" sign you saw just as you were entering the shuttle.

And when the President—the President of the United States of America—said, "Two Sons of Auburn..." as he welcomed you home. How our hearts leapt with joy and with pride!

That it all happened on the Fourth of July made it much better. We were Auburn people and we were Americans too, justly proud of both.

The thing that made it so special to us as Auburn people was that both of you have experienced the same things we have experienced, the love, the joy, the warmth, the specialness of being an Auburn man or an Auburn woman.

The late night walks through Samford Park making our way back home to the dorm room or apartment to study just a little more...

The "Well, that's enough for tonight" feeling that meant it was time for a quick—and sometimes not so quick—trip to The Shack or The Casino...

The fact that you, two astronauts, may have participated in panty raids on Auburn Hall or Alumni Hall...The fact that you may have been a member of Dean Foy's Panty Raid patrol, the group of "men" and student leaders assigned to protect the dorms. As president of the student body, Ken Mattingly, you certainly were a member of Dean Foy's brigade.

The fact that you may have studied Shakespeare under Professor Ted Hoeffner in Samford Hall or learned about government from 'Fessor Jack or "Whiskey Jack" in the shop buildings.

The comment you made, Hank Hartsfield, about Dr. Howard Carr, how he was an inspiration to you, how he encouraged you and spurred you on to your absolute best in your physics courses...

What you said, Ken Mattingly, about Fred Martin in Aerospace Engineering, about the lessons he taught you, some you weren't very eager to learn, but some that have been among the most important you have ever learned. You are good friends today, you said, because of what he forced you to do in the classroom...

Those comments are a tremendous compliment to Auburn and to the Auburn faculty. There is more than book-learning at Auburn. There is common sense. There is caring, compassion and concern. Above all, there is love.

I called you, Ken Mattingly, and asked what you remembered about football. You didn't remember much, but that's all right. You remembered the important things. You remembered the fun you had as a Delta Tau Delta on football weekends...You remembered building the Homecoming floats...You remembered walking through town and across campus with your date on the way to the game...You remember how the police closed off the streets around Toomer's Corner for pep rallies...You remembered Coach Jordan.

You remembered the right things. You remembered the things Auburn people remember.

We were proud of you, gentlemen, from the magnificent blastoff to the perfect landing. We must admit, however, that we were relieved when it was all over. For your safety, yes, and for other reasons, too.

We must admit that the possibility of another "Auburn Joke" was ever present. Had you made the slightest mistake, we would never have lived it down, but you were perfect, picture perfect.

Auburn is no Harvard, MIT or Alabama...

Thank God for small favors...

Today, gentlemen, we thank God for you, for your safe return, for your journey, for what it meant to our country, for what it meant to Auburn and for what it meant to us.

We are proud of you—And we hope you are proud of us.

Auburn Football Illustrated
Auburn vs. Nebraska
October 2, 1982

Astronauts Ken Mattingly and Hank Hartsfield are frequent visitors to Auburn, their alma mater. This tribute came on the day they were honored for successfully completing the last test flight of the Space Shuttle Columbia. It was and, to date, still is, the only time the space shuttle was piloted by two astronauts from the same school.

Role Models

Auburn athletes are not just talking about the new NCAA academic requirements. They are doing something about them.

Five Auburn athletes—Bo Jackson, Lionel James and Randy Campbell from football and Beth Bryant and Mark Cahill from basketball—went to Boykin Street in the Auburn city school system and talked with about 250 fifth graders about the importance of academic excellence as well as athletic excellence.

James was the nation's leading punt returner last year. Jackson was Auburn's leading rusher last season, and Campbell, a quarterback, came out of nowhere to lead Auburn to a 9-3 season and a victory over Boston College in the Tangerine Bowl.

Bryant was a forward on the Auburn women's basketball team which was invited to the NCAA Tournament for the second year in a row. Cahill was a forward on the Auburn men's team which had its best record in seven years.

The program was arranged by Cathy Donald, one of the fifth-grade teachers at Boykin, who became concerned that her students were placing their athletic dreams above academic reality.

The new NCAA academic standards require a freshman to make at least 700 on the SAT or a composite of 15 on the ACT for initial eligibility at a Division 1 member institution, effective August 1, 1986.

"They all wanted to be athletes," said Donald, "but they didn't seem to realize that their school work would play an important part in their opportunity to be an athlete. Very few people go from high school to the pros without going through college first, and even then, a very small number actually succeed in the pros."

Here is what the Auburn athletes told the students:

Randy Campbell: "If you are serious about wanting to play college football or basketball, the first thing you have to do is to be serious about the quality of your education. You can't wait for the ACT test or the SAT test. You have to worry about your next test. Be determined to do as well as you can do on that test. Work to improve your scores on every test. Work as hard on improving your test scores as you do on improving your athletic skills.

"Keep your dreams in proportion. Don't let your dreams get out of touch with reality. I'm serious about my education because I know I'm not going to play professional football. I know my future depends on my education, not my football."

Mark Cahill: "Wanting to be an athlete is not enough. Getting an education is part of being a college athlete. With the new NCAA rules and regulations, a lot of coaches won't even look at you if you don't have the grades. They can't afford to.

"It's great to have dreams of being a pro, but you can't live your life on four years, which is about what the average pro career is. When I was in the fifth grade, I dreamed of playing pro ball, too, but you can't live your entire life for four years. A couple of knee operations put a dent in my dreams. Now I've got to fall back on my high school and college education."

Lionel James: "When I came through elementary school and junior high school, I didn't pay much attention to my academic work. But when I was recruited in high school, I realized that coaches were looking at my academic work as well as my athletic accomplishments. If you haven't proven yourself in the classroom, you may not have a chance to prove yourself on the field.

"To succeed, you have to be determined. If you should fail in the classroom or on the football field, you have to be determined to keep going until you succeed."

Beth Bryant: "To be a good athlete, you first have to be good in the classroom. In elementary school, junior high and high school, you have somebody looking after you, making you go to class and study. You have to do that on your own in college. You have to develop good attitudes about class work when you are young, the same way you have to develop good attitudes about your work on the field."

Bo Jackson: Jackson, who turned down a reported six-figure contract with the New York Yankees to play football at Auburn, also had a few words for the fifth graders on how to live their lives and make decisions:

"Don't go out and do what your friends tell you to do," he said. "Be yourself. Be the boy or girl, the man or woman you want to be. Live life like you want to live it. If you get in trouble on down the road, your friends won't be there to take the blame for you. You are responsible for your own life and your own decisions."

Bo Jackson asked how many of the fifth graders wanted to be athletes. Virtually all of the boys raised their hands. Few of the girls did. That caught Bryant's attention. She pointed out that she was paying for her college education through her athletic endeavors, and she encouraged the girls to give athletics a try.

"Nobody expects you to be the best," she said. "They just want you to be the best you can be. It starts in school. The more you put in to your class work, the better off you will be on the court. Pride is not something you can turn on or off. It starts and ends in the heart."

Was the visit to Boykin a success?

"They seemed really interested," said Bryant. "They all wanted to ask questions, and I was really surprised at how attentive and how interested they were. Some of them wanted to know how many hours we were taking."

"If it helped one person, it was worthwhile," said Cahill. "If we helped change the direction of one life, maybe that one person can help change the lives of his classmates and friends on down the road."

For the record, Cahill's major is in business management. James is in engineering, Campbell is in industrial management, Bryant is in pre-med and Jackson is in educational psychology and geography.

Although the presentation to the fifth graders was not a project of the Auburn athletic department, it was in keeping with the philosophy of Auburn athletic director and head football coach Pat Dye.

"If the new NCAA rules stand as written," he has said, "our elementary, junior high and high school teachers and coaches are going to have to do a great job of teaching young men and women to make them eligible to receive a college scholarship."

Dye's comments are what prompted the program for Boykin's fifth graders.

The NCAA News
Auburn University Press Release
April 20, 1983

The Yoke is Lifted

It should be pointed out, I suppose, that this piece is not being written as Sports Information Director, but as an Auburn man. True Blue, through and through.

And I say that unabashedly and unashamedly.

It seems like only yesterday that tears of joy flowed so freely down my cheeks as the final seconds of the game ticked away in Birmingham. Need I say which game?

It was over. Not the game, but the long drought. It was finally over. We could laugh again. We could cry again. We could smile again. Spring had finally come.

Our winter of discontent had passed and there we were, one big, happy Auburn family, laughing, crying, yelling and screaming, celebrating the end of a reign of terror, the likes of which Auburn has known only once before in the history of its athletic program. That was the 15 years in a row that Georgia Tech beat us, 1940-54.

Auburn finally beat Georgia Tech 14-12, and Auburn people celebrated. Auburn beat Georgia in 1942, 27-13, and we celebrated then, too. We celebrated when we beat Alabama in '49, '63, and, yes, in '72.

Our celebration in Birmingham was all of those celebrations rolled into one. By nature victory celebrations are a combination of the present and the past. One combines with another, then another and another until they blend together to become a school's history, its heritage, its tradition.

As we celebrated our victory over Alabama that November day, eight and a half months ago, we were joined by all those Auburn men and women who had done similar things on similar occasions in the past. It was not the first time a goal post had been torn down and it won't be the last. We were becoming, as those before us had, a part of Auburn football tradition, legend and lore..

To understand what this year could mean to Auburn people, one must first understand the feeling and emotion that was in Legion Field that day.

For the most part of 25 long years, we had anguished in Alabama's giant shadow. We had stood by silently and politely as they told Auburn joke after Auburn joke. We smiled and we laughed.

We tried to turn the tables by telling an Alabama joke, but it was not the same, not really. Inside we died, again and again.

Now, after 10 long years, we had finally beaten them. The iron boot of tyranny had been lifted. It was yanked off by a group of young men who simply refused to be beaten. They had won the game in the fourth quarter, the quarter that had so often spelled our doom in the past. This time the fourth quarter was ours, and with it, the game.

Winning it that way was worth almost as much as the one precious point that spelled the difference in another year of drought and famine and a year of fullness and plenty, the year we have enjoyed.

That one precious point.

Because of it, Auburn is talking national championship and Alabama is talking of spoiling Auburn's year. Had it gone the other way, we would still be an up and coming football team but one that could be great — if we could beat Alabama.

What a difference that one precious point did make!

Auburn is seen as the pre-season favorite to win the Southeastern Conference championship in virtually every pre-season publication. It is a position to which we are not accustomed.

If the truth was known — and it seldom is — most longtime Auburn fans would prefer that we were ranked lower, somewhere around the middle, where we could rise up and strike down one of the favorites as we did in the past.

That is the position which we are accustomed to striking for oh-so many years.

But no more.

This is a new day, a new time.

Coach Dye has made it plain.

"We want to develop our program to the point where it will not be a question of whether or not Auburn will be good, but a question of how good Auburn is going to be...

"When we have the kind of football program Auburn wants to have and the kind Auburn deserves to have, pre-season publicity and high expectations will be an everyday thing. Sooner or later we will have to learn to live with it. What better time to start than right now?"

Will Auburn win the national championship this year?

Time will tell.

This one thing is certain: We have a shot at winning it and that's more than we have had in a long, long time.

The yolk was lifted from our necks last November.

The sky's the limit now.

The Auburn Plainsman
August 18, 1983

Auburn won the SEC championship in 1983, defeated Alabama for the second year in a row, and defeated Michigan 9-7 in the Sugar Bowl.

Greg Pratt, 1962-1983 _____

AUBURN FULLBACK GREG PRATT DIES

AUBURN—Auburn fullback Greg Pratt was pronounced dead at East Alabama Medical Center today at 2:35 p.m.

Pratt, a junior from Monroe High School in Albany, Georgia, collapsed in the dressing room after a morning workout. Auburn trainers worked with him and then called paramedics. Pratt arrived at East Alabama Medical Center at 1:31 p.m. and was pronounced dead just over an hour later by Lee County Coroner Jon Williams.

Pratt had undergone a normal athletic physical Saturday morning.

After physicals, the players were tested for time on a series of four 440-yard runs with a 90-second rest in between each run. There was no indication from the physical that Pratt could not run in the test which is a normal part of Auburn's first day of practice each fall.

Pratt was the only one of the top 44 players who did not complete the test in the required time.

Going into the fall, Pratt was in a close race with Tommie Agee for the starting fullback job. He was projected as the starter as Auburn entered fall practice.

(This release is accompanied by a page of comments from Coach Pat Dye—his comments to the media when he met with them to inform them of Greg's death.)

*****   *****   *****   *****

COACH DYE'S COMMENTS ON GREG PRATT

"I guess at 2:30 or 2:25 the doctor came out of the emergency room and told me that Greg had died of cardiac arrest. They will probably give us a little more detail after an autopsy is performed.

"Greg was running the 440's in our normal physical conditioning tests that we run every year when the players return. He finished the last 440. The trainers were with him because he had a difficult time finishing the last one. They stayed with him after they brought him back to the Coliseum from the baseball field where they were running. The trainers put him in the shower and were talking with him while he was cooling down.

"He was having a difficult time breathing at which time Herb Waldrop, our trainer, called the paramedics. They got to the Coliseum immediately. He had actually stopped breathing, and they began to perform the necessary things. I think they got a heartbeat a couple of times, but I don't think anything significant. In the meantime the emergency squad arrived and took him to the hospital. I guess they worked with him for a couple of hours trying to get a heartbeat. Then the doctors came out and told me that it was over.

"There is no question it's a tragedy to his family. Our prayers and sympathy go out to them. It's a tragedy for Auburn University and our football team—the people who knew him and loved him. He was a fine young man in every respect. He was a credit to his family, his community and to Auburn University during the time he was at Auburn and we will surely miss him.

"We sent our airplane to pick up his mother as soon as we sent him to the hospital.

"I've already spoken to our squad. It's a very sad time for all of us.

"He had a problem last year. Of course he didn't run them (440's) last year. He ran part of them. We took him to the hospital then. It was serious then, but it wasn't anything like the nature of today.

"He worked hard all summer. He took a physical this morning and there was no indication that he couldn't go out and run. As a matter of fact, overall, this is the best conditioned football team I've ever been around in my life. He's been working out with them all summer.

"I've been in the game 32 years—this is my 32nd year—and this is the first time I've ever seen anything like this as a player or a coach."

Auburn University Press Releases
Saturday, August 20, 1983

On Monday, Aug. 22, Lee County coroner Jon Williams released the autopsy report. He ruled a heat stroke to be the cause of death and the manner of death accidental.

Fall practice never starts at Auburn without those who were there thinking about Greg Pratt and that hot August day when football was put into perspective.

The Bear Comes Home ————————

The day was clear and cold, a high of 43, a low of 33, one degree above freezing. A sharp 15 mile-per-hour wind made the day seem colder than it actually was to the 44,000 who had come to sold-out Legion Field to see another renewal of the Auburn-Alabama game.

Auburn entered the game unbeaten, ranked No. 2 in the nation. The Tigers had gone 23 games without defeat. They were seeking to make it 24 against Alabama. The Tide was 5-3-1. It was an enviable record since the five victories assured Alabama of its first winning season in five years.

Auburn entered the game a seven and one-half point favorite. That was the line on Monday, and it did not waiver during the entire week. The Tigers had won four in a row from Alabama, but no one thought this one would be easy. The Crimson Tide had lost three times, but nobody—nobody—had outplayed them or out-hustled them.

Auburn's Shug Jordan put it this way: "We expect nothing but a rough and tough football game from a well-coached opponent. We know they will scramble and hit. However, we fully expect our boys to be prepared to give the same type effort."

Alabama's Bear Bryant said, "We know we will be playing a great football team. It will take everything we've got."

Alabama worked out in Tuscaloosa, ate at Friedman Hall and bussed to Birmingham Friday night. Auburn, following the tradition of the day, worked out on the Plains and came to Birmingham by train early Saturday morning.

Scalpers were getting an "unbelievable" $20 for a $4 ticket and Birmingham police officials vowed to continue their crackdown on such illegal activity "right up to kickoff and beyond" if necessary.

Kickoff was at 2 p.m. This is how Benny Marshall, sports editor of *The Birmingham News* and a member of the Alabama Sports Hall of Fame, described what he saw:

"Alabama's flaming Crimson Tide turned the fourth quarter into a fierce Auburn fight for survival Saturday, but down deep in the shadows, the Tigers still had the stuff that had taken them to 23 football games without defeat.

"They made it 24 by 14 to 8 on a chilly Legion Field afternoon that went from humdrum to hysterical down the home stretch and sent Auburn marching toward 1959 with a second straight undefeated season."

Auburn scored midway of the first quarter on a three-yard pass from Richard Wood to Jimmy Pettus. It was 7-0 at the half. The Tigers stretched that lead to 14-0 in the third quarter when Jimmy Reynolds cracked over from the one-yard line.

The Tigers drove to the Tide two-yard line in the third quarter, but Alabama held and the Tide was beginning to turn. Using the Utah pass, a surprise Bryant had brought into the game just for Auburn, Alabama began to dominate the game. The Tide scored on a nine-yard run by Marlin "Scooter" Dyess. Bobby Jackson passed to Gary O'Steen for two points and with 7:07 to play, the Auburn-Alabama game turned into what Pat Dye calls a war.

As the battle waged, Shug Jordan's expression never changed according to Don

Brown who covered both sidelines for *The News*. On the Alabama sideline, Bryant, was in sharp contrast.

"Bryant, his old brown hat low over his eyes and wearing high rubber boots with his trousers tucked in, was everywhere at once. He shouted, clapped, walked up and down constantly, never stopping. Bobby Luna shouted encouragement to the Alabama team. 'You are better than they are,' he shouted, 'You are better than they are...Every one of you is better than they are...'"

Alabama marched from its 27 to a first down at the Auburn 28 late in the game.

The clock showed one minute 26 seconds to play when Alabama lined up," Marshall wrote, "but the mightiest defense in the nation rolled up some sleeves, pulled out some extra muscle and brought it on home."

After the game the crowd was limp, spiritually and emotionally drained on both sides of the field. There was still Saturday night in Birmingham, however.

Gospel singer Wally Fowler was sponsoring an all-nite singing at the Municipal Auditorium and next to Legion Field WVOK was sponsoring a "Big Dance" featuring three bands. Admission was 75 cents.

It's been a long time now, more years than the mind and mid-section care to remember, but that's the way it was 25 years ago, the last time Alabama brought a new head coach to Birmingham to play Auburn.

Auburn Football Illustrated
Auburn vs. Alabama
December 3, 1983

From Tragedy to Triumph ⸻

It is difficult to say when Auburn's championship season began.

Certainly it began before the Southern Mississippi game. Certainly it began before Greg Pratt's tragic and untimely death during physical examinations before practice.

Just when it began, we may never know.

It could have begun when Pat Dye came to Auburn in January of 1981.

"We want to give Auburn people a championship football program with the class and integrity Auburn people deserve," Dye had said. "We would like to put Auburn Football back where it was in the fifties, late sixties and early seventies. I remember when Auburn put on those blue jerseys and put the fear of God in people. We want it to get to the point where it's not a matter of whether or not Auburn is going to be good, but of how good Auburn is going to be..."

It may have begun even before that. Coaches cannot put character and class in a player. Coaches can only try.

Auburn was supposed to be good in 1983. The Tigers were a virtual consensus choice to win the SEC championship and Auburn players dominated pre-season all-conference teams.

A year ago, when Auburn went 9-3 and beat Boston College in the Tangerine Bowl, there could have been the element of surprise, perhaps disbelief in opponent's preparations for Auburn.

Not this year. Not in 1983.

The Tigers were supposed to be good in 1983 and everyone knew it. One magazine—*Playboy*—even picked Auburn to win the national championship.

Auburn's challenge going into 1983 was entirely different from what it had been in previous years.

They were supposed to be good. Now they had to be good.

It would be a difficult task.

The schedule was formidable, perhaps awesome. It contained the toughest conference schedule in the SEC, and out-of-conference games included games against three of the nation's Top 10 football teams, Texas, Florida State and Maryland. The NCAA rated it the toughest schedule in the country.

People knew Auburn was supposed to be good, but the schedule was too tough, they said. "Poor Auburn," was the word. "They've finally got a good team and the schedule is too tough to do well."

But they didn't know Pat Dye.

"You can't be scared," he is fond of saying. He lives that way. So do his teams.

There was great anticipation and excitement when the players reported on Friday, August 19. Physicals and picture-taking were scheduled for the next day.

So was tragedy.

After undergoing normal athletic physicals, the team went to the Auburn baseball field to run a series of 440-yard runs to give trainers an indication of what kind of physical condition the team was in so coaches would know how to arrange practices in the heat of August.

Fullback Greg Pratt ran those 440 runs—a series of four with a ninety second rest in between—but he collapsed after the final run. He was treated on the field and taken to the Coliseum to recuperate. When he continued to have difficulty breathing, he was taken to the hospital where he died.

He was 20.

The days and weeks ahead were uncertain. Life has to go on, however, and life went on at Auburn. Each player, in his own way and in his own time, came to grips with the death of a friend and did the only thing humans can do—go on.

Greg was remembered by every coach and player. A black patch with 36, Greg's number, was worn on every helmet. Players remembered in other ways, too personal to discuss or mention.

Life went on.

Auburn opened the season with a convincing 24-3 win over Southern Mississippi. Texas was next and the game was promoted to be the biggest game ever played at Auburn. Both teams had been predicted to win the national championship. CBS televised the game to most of the United States, but by halftime, Auburn fans wanted to pull the plug. Texas led 20-0 at the half and went on to win 20-7. That was only the beginning.

The Alabama press was filled with stories the next week implying that Auburn's success in 1982 was a flash-in-the pan. Talk was rampant that Randy Campbell was through as Auburn's quarterback and the dinosaur of modern football, the wishbone offense, would certainly be junked after what happened against Texas.

The Auburn Tigers listened. They listened and they leaned on one another. They were a shaky favorite at Knoxville, but won 37-14. They were behind and looked to be down and out against Florida State, but when the big play was needed, Campbell, Lionel James, Bo Jackson and friends made it. The same applied to the defense. Donnie Humphrey, Gregg Carr and friends made it happen, too. Auburn was a come-from-behind winner, 27-24, and the Tigers were off and rolling again.

Kentucky fell, so did Georgia Tech, Mississippi State, Florida and Maryland. The toughest schedule in the country was challenging, but it was making Auburn a better, more confident football team.

The conference schedule was difficult, but it was to Auburn's advantage. The contenders were Florida, Alabama, Georgia and Tennessee. Auburn was the only team to play them all. Auburn whipped them all and thereby forged its own destiny, a destiny that carried the Tigers to Auburn's first SEC championship in 26 years, a No. 3 national ranking and a berth in the Sugar Bowl opposite Michigan.

When Pat Dye was a junior at Georgia in 1959, the team he played on overcame all the odds and won the SEC championship.

It was said at the time: "They believed in themselves, their destiny they knew and they had the stuff to make their dreams come true..."

Now that can be said about the team he coaches.

The 1983 Auburn Tigers were supposed to be good, and they were good.

There were supposed to be a lot of outstanding football players on the 1983 Auburn football team, and there were.

Five made All-America teams. Bo Jackson made virtually every All-America team and he is only a sophomore. He established himself as one of the leading contenders for the Heisman Trophy in 1984. After Jackson gained 256 yards rushing against Alabama, football fans across the country, from New York to California were talking about Bo Jackson. At 20, his name was becoming a household word.

Defensive tackle Donnie Humphrey, who refused to let a knee injury end his football career, came back for his fifth year and he too made All-American.

Others making All-America teams, second or third string, were linebacker Gregg Carr, defensive tackle Doug Smith and offensive lineman Pat Arrington.

Ten Auburn players made the AP or UPI All-SEC team, Carr, Jackson, Arrington, Humphrey, Smith, defensive end Gerald Robinson, cornerback David King, offensive guard David Jordan, noseguard Dowe Aughtman and halfback Lionel James.

Pat Dye was named National Coach of the Year in Division 1A by Chevrolet and TBS. He was named SEC Coach of the Year by *The Knoxville Journal* and *The Birmingham News*.

He spoke for all of Auburn's honored players when he said, "This award is not for me. It's for the coaches and players I work with everyday."

What made Auburn, 1983, a good football team?

Talent was certainly a big part of it. So were discipline, desire, dedication, preparation, all of the intangibles.

The 1983 Auburn football team was a good football team because the players who made up that team leaned on one another and found strength in their hours of need. They were good because they believed in themselves, their destiny they knew... And they had the stuff to make their dreams come true.

Sugar Bowl Media Guide
December, 1983

Al Del Greco kicked a 19-yard field goal with 23 seconds remaining to give Auburn a 9-7 win over Michigan in the Sugar Bowl and make the 1983 team the first team in Auburn history to win 11 games in a single season. Captured forever in the last frames of a highlight film for that season is the image of Terry Walker, Greg Pratt's roommate, saying "This one's for you, Greg....This is for you..."

College Football at its Best ─────────

Gregg Carr has seen the best and worst of college football.

He has seen the winning and the losing.

When he was young, he saw the losing. As he has grown older, he has seen the winning. There is no doubt that the winning is more fun, but to appreciate the winning, you have to remember the losing, the days when times weren't as good.

Carr came out of Birmingham's Woodlawn High School in 1979 as a can't-miss prospect. He had grown up an Alabama fan, but as he grew older and his day of decision neared, he turned to Auburn.

"I just liked the campus," he said, "and the people. They seemed so genuine and friendly. They really cared about you as a person."

Score one for Auburn and recruiting, but how quick Carr would score became another question. First there was a bout with mononucleosis. Then, just as he was recovering from mono, there came a knee injury, ligament damage.

As things would turn out, that was a good year to miss. Auburn did not have a good season, and when it was over, a coaching change was made. What seemed to be a detriment in 1980 had actually been a blessing. Instead of graduating last year, Carr is back for another season. Mono and a knee injury kept him out of 1980, but they enabled him to come back in 1984 as an All-America football player and one of the stalwarts on a team that is picked by many to win the national championship.

Looking back, Carr remembers.

"Naturally I was disappointed when I got hurt," he said. "I didn't get a chance to contribute and standing on the sidelines was a helpless feeling."

Carr felt helpless in the fall of 1980, but at the start of 1981, he felt uncertain, too. Everybody associated with the Auburn football team felt uncertain. There was no way to know what the new coach, Pat Dye, would bring.

"We weren't sure of anything when Coach Dye came in," Carr said, "but we did know that we were going to have to work. He said spring practice would be like 'going through a briarpatch in a storm.' He said it was going to be tough and he didn't give us any false ideas.

"He told us that if we weren't dedicated to hard work, that if we weren't dedicated to Auburn, it would be best if we went elsewhere."

Carr liked the sound of the words "hard work." He had never been afraid of hard work and if that was what it took to succeed under the new coach, then Carr would fit right in.

To say that he has "fit right in" in the three years that have followed would be an understatement.

He has led the team in tackles two years running, was a unanimous AP All-SEC selection and second team AP All-American in 1983, and is a *Playboy* All-American this year. He is the defensive leader on a team that is picked to win the national championship this year.

"Team goals always come ahead of individual goals," said the soft-spoken Carr, who has been compared to Clark Kent, but his play this year is just as valuable to

Auburn's national championship hopes as that of Heisman Trophy candidate Bo Jackson. Jackson is the offensive leader, Carr, the defensive leader.

"I didn't come to Auburn to win a national championship," he said. "People at Auburn weren't talking about national championships then. I came to Auburn because I could get a good education and play football.

"People ask me what Coach Dye has done for Auburn. That's what he's done—he's made it possible to get a good education and win the national championship, too."

Auburn University Press Release
August 16, 1984

Auburn did not win the national championship in 1984, but Gregg Carr got his "good education." At the end of the 1984 season, he was named one of the NCAA's Top Five scholar-athletes. After a successful pro football career with the Pittsburgh Steelers, Carr enrolled in medical school at UAB. Dr. Carr married Juli Barnes, an Auburn cheerleader from his playing days, and from all indications, they will live as "happily ever after" as this life permits.

Marching On —————————————————————————

The last two football trips have not been that outstanding from the standpoint of results, but there have been some memorable moments.

First, there was New York and a midnight ride with a group of sports writers on the Staten Island Ferry, still the best buy in New York for fifty cents.

The Staten Island Ferry is a 20-minute ferry ride from the tip of Manhattan to Staten Island and back, 20 minutes over, 20 minutes back.

It is memorable not because of the ferry ride or the glorious view of Manhattan at night, but for what it passes—the Statue of Liberty.

To a man of my generation, some of our earliest memories are of our fathers telling us about the great and wonderful world beyond our hometown. I vividly remember my father telling me about his only trip to New York. He passed through the city on the way home from World War II. When the troop ship pulled into New York harbor and the Statue of Liberty came into view, there was not a dry eye on the ship, he said. Grown men wept openly at the sight of home. He was among them.

I have seen the Statue of Liberty many times before, but this time there was a different feeling. Age? Maturity? Perhaps. Perhaps it was because the torch, the symbol of what our country is all about, was on the ground beside the statue, lying there like a piece of twisted metal. Not a word was spoken as we glided silently by. Perhaps we all had the same feeling. Several spoke of it later that evening.

> *Give me your tired, your poor,*
> *Your huddled masses yearning to breathe free,...*
> *I lift my lamp beside the golden door!*

It is up to us, all of us, not only to put that torch back in her hand, but also to keep it there.

Then came Texas and the Alamo.

The Alamo—the mission that became a fortress and an everlasting shrine.

For 13 days, Col. William Travis, an Alabamian, and his small band of men including Jim Bowie and Davy Crockett held back the greatest army in the Western world. One hundred and eighty-five men holding back 5,000.

Santa Anna, of course, ultimately breached the wall and killed the Alamo defenders to a man, but what a price he paid. He lost a third of his army, over 2,000 men. Of the 685 members of Mexico's most prized unit, 665 were killed.

It is said that when the Alamo fell, the defenders fought so fiercely in hand-to-hand combat that there were piles of Mexican bodies around each Alamo defender when he died.

Santa Anna was so incensed at the fury of the battle and the losses he sustained that he ordered the bodies of the Alamo defenders mutilated and burned.

It is trite and perhaps somewhat corny to say this—truth is often that way—but the same emotion, determination and spirit displayed at the Alamo is what we need to overcome our present state of disappointment and defeat.

As Walter Lord wrote in his book about the Alamo, *A Time to Stand*, "Even heroes

get discouraged. All men know such moments...perhaps in the end the hero is the one who marches on..."
It is time for us to march on.
The battle of 1984 is just beginning.

Auburn Football Illustrated
Auburn vs. Southern Mississippi
September 22, 1984

Wreck Tech _____

Wouldn't it be a shame if Auburn and Georgia Tech ever stopped playing each other?

Think what all of us would miss. Think what college football would miss.

The Auburn-Georgia Tech series started in 1893, the second year of college football in the Deep South. Georgia Tech was the fifth team Auburn ever played. Auburn was the third team Tech played.

Auburn-Georgia Tech is older than Georgia-Georgia Tech, and Auburn-Alabama dwarfs to insignificance when compared to the tradition and history of Auburn-Georgia Tech.

Auburn and Georgia Tech have played 86 times. Only Auburn and Georgia have played more—87. Auburn-Georgia Tech is the 10th oldest series in college football today. Auburn-Georgia is the eighth oldest.

Auburn and Georgia Tech have been bitter rivals from the start, going back, perhaps, to the professional jealousy between the two schools' engineering students and graduates.

The first Auburn and Georgia Tech game was played in 1892 in Atlanta. Auburn was a winner 26-0 in its third game in four games. The bulk of that first season was played between November 22 and November 25. Auburn lost to Trinity (now Duke) 34-6 on November 22, lost to North Carolina 64-0 on November 23 and beat Georgia Tech 26-0 on the 25th. It was part of a round-robin football tournament sponsored by the Atlanta Athletic Association. North Carolina and Virginia—the ACC—played for the championship on November 26.

Georgia students cheered for Georgia Tech in that first Tech-Auburn game. You know, the way we do when we *always* cheer for Alabama except when they are playing Auburn.

In the next game, however, the Georgia students cheered for Auburn—as they are doing today. Seems as though the Tech students had thrown rocks at the Georgia team in the first Tech-Georgia game. Bad blood from the start.

John Heisman, the man for whom the Heisman Trophy is named, coached at Auburn from 1895 through 1899. Georgia Tech never beat him. Heisman won 45-0 in 1896, 29-0 in 1898 and 63-0 in 1899. Tech never scored on Heisman's Auburn teams and, interestingly, all of those games were played in Auburn as all of the later games would be played in Atlanta.

The 1896 game is of special note. That game gave birth to Auburn's "Wreck Tech Pajama Parade." Auburn students, it seems, greased the railroad tracks the night before the Tech team train was due in Auburn, and the next morning, when it tried to stop, the train slid all the way through Auburn and halfway to Loachapoka 10 miles away. The Tech team had to walk back to Auburn, and Auburn won the game 45-0, much to the glee of Auburn students. It is not known if John Heisman was aware of or was involved in the prank.

Two years later, school officials threatened to dismiss any student caught trying to grease the tracks. Upperclassmen threatened to roadtrip any underclassman who did not grease the tracks.

In a classic case of one-upmanship, the underclassmen slipped out of their rooms the night before the game and panic-stricken school administrators were relieved to see a big pep rally at the train station rather than another track greasing. Every Auburn student was at the train station that night as virtually every Auburn student was at the "Wreck Tech Pajama Parade" Thursday. It was the 88th year in a row that Auburn students had marched in their pajamas before the Georgia Tech game, and it has become one of college football's most colorful traditions.

Each team has known the agony and the ecstasy of this long and colorful series. There were times when Auburn thought it would never beat Tech again, and there have been times when Tech thought it would never beat Auburn again, but through it all, the Auburn-Georgia Tech series is virtually even, Auburn 43-Tech 39 with four ties.

It would be a shame if these two schools ever stopped playing. We—Tech and Auburn—owe it to ourselves and to college football to keep this series alive. We owe it to the legend, lore and traditions of college football.

> *Auburn Football Illustrated*
> October 20, 1984
> Auburn vs. Georgia Tech

Georgia Tech dropped Auburn and ended the series after the 1987 game, won by Auburn 20-10. It was Auburn's 45th win in the series and the Tigers' ninth win in a row over their once ancient rival. There are no plans to resume the series.

Marvin

They buried Marvin Price last Friday.

Coming out from the flowers on his casket was an Orange and Blue ribbon. On that ribbon was the word "Auburn." Underneath there was a football.

For some it would have been gaudy, showy, inappropriate. For Marvin Price, it was just right.

Marvin Price never played football here. He never attended Auburn. His brother did, and he went on to become a pharmacist. He owned the little country drug store where Marvin worked all those years, 45 in all.

There was no better Auburn man than Marvin Price. Even though he had no direct tie with Auburn, he had purchased season tickets since 1958, the year the season ticket program started.

In all those years, he asked only one favor. He needed seats on the "cripple row." His legs, worn out by years of 12 and 14-hour days, could not climb steps anymore. His request was granted. Section 3, Row 26, Seats 1-2.

It hurt him deeply when the GAF-10 contribution went up from $250 to $400. He was retired and living on a fixed income. He had an invalid wife. That meant cutting from 10 season tickets to six. Still, however, he kept buying. When he couldn't come to the game, he made sure some good Auburn man did. His Auburn ticket order was like his church pledge. It had to be paid and the tickets had to be ordered. To Mr. Marvin, there was a lot of similarity in the church and Auburn. Both were to be loved and revered, honored and respected.

He liked to come to the games early, to "get a feel for the campus" by eating at the Union Building, walking across Samford Park and standing at Toomer's Corner for awhile to "take it all in." Jordan-Hare Stadium on a Saturday afternoon was his favorite place on earth.

He spent many a long afternoon, Mr. Marvin did, pounding the hard concrete floors of the City Drug Store in Gordo. Standing behind that soda fountain, he was fair game for the Alabama fans and they took their shots.

When Auburn was losing, they would come in just to ask, "How's Auburn doing?" They would snicker when Mr. Marvin would say, "Not too good just now..." When Auburn was winning they were never to be found, choosing to stay with their own kind up the street at Elmore Supply. The young ones were the worst. They would try to goad Mr. Marvin into saying something about Alabama. He never would. He had made his choice.

His last trip to Auburn was October 5 for the Ole Miss game. He and his new wife spent the night at the Holiday Inn in Lanett. They could not get a room in Auburn. Those who knew him say he talked about the game for days. He was convinced Auburn was on the road to a great season.

He died peacefully. His last thoughts may well have been about the upcoming Georgia Tech game. He hated Tech. Tech was right next to Alabama on his list.

M.R. Price's name will never be recorded in the annals of Auburn history. He never gave a scholarship, he never built a building, he never did any of the things that cause people to be remembered.

All he did was give Auburn his love and loyalty for more than 70 years. It is entirely appropriate that his casket bore Auburn colors. For he was a great Auburn man.

Auburn Football Illustrated
Auburn vs. Mississippi State
October 26, 1985

Toomer's Lemonade

You can't take the heart and soul out of an institution without changing it. Such is the case with Toomer's Drugs, an Auburn institution that has anchored Toomer's Corner for ages.

The store is still there, the stock is virtually the same and they will probably continue to sell lemonade, but the heart and soul is gone and Toomer's Corner will never be the same. Mac Lipscomb is retiring.

Mac bought the drugstore from Mr. Shell Toomer himself back in 1952. He has overseen downtown Auburn's most cherished and well-known institution for 25 years and he has overseen it well. He has been true to the Spirit.

Mac has served as an unofficial spokesman for Auburn tradition and the Auburn Spirit for years. News media from across the country know about our tradition of rolling Toomer's Corner. Keith Jackson made mention of it on national television when Auburn beat Alabama 23-22 in 1982, and what a celebration that was. They know about it because Mac Lipscomb probably told them about it.

When out of town news media come to Auburn and ask how Auburn students celebrate a big victory, our response is simple—"Go see Mac Lipscomb at Toomer's Drug Store at Toomer's Corner. He can tell you better than anybody."

An hour or so later, they will return to the sports information office all smiles. We know without asking what Mac has told them. He has told them that Auburn is the most wonderful place in the world. And more often than not, he has given them a free lemonade, the on-going symbol of Toomer's Drugs. Years later, after the details of the game have been forgotten, they ask about Toomer's, about Mac and about Toomer's lemonades.

"Are they still making those lemonades?" they will ask. "That was the best I've ever had..." Toomer's, you see, makes its lemonade the old-fashion way. They squeeze the lemons.

But Mac will soon be gone. The lemonade may still be there, the chipped white walls of Toomer's may still be there and the faded blue letters atop the store—letters which have never all been standing at the same time—may still be there, but Mac won't be there and Toomer's will never be the same.

Mac Lipscomb, you see, is as Auburn as an Auburn man can be. He was born here, grew up here, married here and raised his children here. He was part of the Auburn experience. He made Auburn a better place to live and to learn. He taught people about life. Students who came his way were better for the experience.

He felt a responsibility being the owner of Toomer's Drug Store. He knew it was an Auburn institution. He wanted to stop selling lemonades a long time ago because he was losing money on them, but he didn't because "Auburn people expect a lemonade when they come in Toomer's." He knew people expected Toomer's to be the same whenever they came back to Auburn. Nothing thrilled him more than when an alumnus came in and said, "Hello, Mr. Lipscomb, Do you remember me? I'm old so-and-so who used to..."

Whether he recognized them or not, within minutes Mac would be in joyous reunion with them as they relived the best days of their lives, their days at Auburn.

Simply put, Mac Lipscomb is one of those people who make Auburn Auburn. He was the heart and soul of an Auburn institution.

Old soldiers never die, however, they just fade away and so it will be with Mac Lipscomb. Though he won't be at Toomer's anymore, he will still be very much a part of Auburn. Look for him now at the Auburn Grille. He'll go there everyday at lunch just to see what is going on in Auburn and at the University. He'll hold court there for anyone who will listen. The young ones, the wise ones, will listen. The others will never know what they missed. It will be their loss.

Mac said something once that has become truer and truer with the passing years.

"People are always talking about wanting to move back to Auburn," he said. "People who go to school here want to stay here or come back here.

"But," he said, "You never hear about anybody who wants to move back to Tuscaloosa or Athens."

Maybe, just maybe, it's because those places don't have a Mac Lipscomb to keep the home fires burning.

Auburn Football Illustrated
Auburn vs. East Carolina
September 20, 1986

Mark Morgan, Mac Lipscomb's successor at Toomer's Drugs, is an Auburn man, too, and in more ways than just degree. He, too, understands the unique and special place Toomer's Drug Store holds in Auburn tradition, legend and lore.

Lemonade is still being served at Toomer's, as it has been since 1896 when John Heisman was coaching here, and it was the day Auburn played its first home football game, the day the Georgia Tech football team walked up College Street amid the jeers and cheers of the Auburn students who had greased the tracks and sent the Tech train sliding halfway to Loachapoka. Almost 100 years later, lemonade is still being sold on Toomer's Corner.

Some things, thank God, don't change.

Where We Have Been, Where We Are Going...

It is an old story, but it is a story worth retelling if you are an Auburn man or an Auburn woman.

To understand where we are and where we are going, we must understand the past, where we have been and what brought us to this day. Only then can we appreciate where we are and where we are going.

To Auburn men and women of my generation and older, this is a well-known story, one of pride and accomplishment. Unless younger generations of Auburn fans come to know the story and to understand it, it is a story that will become lost in antiquity. We are talking about the story of Auburn Football, where we have been, where we are and where we are going. At no point in our history are these truths more evident than today.

We begin in the 1920's. Wallace Wade and Frank Thomas were at Alabama, and the Crimson Tide was well on its way to becoming Dixie's Football Pride. Alabama played in the Rose, Sugar, Cotton and Orange Bowls. Howell, Hutson, the great names of Southern football, were synonymous with Alabama. Tennessee, under the great Bob Neyland, was Alabama's chief competitor. The Vols were 31-2 from 1938 through 1940. Nobody else was close. Georgia, under Harry Mehre and Wally Butts, and Georgia Tech, under William A. Alexander, were also enjoying great success.

And Auburn? We were struggling. The days of Heisman and Donahue were over and gone. These were years of crisis and struggle for Auburn's athletic program, years of seeking identification, purpose and leadership. The athletic department was in bad financial shape with little chance to do much better. There was no stadium to speak of—all of our games had to be played on what is now the Haley Center parking lot. Bleachers lined both sides of the field. No team wanted to come to Auburn and who could blame them. Things were so bad that Auburn became a road team, playing any and everybody on the road, hoping to get a victory, happy to get a big paycheck. It might be stretching the truth to say that Auburn was the Chattanooga of that day, but it would make the point.

Auburn rarely played a home game and if it did, it was against the likes of Spring Hill, Howard or Erskine, hardly the football powers of the day. But then neither was Auburn. For several years even the Homecoming game was played on the road.

Something had to be done. Coach Jack Meagher may not have been the first to recognize it, but the success of his teams in the late thirties gave Auburn people reason to hope—and reason to build a new stadium. It was dedicated at the next to last game of the 1939 season, a 7-7 tie with Florida. It was Auburn's first home game in almost four years.

Football was disbanded at Auburn during World War II, and when it resumed, Jack Meagher did not return. Dark days set in again. Even a stadium was not enough to help Auburn. The program hit rock bottom in 1950. The Tigers were 0-10-0. They lost to Southeast Louisiana, Tulane and Clemson in Auburn. Again, something had to be done.

You know the rest.

Jeff Beard was named athletic director in 1951. He hired Shug Jordan to be the head football coach. Joe Sarver took over the alumni office, and President Ralph B. Draughon gave them all the support they needed. The first order of business was to beat Georgia Tech. Tech, for financial reasons, had forced Auburn to play in Atlanta's Grant Field every year since 1902. Auburn had not beaten Tech in 10 years. Beating Tech was Auburn's No. 1 priority. Jordan said he would not try to move the Tech game out of Atlanta until Auburn had won in Atlanta. The Tigers won in 1955, then again in 1957, 1959 and by 1960, the Tech game was in Birmingham. It came to Auburn for good in 1970. After next year's game, Auburn is going off the Tech schedule at Tech's insistence. The record since 1955 is 21-9-1, Auburn's way.

The Auburn-Georgia game was played in Columbus. It went to Athens in 1959 and came to Auburn to stay in 1960.

Schools like Tennessee refused to schedule Auburn in the early days. What did they have to gain by playing Auburn, they asked. And, frankly, there was little to gain. Tennessee agreed to play Auburn in 1956, but they refused to play in Auburn. Our stadium held 34,000. It was still not worthy of the Vols. They came once, in 1974, when it held 61,000, and they came for good in 1980.

That Tennessee is here today is proof of how far Auburn Football has come. That Georgia Tech and Georgia are coming this year is still further testimony to Auburn's growth and development. The concrete and steel rising over the East Stands is still more evidence. In less than a year now, Auburn's Jordan-Hare Stadium will hold 85,000 fans. It will be the fifth largest on-campus stadium in the country.

There is only one Southeastern Conference opponent that has yet to come to Auburn. I am forbidden to write about that. This is not the time nor the place. But when that one remaining school does come—and it will come—-then our circle will be unbroken and our joy complete.

Auburn Football Illustrated
September 27, 1986
Auburn vs. Tennessee

That one remaining school, The University of Alabama, came to Auburn on December 2, 1989, and Auburn's joy was complete.

Sentimental Journey

Just over a year ago I shared with you the death of an Auburn man, Marvin Price, in this space. His casket was covered with orange and blue mums. It was appropriate because there has never been a better Auburn man.

I write to you of Marvin today. A boyhood friend, Rear Admiral E. F. May of Foley, tells us of where and when Marvin's great love for Auburn began. It is a story worth retelling, especially today, since Marvin's beloved Tigers are playing arch-rival Georgia Tech once again.

Here is the story of an Auburn man's love affair with Auburn. His friend begins, appropriately, by saying, "I can tell you where it all began..."

"Marvin and I were friends from childhood to his death. We burned corn-stalks in the field on Halloween. We flew kites. We played baseball, basketball, and football on the Gordo High School teams and graduated together. Our senior year we and the late Dr. Downing went to Birmingham for a state high school seminar of some sort as our school's representatives. It was a Thursday-Friday and Saturday affair.

"On Friday p.m., we asked Downing to take our notes and prepare our report. Marvin and I walked to the freight yards, hopped a box car to Atlanta, stayed at the YMCA and got tickets to the Auburn-Georgia Tech game. It was easier in those days-65 years ago.

"We placed bets on Auburn and lost (Georgia Tech 34- Auburn 0). We were stuck in Atlanta with $5 each to get back to Gordo. We told our tale to two Auburn students who sneaked us aboard the Auburn special train. We were thrown off twice, but students pulled us aboard through windows as the train started.

"We spent the night in the dormitory at Auburn. The next morning a pla-toon of Auburn students escorted us to a freight train, talked to the conductor and we hoboed home.

"I won't recall other experiences we had, but we never lost touch...and Auburn was always an important part of our lives."

You will note that Admiral May, now retired, does not note what kind of welcome they received when they arrived home.

Much has changed since that little adventure, but the more things change the more they remain the same.

Auburn people have always been special. Maybe it's the Land Grant background, maybe it's soil, maybe it's the specialness of Auburn people. Whatever it is, it has been passed down by Auburn men and women from generation to generation.

As Admiral May and Marvin Price learned so long ago, "An Auburn Man Needs No Introduction."

It is as true today as it was the day they hoboed home from Atlanta.

May it ever be so.

Auburn Football Illustrated
Auburn vs. Georgia Tech
October 18, 1986

On Knowledge and Wisdom _____

We were riding back from Jacksonville, Trey Gainous and I, on a dark and stormy night. We were talking to keep each other awake. Trey was driving. He had received an award from the Boy Scouts of America, a role model award, signifying that Trey Gainous—our Trey Gainous—was a role model for young men to follow. His was a life, an example, by which others could pattern their lives.

The conversation had turned to school and a test he had later in the week. He was in Building Science and the test was in Structures or some such course. My area of expertise is in words and feelings. He was a builder, but the conversation stirred a question that had been on my mind. Just that day I had written a release about the new stadium addition, the one in which many of you sit today. How long, I wondered, would it last? How long would we be able to use it? Fifty years? 100 years? 150 years? After all, $15.5 million is a lot of money.

That question was put to Trey. You know him as a punt returner, a receiver and an outfielder. I knew him as my friend, my friend in building construction. That is one of the pleasures of this job.

"How long," I asked, "would the new upper deck last? How long would it be usable?"

Trey reached into his pocket and took out another dip. We were, after all, a long way from Auburn and a little Skoal would help keep him awake. "I don't really know," he said, "but if I am right—and I think I am—concrete never reaches its full strength..."

He began to discuss PSIs—pounds per square inch—which is the amount of weight or pressure concrete can withstand. He explained how concrete is made, how it is strengthened or weakened by the amount of water used to mix it. He told me about how fly ash, something I knew about from my days at Housel Hardware in Gordo, was used to make concrete seal better.

I had known a little about concrete from my boyhood days working on a delivery truck for the family hardware business. My education consisted mainly of hauling 90-pound sacks of the stuff, shoveling sand and making sure nobody topped off the stacks. That means taking all the sacks off the top rather than going to the floor stack by stack. Ninety-pound sacks of cement are heavier when you have to pick them up off the bottom rather than pull them off the top, but I had never had a lesson in concrete like this.

But how long, I asked, will that new stadium addition last? A hundred years? A thousand years?

"If I'm right," Trey said, "it will last forever."

"Right!" I thought. "Forever..." As much as I liked Trey Gainous, as much as I loved him, I was convinced he had been playing too much baseball and not going to class enough. A stadium that lasts forever...Bah...Humbug! Too much Skoal was affecting his mind.

A few days later Mack Freeman, a good Auburn man who was the architect of the new stadium addition, stopped by the office. I asked him the same question I had asked Trey a few days earlier.

How long would that new stadium last? Fifty years? 100 years? How long?

The way Mack smiled, I knew I had asked a dumb question. I wasn't prepared for his answer.

"Let's put it this way," he said. "If people in years to come, come back and look at our stadium addition like we go back and look at the Colosseum in Rome, our stadium will be in better shape then than the Colosseum is now..."

"Mack," I said, with shock and more than a little dismay, "you're telling me that stadium is going to be there 2,000 years from now..."

"That's right," he said. "Concrete never reaches its full strength. As it gets older it gets harder. Theoretically, the new addition of the stadium will stand forever, barring a natural disaster of sort."

A stadium that will last forever...unbelievable...yet, if it is true—and we have no reason to believe that it is not true because I have checked the information again and again—the possibility is mind boggling. We are building structures today that will last forever...

As you ponder that thought on this Homecoming Day, 1987, think about something far more important, more relevant and more lasting. More lasting, perhaps, than forever.

If we are building a stadium that will last 2,000 years, what are we, as Auburn men and Auburn women, doing to insure that the Auburn experience we hold so dear, that we consider so special in our lives, will remain special for our children and our children's children?

What values, traits and characteristics should we choose to pass on to those who follow us? And how do we pass on those values?

I shall not attempt to answer those questions. There are as many different and correct answers as there are Auburn men and women.

I will, however, share one thought with you, and in doing so, you will get an insight into why I believe Auburn is special. The thought is not original with me. It comes from Louis L'Amour and his book *Last of the Breed*, not a great scholarly work, but great truths do not have to come from great scholarly works.

He is talking about wisdom.

"What is wisdom?" he wrote. "I have often wondered, and I am not sure. Understanding of life and men, I presume. It goes beyond mere knowledge as knowledge goes beyond information."

A person can have knowledge, but not wisdom. Wisdom is the understanding of life and men, but it is more. Wisdom is perspective.

Auburn imparts wisdom. And it is wisdom, not just knowledge, that we must impart to those who follow.

Someone once said, "Our children are the living messages we send to a time we will not see."

As Auburn men and women, we are truly blessed for we have not only our own children, we also have Auburn.

What messages will you choose to send to a time you will not see?

Think about it on this Homecoming Day, 1987.

And act accordingly.

Auburn Football Illustrated
October 24, 1987
Auburn vs. Mississippi State

Joe Mack and Otto Macnab

There have been some interesting new developments on the recruiting scene concerning the recruitment of Joe Mack and Otto Macnab, developments that are quite troublesome to Auburn.

We have been forced to back off recruiting these two fine young men because of alleged NCAA and SEC rules violations. Unfortunately the alledged rule violations took place right here in this column three weeks ago.

Those of you who are regulars at Auburn home games will recall that the two young men were mentioned in the space by name and you were told that they possessed all of the assets we look for in our athletes, from a physical standpoint and from an intangible standpoint.

Because their names were mentioned in the column, we had to stop recruiting them. At least two schools in the SEC turned us in for recruiting violations and we were called on the carpet to answer to the SEC. Because of this unfortunate event, neither of these two young men will ever get the chance to play at Auburn.

But there's a catch—neither will they play for anyone else in the SEC.

Otto Macnab and Joe Mack do not exist. They are characters in two best selling books. Joe Mack is the hero in Louis L'Amour's *Last of the Breed* and Otto Macnab is one of a multitude of characters in James Michenor's *Texas*. He is also a hero.

Yet, two SEC schools turned us in for a recruiting violation because they were mentioned in this column!

What we don't know is more amusing than what we do know. We do know that we were turned in, but can you imagine the conversation and consternation that must have gone through recruiting meetings? "Who are these guys that Auburn is recruiting? How come they know about them and we don't? Let's get to work on it and find out all we can on this Mack guy and Macnab..."

Bob Barrett, Associate Commissioner of the SEC who works with enforcement and compliance with the rules, was justifiably upset when he read the column. When he heard the truth, he laughed. "Wait 'til I tell these guys this," he said.

Bob did not reveal who turned us in, but he did reveal what they said when informed that Otto Macnab and Joe Mack were fictional characters. Unfortunately, what they said is unprintable here, because this is, for the most part, still a family publication. Suffice it to say, they laughed too in the end.

The note about Macnab and Mack was included to show just how ridiculous recruiting talk can be. Telephones rang off the hook at Auburn wanting to know who Macnab and Mack were. Their names were mentioned on sports talk shows around the South and scouting services were checking their files to see who these players were.

And Auburn was turned in to the SEC and to the NCAA for rules violations.

There is a message here, and it should be clear.

Recruiting is sometimes a dirty business and somebody is looking at everything we do, even scanning the pages of this program, eager to catch us in the smallest mistake, the slightest miscue. There's a game going on out there, and it's as serious to its participants as the KGB vs. the CIA. These players are playing for keeps. They aren't picking on us. We play the game too.

And you, alumni and friends of Auburn, don't need to get caught up in it. It's more than you can handle. It is more than you can comprehend and more than you can understand.

The SEC and NCAA have clear-cut rules about the involvement of alumni and friends in the recruiting process. You are not to be involved. You are to stay out of it and leave the recruiting to the coaches.

Let this story of Joe Mack and Otto Macnab be a lesson to each of us. If we were turned in for a mention in a column of a football program, think how much closer the recruitment of a real student-athlete is being watched.

The slightest mistake on your part, no matter how innocent, could cost us the opportunity to recruit a student-athlete who wants to come to Auburn.

Before you do anything, anything at all, call Coach Dye's office and check it out.

Remember...Big Brother—or someone—is watching you.

> *Auburn Football Illustrated*
> Auburn vs. Florida
> October 31, 1987

The Lady in Crimson _____

There is a lady I would like to meet somewhere here in Legion Field. She is wearing Crimson and White.

I would like to meet her, thank her and tell her she is what this Auburn-Alabama rivalry should be all about.

For the whole story, we have to go back a year ago to November 29, the day of the Alabama-Auburn game. Auburn had just won 21-17. Auburn fans were ecstatic. Alabama fans were in shock and disbelief. The annual agony and ecstasy. The faces and colors may change, the feelings never do.

Coach Dye was in the Auburn dressing room. He had just told his players to think about the players in the dressing room next to them. "We know how they feel," he said. "Give them all the credit in the world. They deserve it..."

It had been a hard year for the Dye family. They had endured rumors and innuendoes no family should have to endure. Coach Dye wanted his wife, Sue, to share the moment with him.

"Find Sue," he said, his eyes misty. "I want her to be at the press conference with me."

Finding Mrs. Dye was easy. Getting her to the press conference was not easy. Because of the configuration of the Legion field dressing rooms, there was only one way to get a lady to the press conference—right through the Alabama fans.

They were as sad as we were happy. I held Mrs. Dye's hand. She held her daughter's hand, and, one-by-one, in single file, all holding hands, we worked our way through the Alabama people waiting for their sons, their brothers, their boyfriends. Their sadness was evident. Having been where they were a year earlier, I knew how they felt...and I had empathy for them. Not sympathy. Empathy. Sympathy means agreement. Empathy means understanding. I understood how the Alabama people felt, and having been there before, I felt for them. The emotions of loss are never pretty and they are always the same, in everybody's heart and on everybody's face. It matters not whether they wear orange and blue or crimson and white, the emotions are the same.

We did not identify ourselves as we made our way through the shoulder to shoulder mass of Alabama people. It would have served no purpose. Suddenly, from my left, there came a voice and a hand.

"Are you David Housel?" the woman asked.

"Yes, I am," I said, still moving forward.

"I know how much this means to you," she said. "Congratulations..."

I took her hand, kissed it and moved on. There was no way to stop, to speak or do more. The crush was too great.

I have thought about that lady often during the last 12 months. I wish I knew who she was. I wish we could visit. I want to talk with her and tell her how much I admire her and how much I appreciate her perspective on this game we are about to watch. She was an attractive lady, on the older side of middle age. She had graying hair and she wore Crimson. That is all I know, but I shall always remember her, and I shall always love her and what she represents.

Two years ago, in 1984, I had felt her same heartache. Alabama, you will recall, had beaten Auburn 17-15 and the "Wrong Way Bo" jokes were born. That was a hard loss to take. I started out our dressing room door, but stopped. I desperately needed to get some perspective on the loss. For some unknown, unexplainable reason, I went out the interview room door and faced the Alabama mothers and fathers awaiting their conquering heroes.

My eyes met some of theirs and I congratulated them, sincerely, but with a broken heart. Some of them seemed to understand.

As I started under the west stands, someone called my name. It was a preacher from my hometown. He began to jump up and down as if he were a jumping jack at a circus. It wasn't enough that Alabama had won, he had to ridicule Auburn and make fun of my loved ones at our lowest hour. What followed was not one of my finest hours.

As calmly as I could, I told him that I had not seen him for two years—years in which Auburn had won. When Alabama won nine years in a row, he was always waiting for me when I went home for Christmas. The two years Auburn won, it was as if Christmas didn't happen. He was not to be seen and I did not seek him out.

"I'll talk football with you," I said, "but only if you are willing to talk when you lose as well as when you win." We have not spoken since that day.

I am not being critical of Alabama people when I cite that example. Nobody has a monopoly on bad fans—Auburn has them too—and I am not saying my friend is a bad fan. I'm just saying that we let a football game come between us.

And all too many of you will let this football game affect you the same way. Family relationships will be strained forever because of the outcome of today's game. Some business relationships will be broken forever because of today's game. It is senseless and it is stupid, but that's the way some of us are.

Coach Dye said it before last year's game. "People take this game too seriously. They let it affect their lives too much. Auburn is going to have a good football program no matter who wins the game and Alabama is going to have a good football program no matter who wins the game..."

Dr. Joab Thomas said people feel their manhood or dignity is threatened when Alabama loses a game. He was talking about Alabama fans, but he could have been talking about Auburn fans just as well. Change the name, we are all the same.

It would serve us all well to remember the example of the lady in Crimson last season.

That and the Golden Rule: Do unto others as you would have them do unto you.

Auburn Football Illustrated
Auburn vs. Alabama
November 27, 1987

The Lady in Crimson never came forward. Two years after this column was published, the preacher and I began talking again. We talk football now, but only occasionally, and ever so politely.

Tradition

Tradition as we know it in the Deep South began here at Auburn in 1892.

A group of Auburn students, tired of playing themselves in the new game called football, issued a challenge to their counterparts at the University of Georgia.

Georgia accepted the challenge and on February 22, 1892, football as we know it was born in the Deep South. The South—and Auburn—have never been the same.

Almost 100 years have come and gone since that first game—won by Auburn 10-0—and college football is an integral part of life in the South and life at Auburn.

Throughout the years, since that very first game, Auburn has been an integral part of football in the Deep South. Some years have been better than others, but when it is all added up and totaled, Auburn Football has been synonymous with success. Tradition. Class. Integrity. Winners...All are words used to describe Auburn Football.

No school in the country has a more colorful tradition, legend and lore than Auburn. Some schools may have won more games, but in the things that make college football special, Auburn is at the head of the pack. It has always been that way.

For tradition's sake, then, let's take a look back down through the years at Auburn Football, how it all began, how it was preserved and how it is today. Today, as Auburn embarks on her greatest era.

They traveled in trains and horse buggies to that first game in Atlanta's Piedmont Park. Georgia's mascot was a goat with red and black ribbons. A manager clad in Orange and Blue served as Auburn's mascot.

It rained at that first game, but 5,000 fans still showed up. The loyalty and devotion which would characterize Auburn fans was evident from the very start. Auburn won the game 10-0, scoring two touchdowns—which counted four points each—and converting one extra point attempt which counted two points. Both Auburn touchdowns were set up by Georgia turnovers. Auburn's reputation as an opportunistic football team was established in that very first game. That, too, is an Auburn tradition that carries through to this very day.

One of the leaders on that team, the quarterback, Clifford Leroy Hare, "Cliff" Hare, went on to become Dean of Chemistry and Faculty Chairman at Auburn. He is one of two men for whom Auburn's Jordan-Hare Stadium is named. The other is Ralph "Shug" Jordan, Auburn's most successful football coach; but more about him later.

Cliff Hare, who became Dean Hare, believed "Athletics make men strong, study makes men wise and character makes men great." Those words have become hallmarks of Auburn Football and the Auburn athletic program. "Athletics make men strong, study makes men wise and character makes men great..."

John Heisman, the man for whom the Heisman Trophy is named, was probably Auburn's first great football coach. The legendary Heisman coached here from 1895 through 1899, compiling a record of 12-4-2.

Heisman was a great Shakespearean actor. He never quite escaped the Shakespearean role, even when he was coaching.

He described the football as "a prolate spheroid—that is, an elongated sphere—on which the outer leathern casing is drawn tightly over a somewhat small rubber tubing."

As eccentric as his description may have been, there was never any doubt about Heisman's intensity when it came to football. "Better to have died as a small boy, than fumble this football," he said.

Defensively, Heisman told his players to "Thrust your projections into their cavities, grasping them about the knees and depriving them of their means of propulsion. They must come to earth, locomotion being denied them." In today's terminology, we call that a tackle.

Heisman was an innovator of the game. He pioneered many of the things we take for granted in football today. "Heisman's forward pass" and the hidden ball play were two of his many innovations.

He went on to coach at Clemson, Georgia Tech and Pennsylvania. When he retired from coaching, he became athletic director of the Downtown Athletic Club of New York City. That club honored him in 1935 with the presentation of the first Heisman Trophy which is given annually to the outstanding college football player in America.

Two Auburn players have won this most prestigious award, Pat Sullivan in 1971 and Bo Jackson in 1985.

Mike Donahue, "Iron Mike," as he was called, became Auburn's head coach in 1904. Fans were disappointed when he first arrived at Auburn. They had hired an Irishman to head up Auburn's football fortunes. They had hoped to have a John Wayne type figure, but when Donahue stepped off the train, they realized they had more of a Mickey Rooney than a John Wayne. Looks were deceiving, however, and the Donahue era of Auburn football continues to rank as one of the greatest eras college football has ever known. His teams were known for defense, still a great Auburn tradition, and when he left Auburn in 1922, the Tigers had compiled a 97-35-4 record and won four Southern championships.

Heisman and Donahue were given much of the credit for putting Southern football on the map. And if Southern football was on the map, Auburn Football was the focal point.

"You were nobody until you had beaten Auburn," Atlanta's Ed Danforth wrote. "That was the place card at the head of the table."

Being at the head of the table has been and is Auburn's goal every year. As Coach Pat Dye says, "We want Auburn football to get to the point where it's not a question of 'Is Auburn going to be good,' but a question of 'How good is Auburn going to be.'"

Auburn's first bowl game came in 1937. It remains a historic bowl trip, the likes of which only one other college football team has ever taken.

Auburn was invited to play Villanova in Havana, Cuba, as part of the Cuban National Sports Festival. It was and still is the first and only post-season bowl game ever played on foreign soil.

Auburn looked forward to the trip, but uncertainty began to arise when an army general named Fugilanio Batista overthrew the Cuban government. The game was almost called off because Batista's picture was not in the game program, but a quick printing job and assurances from Batista that peace would prevail let the game go on.

Auburn and Villanova played to a 7-7 tie. Guns and soldiers were very much in evidence, but the game was played and Auburn, Villanova and revolution entered college football's history books.

The next year, Auburn went to the Orange Bowl, the third Orange Bowl to be played, and the defensive performance of Coach Jack Meagher's Tigers put on that day continues to rank as one of college football's best bowl performances. Auburn held Michigan State of the Big 10 to two first downs and 57 yards total offense enroute to a 6-0 victory.

There were several bright moments for Auburn football fans in the forties, the 27-13 win over Rose Bowl-bound Georgia in 1942, the most notable, but for the most part, the decade of the forties were war years. College football was played, but the people's thoughts and minds were in far off Europe and Japan where America's young men were fighting and dying for freedom.

With the fifties came Ralph "Shug" Jordan and Auburn returned to the glory days it had known in the days of Heisman, Donahue and Meagher. Jordan's teams won 176 games in his 25 years on the Plains and played in virtually every bowl. Auburn players won virtually every major award, including Zeke Smith's Outland Trophy in 1958 and Pat Sullivan's Heisman Trophy in 1971.

Jordan's 1957 and 1958 teams were undefeated, going 24 games without defeat, and the 1957 team won the national championship.

It was under Jordan's leadership and that of athletic director Jeff Beard, that Auburn's athletic facilities, now rated as fine as any in the country, had their beginnings.

What is now Jordan-Hare Stadium was opened in 1939 with a seating capacity of 7,200. The capacity increased to 21,000 by the time Jordan and Beard, both Auburn alumni, came on the scene in 1951. They had a dream of seeing Auburn play all its home games on campus.

There were three major stadium expansions under their direction bringing the capacity to 64,000. Another major expansion in 1980 brought the capacity to 75,000, and teams like Texas and Nebraska scheduled home-and-home series with Auburn. Every SEC team but one made regular visits to Jordan-Hare Stadium, and in 1989 that team will make its debut. When that day comes, the dream shared by Jordan and Beard will be complete.

What may become the greatest era of Auburn Football began in 1981 when Pat Dye was named head coach and athletic director. It took him but one year to get his program established. Auburn beat Boston College and eventual Heisman Trophy winner Doug Flutie in the Tangerine Bowl in 1982. The 1983 Tigers won the SEC championship and defeated Michigan 9-7 in the Sugar Bowl. In 1987, Auburn claimed its second SEC title under Dye and played spoiler to Syracuse's national championship hopes in the Sugar Bowl.

With Dye at the helm, Auburn has won more games than any other school in the SEC since 1982, and the Tigers have appeared in New Year's Day Bowl games four of the last five years.

In keeping with tradition, Auburn players are among the most honored in all of college football. Dye and his staff have produced 12 All-Americans, 39 All-SEC players, a Heisman Trophy winner, two semi-finalists for the Lombardi Award and 32 players have gone into pro football.

More importantly, Auburn has won as Auburn has never won before. Dye's teams have averaged better than nine wins a season and his last three senior classes have been the winningest senior classes in Auburn history. The 1985 Auburn seniors won 36 games and the 1986 and '87 seniors won 37 games. This senior class has a chance to break that mark. Jordan-Hare Stadium has continued to grow under Dye as well. In 1987, the addition of an upper deck and executive suites on the east side of the stadium brought the seating capacity to 85,187, making Jordan-Hare the fifth largest on-campus stadium in the country. When filled to capacity, as it is expected to be at least three times this year, Jordan-Hare has the distinction of being one of the largest cities in the state of Alabama.

Coach Dye has succeeded because of a strong belief in the work ethic, a belief shared by Auburn men and women down through the years. Dean George Petrie, Auburn's first football coach, put it this way when he wrote the Auburn Creed, "I believe that this is a practical world and that I can count only on what I earn. Therefore I believe in work, hard work."

Coach Dye puts it this way: "We may not be the best football team in America, but there is no reason we can't be the best conditioned, best prepared team...."

College football tradition as we know it in the Deep South began here at Auburn in 1892. Ninety-six years later, it continues to flourish here on the Plains.

And there is no sign it is about to change.

—Some of the material for this story was taken from War Eagle, A Story of Auburn Football *by Clyde Bolton.*

Auburn Football Illustrated
September 10, 1988
Auburn vs. Kentucky

Mamma

Many times over the years, I have written to you in this space about the special-ness of the Auburn family, what it is like to be a part of it, to feel its warmth and com-fort, its love and affection.

I thought I knew what I was writing about, but I really did not know, not until last week, when I lost my Mamma. She was my mother, but she was more than that. She was my Mamma.

She was not a perfect woman, but she was a woman of uncommon good. You can tell a person by the things they love. My Mamma loved her family, her church and Auburn.

How she did love Auburn!

When she had her first stroke in 1977, Auburn was a symbol of hope. Before she could even pronounce the word "Auburn" again, she wanted to know if she could "go down there" for a football game. It was June, and if she could be at Auburn in the fall for a football game, she knew she would be all right. She made it, too, for the Florida game in October of that year and a 29-14 Auburn victory.

The first stroke affected Mamma's ability to speak clearly and walk freely, but it did not affect her ability to love and to show concern and affection.

When Coach Sonny Smith's wife Jan, a woman she had never met, suffered a stroke in 1985, it concerned her greatly. She wrote Jan several times to encourage her. "If I can do it," she wrote, "you can do it." She never failed to ask about Jan and how she was doing.

Mamma loved to come to Auburn. Though she could hardly see in later years, she loved to be a part of the crowd, to feel the excitement. Her last trip here was October 18, 1986 for the Georgia Tech game. It just happened to be my 40th birthday and, as always, "her baby" took care of her as best he could.

I remember the first time she ever came to Auburn, in November of 1960 for the Homecoming game against Mississippi State. She got up early as she always did and fried chicken. There's nothing better than Mamma's fried chicken at an Auburn foot-ball game. Little did we know then, but we and thousands of others, were starting what would become an Auburn tradition in the eighties, tailgating.

I remember well the trip home that night. Like most other Auburn fans, we lis-tened to the LSU game on WWL radio out of New Orleans during the long drive home. When the game was over and she thought her boys were asleep in the back seat, she talked to my father about the real reason they had come to Auburn that day. She wanted to expose her oldest son, who was 14 at the time, to college and to the college atmosphere.

Twenty-eight years later that oldest son is Sports Information Director at Auburn and he's writing to you, telling you how much he loved his mother and why.

Mamma loved Auburn Football and she hated Alabama. She came by both natural-ly. She didn't lie. She never said, "I'm always for Alabama except when they play Auburn…" She gave it to 'em straight: "I hope you get whipped this weekend," she would say, and there was no doubt that she meant it.

The maddest her son ever got was that same year, 1977. We lost to Alabama again that year, as we usually did in those days, but what made me mad was the way two Alabama fans treated my Mamma. She still could not express herself well because of the stroke, and two Alabama fans began calling her on the telephone again and again, ridiculing Auburn and making fun of her because she did not, could not, defend Auburn. Finally their cruelty made her cry.

But she could dish it out, too. In February of 1987, after her second stroke, Wayne Atcheson, Sports Information Director at The University of Alabama, visited her at West Alabama General Hospital near Tuscaloosa. As I was introducing Wayne to my Daddy, I mentioned that he was the SID at Alabama. Mamma, who sometimes had the ability to hear what she wanted to hear, rose from what appeared to be a deep sleep, shook her good hand at Wayne and said in clearest tones, "We're gonna whip you next year." She then closed her eyes and went back to sleep, leaving a stunned son and a befuddled SID from Alabama.

But whip them we did, and Mamma was a very happy lady last November.

She loved to go to bowl games. "Going somewhere after Christmas," was the way she described it. The Gator Bowl in Jacksonville was her favorite. Some of you may have met her. She liked to hold court in the lobby of the old Robert Meyer Hotel, and she never met a stranger, not when it came to her beloved Auburn Tigers.

Like many of you, she adopted Auburn. She did not go to Auburn and she was not an Auburn graduate. Her degree was from Livingston, "Miss Julia Tutwiler's School for Female Women," as she used to call it. But as Coach Jordan once said, "The people who adopt Auburn by choice are sometimes more loyal and devoted than some who went to school here..."

My Mamma was one of those people.

My Mamma's gone now, and I tell you about her tonight as an expression of my appreciation, and that of my family, for your outpouring of love and concern in our time of sorrow.

You will never, never know how much it meant to us.

You taught me or at least brought me to a new and deeper understanding of what it means to be a part of the Auburn Family, surely the greatest, most loving, most caring family on earth.

Thank you. From the bottom of our hearts, thank you.

Auburn Football Illustrated
Auburn vs. Kansas
September 17, 1988

Big Gene Lorendo — a Father, a Man ____

When George M. Cohan left home to pursue a career in theater, his father thought his son was throwing his life away.

"Goodbye, Mother," Cohan said as he left home. "Don't worry about me. I'm on my way to New York to sell my songs and plays and get a job in a Broadway show. Dad doesn't think I will amount to anything, but keep on praying for me and everything will come out all right."

Cohan said that in 1893. Now, almost 100 years later, Cohan is still regarded as one of America's great musical talents. He produced, directed or starred in 166 stage plays and his contributions to Americana are legendary. *You're a Grand Ole Flag*, *Give My Regards to Broadway*, *Yankee Doodle* and *Over There* are just a few of the songs and tunes he gave to his country's heritage.

In Auburn, Alabama, 80 years later, another father and another son faced a similar parting. "Big Gene" Lorendo was a football coach at Auburn, the epitome of what a football coach was supposed to be: mean, rough, tough and gruff. You didn't give no lip to "Big Gene."

He had two sons. One, Mac, was a football player. He would go on to become an All-SEC offensive lineman for the 1972 Auburn Tigers, the Amazins', as they would come to be known, because of their iron will to win and their "never-say-die" attitude. People expected Big Gene's sons to be football players. It was the natural, expected thing.

The other son, Cam, was not interested in football or athletics. He was interested in a career in the arts, specifically dance, theater, and ballet.

Like George M. Cohan, he was concerned about how his father would react. Underneath his tough and gruff exterior, Big Gene was a loving, caring person. He could tell something was bothering his son.

"What is it, son," he finally asked. "We've always talked. If you want to talk about it, I'm here to listen and to help you."

Cam told his father he didn't want to disappoint him. He wanted his father to be proud of him, but he really was not interested in football. What he wanted to do was dance. He...

There was no need to go on.

Big Gene took over from there and what he said insured that the father-son relationship he cherished so deeply would remain intact forever.

"I'm always going to be proud of you," he told his son. "The only way I wouldn't be proud of you is if you didn't do the best you could do. When you quit doing your best, that's the time I get mad at you. You do your best and I'm always proud of you."

The rest is history. Mac followed football and went to the Canadian Football League after becoming a star at Auburn. Cam went on to a distinguished career in ballet and the arts. He now owns his own architectural and interior design firm in New York.

"I came to a new appreciation of dancers and actors watching Cam's career," Big Gene said recently from his home in Minnesota. "I've coached a lot of great football players and been around a lot of great athletes, but I've never seen anybody put more into their work than some of the dancers.

"The physical effort and intensity required to be a great football player is like the effort and intensity required to be a great dancer. You might not think of Baryshnikov as a great athlete, but if you look at his body and his intensity he puts into a performance, it's one and the same.

"The only difference is that one performs on the football field, the other on the stage. The commitment to excellence in the great ones is the same."

Auburn Football Illustrated
Auburn vs. Tennessee
September 24, 1988

Gene Lorendo and his wife, Jane, have moved back to Minnesota, their original home. Mac, an All-SEC offensive lineman in 1972, works for the telephone company in Nashville. Cam is still in New York. Big Gene is proud, equally proud, of them both.

Comeback _____

It's hard to believe it has been 20 years since Auburn won one of the most important games in all of its history. One that was not even a varsity game.

Return with us now to that thrilling day of November 23, 1968. Let us try to capture again the glory, the ecstasy, the hope and promise of that Saturday so long ago that has meant so much to Auburn football then and now.

Auburn had a good recruiting year in 1966 and an even better year in 1967. This was when signing day was in December instead of February. For the first time in a long while, Coach Shug Jordan's staff had dominated the state's "Ten Most Wanted" list two years in a row.

Coming to Auburn in that long ago fall were such players as Bruce Bylsma, whose son, Wayne, is a linebacker on this year's team, Bob Brown, Jere Colley, Larry Hill, Bill McManus, Sammy Oates, David Shelby, Eddie Welch, a quarterback named Sullivan and a receiver named Beasley.

There were freshmen teams back then because freshmen weren't eligible for varsity competition. This highly touted freshmen class was blown away by Florida (John Reaves and Carlos Alvarez) 54-17. The freshmen beat Georgia 40-18, Ole Miss 37-14 and Mississippi State 30-7. Then came Alabama.

There was more interest in this freshman game this year. Alabama had dominated the varsity series with Auburn over the past 10 years, Auburn winning only once since 1959, that in 1963, 10-8. This game, the battle of boys, was supposed to be an indicator of things to come. Would Alabama continue to dominate Auburn or had the Tigers pulled even? A waiting world wanted to know. Or so it seemed on that November Saturday 20 years ago.

The game was played at Tuscaloosa and the first quarter was all Alabama. Five minutes before the half, it was 27-0, Crimson Tide, and Auburn's hopes of changing the balance of power in Alabama appeared dim.

But then a strange thing happened.

One of the players trotted on the field to receive Alabama's sixth kickoff of the first half. As he reached the Auburn huddle on the 40-yard line, he muttered, "Looks like this is going to be a massacre..."

He seriously misjudged the competiveness of his young Auburn teammates. Before he could finish his sentence, one of his teammates had given him a quick hard kick in his posterior.

"No damn way," the teammate said. "If you feel that way you better get your ass out of here right now."

All summer long these young freshmen had heard the talk and suffered the ridicule. "If you want to be a winner," they had been told over and over again, "you should have gone to Alabama. Alabama's a winner. Auburn's a loser."

They had had enough. The time had come for them to speak for themselves, and the give up attitude of one of their teammates crystallized their desire and perhaps their destiny.

The Alabama freshmen taunted the highly touted Auburn freshmen when they came to the line of scrimmage at their own 33-yard line. Sullivan, a future Heisman

Trophy winner, took command. Auburn drove 67 yards for a touchdown. Sullivan ran for 34 yards and passed for 33 yards to Daryl Johnson for the touchdown. 27-7 Alabama.

Alabama lost 12 yards in two plays. A third down snap was high and Auburn got a safety and the ball. 27-9 Alabama.

Auburn got the ball on the Tide 42 with 2:20 left in the first half. "Hold 'em out of here on this play," he told his offensive linemen, "and we'll score." They did and Sullivan found Terry Beasley streaking down the sideline. 27-15 Alabama at the half, but the Tide was turning.

On Auburn's first possession of the third quarter, Sullivan dropped back and there was Beasley again, 27-22 Alabama. The Tide had stopped laughing. So had its fans.

The Tide rose up and stopped Auburn on its next possession, but on fourth and 14 from the Auburn 16, punter David Beverly, a preview of things to come the next season, ran for a first down at the Auburn 32.

Ten plays later, Sullivan passed four yards to future offensive tackle, Jere Colley, for a touchdown and it was 29-27 Auburn.

Auburn kicked off and the defensive adjustments designed by Tom Jones, Jim Hilyer and Herb Waldrop, now Auburn's trainer, held. Auburn got the ball back at the Tide 45 and four plays later it was 36-27 Auburn.

The Auburn-Alabama rivalry turned around that day.

Auburn won three of the next four varsity games, coming from behind all three times, from 17 points behind in 1970 and 16 behind in 1972. Auburn came to win and win Auburn did — just like they had done as freshmen.

November 23, 1968.

Could it have really been that long ago?

Auburn Football Illustrated
Auburn vs. Akron
October 15, 1988

Cultural Literacy

One of the most popular books of the summer was *Cultural Literacy*, a book that looked at the American way of life and analyzed what one would need to know if he or she were to truly understand America.

It was an interesting book, especially the list of names, places, dates and terms that should be understood if one were to be literate about America.

Let's try the same thing today. Call it "Cultural Literacy — An Auburn Perspective," a collection of names, places, dates and terms that must be understood if one is to truly understand and appreciate the Auburn experience.

Alabama
Allnighter
The Amazin's
Anders
API
Archie's Barbecue
Athletics Make Men Strong, Study Makes Men Wise, Character Makes Men Great
The Auburn Creed
Auburn Football Illustrated
AUM
Aubie
Wilford Bailey
Doug Barfield
Jeff Beard
Bill Beckwith
Joe Beckwith
Big Blue Party Store
Biggio Flats
The Blocked Punt
Blue Room
Bombed Out
Bo Over the Top
Broun Hall
Earl Brown
Paul "Bear" Bryant
Jimmy Buffett
Burn the Bulldog Parade
Randy Campbell
The Casino
Dean Cater
Chewacla
Joe Ciampi
Cliff Hare Stadium

Courage
Crash and Burn
'Fessor Craft
Creek Bankin'
D Zone
Dairyland Farms
Dam Slide
Day House
December 2, 1972
December 2, 1989
Dead Day
Dean's List
Vince Dooley
Caroline Draughon
Ralph Draughon
Pat Dye
East Alabama Male College
Joel Eaves
1892
Extension
February 22, 1892
4244
14-13
Dean Foy
Harold Franklin
Rowdy Gaines
Gator Bowl
Harvey Glance
Georgia
Bobby Goldsboro
The Grille
Haley Center
Cliff Hare
Hank Hartsfield
Her-r-r-e come the Tigers!

Hey Day
Doc Hodge
Cindy Holland
Honor
Wilbur Hutsell
Instruction
Integrity
Iron Bowl
J&M
Bo Jackson
Fob James
Madison Jones
Shug Jordan
Kopper Kettle
Auburn Knights
Land Grant University
Langdon Hall
David Langner
Lathe
Legion Field
Loveliest Village of the Plains
The Man With the Moustache
Jim Martin
Maryland Fried Turkey
Ken Mattingly
Jack Meagher
Harold Melton
Mildred and Barbara
Morrill Act
McAllister's Boarding House
Phil Neel
Bill Newton
1957
Northcutt Realty
Olin L. Hill's Going Out of Business
     Sale
On the Rolling Plains of Dixie
Vickie Orr
Panty Raid
Gordon Persons
George Petrie
Harry Philpott
Pitts Hotel
Plainsman Club
Plainsman Park

Punt, Bama, Punt
Quiz
Rat Caps
Research
Rock Slide
Rolling Toomer's Corner
Ross Square
Rush
Samford Hall
Bob Sanders
Sani-Flush
Roy Sewell
17-16
Shepard's Purse
Shine's
Shot Down
Sonny Smith
Zeke Smith
Spencer Lumber Company
Jordan-Hare Stadium
Step-Sing
Streaking
Sugar Bowl
Pat Sullivan
Homer Swingle
Talisi Hotel
The Tea Room
Tigers (origin)
Toomer's Corner
Toni Tenille
27-13
23-22
280
Coach Umbach
Union Movie
Walk-Ons
War Eagle (legend)
War Eagle (mascot)
War Eagle Supper Club
War Eagle Pills
Whiskey Jack
Wreck Tech Pajama Parade
Luther Young
Young's Laundry
"You're So Right, Carl."

Auburn Football Illustrated
Auburn vs. Mississippi State
October 22, 1988

Common Ground _____

If you are still trying to make up your mind on who to vote for Tuesday, here is a fact you might want to consider.

In the last seven years, when Republicans have been in the White House, Auburn has defeated Alabama four times. In the previous four years, when Democrats were in the White House, the Jimmy Carter years, Auburn did not beat Alabama a single time.

Not that that has anything to do with who will make the best President, but it did get quite a reaction from the Washington Auburn Club this summer. And an interesting reaction it was. Half cheers, half "ooooh's," but the cheers did seem a bit louder. It probably had more to do with beating Alabama than presidential politics, but it did start me thinking—which is not always an easy thing to do—and I want to share those thoughts with you on this Homecoming Day.

Auburn has a lot in common with America, not just the land and the freedom, but with the dream and the idea.

A student can come to Auburn and be anything he or she wants to be. He can do anything he wants to do. He can be a farmer or an astronaut, a teacher, a preacher, a bank president, a college president, or an Ag teacher. A doctor or a lawyer. Anything he wants to be. Auburn is a place where dreams come true. All a person needs is a strong will, determination and a willingness to work. Auburn provides the opportunity. The individual provides the rest.

At Auburn, who you are isn't nearly as important as what you are. Being Greek isn't nearly as important at Auburn as it is at other colleges and universities. Auburn people tend to measure each other more by quality and depth of character than by what part of the city you come from or by the clubs and social groups your parents belong to.

Perhaps it is our land-grant heritage, perhaps it is the fact that most of us are just one generation removed from the farm, where people work for what they earn, where they toil with their hands, where they go about the business of living and dying, springtime and harvest every year.

Maybe it is because of the diversity here, a fine arts program and an agricultural program, an engineering program and a liberal arts program, a school of business and a religious affairs program. Culture, agriculture, business, science, education, philosophy, all of the endeavors of mankind are a part of the Auburn experience. Diversity is one of our strengths. It is part of our being, part of our nature.

Throughout most of our history, we have been underfunded in our most important venture, education, and outmanned on the athletic field. Yet, we have prevailed.

Not because of any magic formula or Divine Right. If there is Divine Right in this state, it is not at Auburn. Auburn has succeeded through hard work, dedication, love, loyalty and sacrifice, the same qualities that have made America a great country.

At times, like our country, we have found ourselves split and divided. One faction wants us to go this way, another faction another way. The only thing it seemed we had in common, the common ground Jesse Jackson talked about, was our love for

Auburn. Our tremendous, immeasurable love for Auburn. It was bigger than all of us.

Because of that love, because of that loyalty, we have conquered, we have prevailed. The Dream lives on.

The days of the Funderburk controversy and the Jeff Burger controversy are behind us. So is the argument over who would have made the best president, Harry Philpott or E.T. York. These are part of the natural struggles of the college campus, the normal strains and tensions, Liberal Arts and Agriculture, Engineering and Education, English and Athletics, the faculty and the president, the students and the Board of Trustees. All are part of life on the college campus. Yet, it is out of these struggles and strains that progress comes. And progress is still our most important product. Progress and Education. Throughout history, they have been one and the same.

Yes, we are approaching election day, another of those magic days when the American Dream, the greatest experiment the world has ever known, works again. Some of us will win, some of us will lose. For the next four years, one side or the other will be the loyal opposition. The *loyal* opposition. That word *"loyal"* says a lot.

So it is with Auburn. Down through the years, we have disagreed, argued, cussed and discussed. Mainly we have discussed, and in that discussion we have found common ground. And we have gone forward.

We have gone forward because of our commitment to Auburn.

So it is with America.

So let it be with Auburn.

Auburn Football Illustrated
Auburn vs. Southern Mississippi
November 5, 1988

Excellence is Where You Find It _____

Pat Dye didn't think he would like it.

He was a football coach, not a theater critic, and this was a bit out of his league.

But he always liked the best, and this was the best on Broadway. He'd give it a chance, but there would be no great expectation, just a chance, as he was fond of saying in football, just a chance that he would like it.

It was *Les Miserables*, the story of Jean Valjean and the Bishop's candlesticks, how they changed Valjean's life and how he, in turn, changed the lives of others around him. It is the story of God at work in our lives through each other. It is moving and powerfully done.

As their car pulled up to The Broadway Theater on Broadway and 53rd Street, Dye told his companions not to be surprised if he left at intermission or even before. He didn't know much about theater, and he really wasn't into a French play, not a week after having beaten Alabama 10-0 and winning Auburn's second SEC championship in five years.

He would give it a little while. If he liked it, he would stay; if not, he would go. No commitments on this one. Not from Pat Dye.

Hindman Wall had no illusions. The only question was whether Coach Dye would make it to intermission. Wall remembers it this way:

"Coach Dye made it clear that he might be gone by intermission. He was sitting in the orchestra, and we were in the balcony. At intermission, we looked down to see what his reaction might be and he was already giving us a big thumbs up sign. He loved it, and he was moved by it. It's hard to see that play and not be moved."

Moved Dye was, by the story, by the play and by the performance. He saw and felt things he had seen and felt before, on other fields of human expression.

"I'd heard a lot about plays on Broadway," Dye said recently, "but I never dreamed that watching people who were so talented on stage could be so entertaining.

"The thing that makes it so unique is that I went there with a negative attitude. I didn't think I could sit in a theater seat with a packed house and not feel cramped and uncomfortable, but I never knew there was anybody else there other than Sue and me when I got involved in the play.

"The story and the music were absolutely unbelievable," he said. "How they can take their feelings and put them into music and make you feel it on the stage is amazing. There was never an instant when you thought they had hung on to a scene too long. They would get right into something else that would excite and inspire you. It was a series of highs for me. Each scene was a special time and a special place performed by special people."

Dye's three favorite characters in the play were Jean Valjean, played by country music singer Gary Morris, and two little girls, Cossette, played by Donna Vivino and Judy Kuhn, and Eponine, played by Chrissie McDonald and Kelli James. "To me they were unbelievable," said Dye. "I had no idea anyone could have so much talent and ability and make a character seem so real and so close."

Dye saw a parallel between the actors and actresses on the *Les Miserables* stage and the young men he had recently coached to an SEC championship.

"It's a lot like football," he said. "The emotions on a football team are at an all-time high when you are playing on national television and when you have a packed house for a big game.

"There's no doubt that the audience and the response of the audience has to have a tremendous response effect on the actors to get their adrenalin and motivation going to be able to perform at that level every night. I never dreamed it would be like that. They respond and react to the audience the same way a football team responds and reacts to a crowd.

"You could see the intensity in the actors' eyes and you could feel them respond to the audience and the audience respond to them. It was a beautiful thing to be a part of. They wanted their performance to be the best it could be and it showed. You could feel it watching them and you couldn't help but be inspired," Dye said.

"I've read about people who like to perform live rather than on film or tape and now I can understand why. The rewards are different for a live performer. Sure, they are getting paid for it, but their reward is in the response they get from the audience, and when you have the ability to move people, that's worth more than money."

Dye had the opportunity to visit with the play's star, Gary Morris, in June at the group Alabama's June Jam in Fort Payne. It was no accident that their conversation turned to *Les Miserables*.

Dye told Morris how much he enjoyed his performance as Jean Valjean and remarked how physically demanding the role must have been. "If I had done what you did," Dye said, "I would be physically exhausted."

Morris told Dye it was indeed physically and emotionally demanding, but he added, "It is one of the most rewarding things I have ever done."

"Instead of having 11 or 12 big games a year, he had a big game seven or eight times a week," Dye said. "There's only one chance for a live performer or an actor before an audience and it has to be the best it can be every night."

Again, Dye saw a parallel between Morris' world and his world of college football.

"There's no question that there is a lot of teamwork in putting on a big show like that," Dye noted. "They had more than 11 players, but it's still teamwork. That's the key to it. One person makes a mistake or isn't having his best night and it can affect everybody else on the stage or on the team."

Yet, it was in terms of the actors themselves that Dye saw the greatest parallel to the game he coaches.

"There are a lot of actors," he said, "like there are a lot of football players. But there aren't many great ones. The great ones, the ones who win the awards, the ones who move the audience night after night, are the ones who have paid their dues and paid the price. They worked and worked and worked. They know the meaning of sacrifice and discipline in their lives.

"The ones who are the best are the hungry ones, the ones who feel that hunger down deep in their soul. They want to be the best they can be, and they work every day to be that way. They don't let anything keep them from reaching their ultimate goal. The only thing they fear is not being their best every time they go out. That's something I can relate to and it is something everybody ought to be able to relate to."

Another case of "Excellence is where you find it," on the football field or in the theater.

Coach Dye's next venture into theater? Probably this December, Michael Crawford and *The Phantom of the Opera* in New York. That is unless he decides to drop in on a University Theater production this fall.

Excellence, after all, is where you find it.
On Broadway, at Jordan-Hare Stadium or at Telfair Peet Theater.

Auburn Football Illustrated
Auburn vs. Georgia
November 12, 1988

Dooley and Dye————————————

The question was first asked just over a year ago, in the stadium edition of *The Athens Daily News*. It was asked in a column by a fictitious character named Hap Hazzard as he pondered the events of the day to come.

It was No. 47 of 50 questions he asked himself before the start of last year's Auburn-Georgia game. The question was, "Is Auburn proud of Vince Dooley?"

Today he gets his answer.

It is appropriate that the answer comes today, the day on which Coach Dooley is going after his 200th coaching victory, a milestone reached by only two other active coaches, Bo Schembechler of Michigan and Joe Paterno of Penn State.

Yes, we are proud of Vince Dooley. We are very proud of him and all that he has accomplished, the same way Georgia people should be proud of Pat Dye.

There are those among us who will say that these words should not be written, that we should not say anything nice about Coach Dooley because Georgia will use it against us in recruiting or, worse yet, because Georgia is "the enemy."

Ridiculous.

Auburn people should be—and are—proud of Vince Dooley. He's walked these same hills, seen these same trees and felt the same things we feel when Auburn comes on the field. He is one of us.

A part of Auburn will forever be in Vince Dooley's makeup, just as a part of Georgia will forever be in Pat Dye's makeup. We are all the sum total of our experiences.

Being proud of one of your own, if you are from Auburn or Georgia, doesn't mean you are disloyal to your school or your team. Being proud of someone's accomplishments means you are man or woman enough to recognize accomplishment no matter what color it wears, the Red and Black of Georgia or the Orange and Blue of Auburn.

Those fans who respect and appreciate only what their team and coaches accomplish are missing out on the highest majesty and grandeur of the game we profess to love and understand, the human factor. The ability to rise to the challenge, the ability to overcome the odds, the ability to dream the impossible dream and make that dream come true. That's what football is all about—the human factor.

Vince Dooley and Pat Dye. Consider what these men have accomplished.

Coach Dooley is the nation's third winningest active coach in terms of coaching victories. He is the dean of SEC head coaches. Throughout his 25 years, he has conducted himself with class and dignity. He has been true to the values his old school taught him.

Coach Dye has made Auburn the SEC's winningest team over the last five years and the fifth winningest team in the country. Auburn has won 55 games and two SEC championships since 1983, and the Tigers are in the running for another, depending on the outcome of the game today. No matter who wins today, we are in the Golden Era of Auburn football, and Pat Dye—a Georgia alumnus—made it happen. But he is one of us now, just as Vince Dooley belongs to Georgia.

Both men are doing what their old schools taught them to do best. They're working hard, they're loyal—Dooley to Georgia, Dye to Auburn—and they are representing each other's university with dignity and integrity. And, they are winning.

Two years ago, after Georgia upset Auburn 20-16 here in Jordan-Hare Stadium, Dye and Dooley met in the press interview trailer. As usual, Coach Dooley was magnanimous in victory, praising his team in victory and Auburn's effort in defeat.

As he was leaving, Dye looked at him and said, "If anybody had to do this to us, Coach, I'm glad it was you. I hate anybody had to do it, but if it had to happen at all, I'm glad it was you. You deserve it."

As Dye spoke, the look in the two men's eyes said more than words. There was mutual respect, mutual admiration, a mutual understanding. It was a special moment only they truly understood.

"You go up to Birmingham and Beat Bama," Dooley said, smiling.

"And you Beat Tech," Dye said, smiling too.

A week later they were competing again, this time in recruiting.

Yes, Auburn people are proud of Vince Dooley.

And we hope Georgia people are equally proud of Pat Dye.

Auburn Football Illustrated
Auburn vs. Georgia
November 12, 1988

This proved to be Vince Dooley's last game against his alma mater. He retired at the end of the 1988 season with an overall record of 201-77-10, a record that destines him to the College Football Hall of Fame. He was 11-13-1 against Auburn.

Mr. B.

Bill Beckwith began working in the Auburn Athletic Department in the fall of 1949 as a student assistant in the publicity office. Then, as now, somebody had to cut out and paste the stories in a scrapbook. That was Beckwith's first job at Auburn.

He did it as a hobby at first while holding down a "real" job at a local furniture store. Like most college students, Beckwith, a 22-year-old Navy veteran, was working his way through school on the GI Bill.

When publicity director Jimmy Coleman turned in his resignation in 1950, athletic director Wilbur Hutsell asked Beckwith to do the job "until we can find somebody." In return, Hutsell promised to pay him $80 a month. Beckwith is still waiting for Auburn to find somebody.

Beckwith was acting Publicity Director in 1951, and his first major assignment was to handle the media events around the hiring of a rookie head coach named Ralph "Shug" Jordan. The rest is history.

Beckwith's first major publicity push was Bill Turnbeaugh, better known as "Blind Bill Turnbeaugh," thanks in part to Beckwith's PR efforts. Turnbeaugh could hardly see and Beckwith told members of the media that Turnbeaugh was so blind that he couldn't see the ball carrier, fought off would-be-blockers until he found the man with the ball, then threw him to the ground. Turnbeaugh made second team All-SEC and a legend was born—the legend of Bill Beckwith.

Beckwith was Publicity Director in 1957, and for all of the Tigers' success on the field, Beckwith's handling of the Southern bloc vote had as much to do with Auburn being named No. 1 in the nation as the team's success on the field.

In 1958 Beckwith began what was to become his most valuable and lasting contribution to Auburn, the development of Auburn's season ticket plan. Auburn sold 1,800 season tickets that first year. This year, 31 years later, 75,000 season tickets will be sold, giving Auburn one of the strongest financial bases of any athletic program in the country. In 1970, again at Beckwith's urging, the season ticket plan was tied to contributions to the Greater Auburn Fund (GAF). That made Auburn's base even stronger.

Beckwith is not the most popular man in the Auburn Athletic Department. Any man who has to say "No" as much as ticket managers do will not make friends, but there is no doubt that Bill Beckwith has put Auburn first throughout his 40 years on the Plains.

Beckwith is as much a part of Auburn Football as War Eagle and Jordan-Hare Stadium. He has seen every Auburn football game since 1949, and of the 201 games played in Jordan-Hare Stadium, Beckwith has seen 189 of them.

The times have not always been good, but, as with most labors of love, the good has far outweighed the bad.

Bill Beckwith's most memorable moment in his 40 years at Auburn? Easy. Sometime in August of 1989 when Auburn sold out of season tickets for the first time in history. 75,000 season tickets. It was more than anyone could have ever imagined in 1958 when it all began.

Like all good Auburn men, Beckwith has always dreamed of the day when Alabama would come to Auburn, when, at long last, Auburn would have a chance to show the Crimson Tide some of the Southern Hospitality that has made Auburn famous. It is fitting that Auburn's first opportunity to host the Crimson Tide would come in 1989, Beckwith's 40th year. He has worked so hard and so effectively to bring it about.

His Auburn career, his work and his dedication to his alma mater is a hallmark for others to follow. It is in recognition of his 40 years of service and devotion that the *1989 Auburn Football Media Guide* is respectfully and affectionately dedicated.

Auburn Football Media Guide
July, 1989

A lot of people are called "Mr. Auburn." Bill Beckwith is "Mr. Auburn."

Man of the Hour

It was eight years ago. Auburn was playing LSU. It was a cloudy, overcast day, sprinkled with showers and rain throughout.

For most of us, it was a cold, clammy day. An entirely forgettable day.

For John Murphy, it was his moment of glory, his dream come true. His one great hour on the stage.

Pat Dye was in his first year as Auburn's head football coach. Auburn had won the first game of the Pat Dye era, struggling to a 24-16 win over TCU, hardly anything to brag about, but any win in those days was something to brag about. How quickly we change, how quickly we forget.

But things turned sour after that first win. The next week we would lose to Wake Forest 24-21, blowing a 14-0 lead. Vincent Jackson committed to Auburn that night but it didn't matter. Few of us knew — or cared — who Vincent Jackson was, much less that his nickname was Bo. That was then, not now. Auburn had just lost to Wake Forest. Wake Forest! Our fortunes were indeed low.

Tennessee won 10-7 the next week. Auburn's last drive ended inside the Tennessee one-yard line. There were tears in the dressing room after that game. Losing had begun to hurt again. Winning had begun to matter again.

A trip to Nebraska was next and Auburn lost again, this time in a driving rain-storm. The score was 17-3. Nebraska had to drive only 13 yards for its two touchdowns because of Auburn miscues.

LSU was next and Auburn's new coach had a decision to make. It was obvious that Charles Thomas could not handle the wishbone offense. A new quarterback had to be found. Joe Sullivan, the quarterback of a year ago, was a drop back passer as his brother Pat, now an insurance agent, had been. It didn't matter. Sullivan was too sick to practice or run the offense. He was in bed most of the week with the flu. Ken Hobby, the heir apparent, was hurt, a bad ankle. He couldn't practice. A kid who would probably never play, Randy Campbell, wasn't ready. Four games into the season, LSU was next and Auburn didn't have a quarterback. What would Pat Dye do? What would Auburn do? How much worse could it get?

Into Auburn's hour of need stepped John Murphy. A year before he had been playing football for the Patriots, an independent intramural team made up of everyday, average, normal students who played touch football as a means of recreation. After a couple of games, the Patriots changed quarterbacks. John Murphy wasn't good enough to play quarterback for the intramural league Patriots, much less for the Auburn Tigers.

Yet, there he was, about all Auburn had. He had played quarterback at Vestavia in Birmingham and he had walked on at Tennessee. They, too, told him he wasn't good enough. But John Murphy remembered that Abraham Lincoln never won an election until he was elected president. He remembered that the race doesn't always go to the strongest or fastest man. Sooner or later it goes to the man who thinks he can. John Murphy thought he could, so he walked on at Auburn, still chasing an elusive dream.

On Wednesday before LSU, Coach Dye made the decision. John Murphy, the man who wasn't good enough to play quarterback in the intramural league a year before, would start at quarterback for the Auburn Tigers against LSU.

It was a deeply held secret. Few people knew and even fewer breathed a word of it. Auburn would run what would become known as the designated offense against LSU. Murphy would run the ball or pitch it to Lionel James, George Peoples or Mike Edwards. Sullivan, if he was able, would come in on obvious passing downs and Campbell would be available for spot duty. The play would be called and the quarterback who could run that play would go into the game.

John Murphy ran the ball seven times that day, gaining 18 yards. His long run was six yards. He threw one pass which was incomplete. He scored no touchdowns but Auburn won, 19-7. It was Pat Dye's first SEC victory and it was Auburn's first SEC win in two years. Since that game, Auburn has been the winningest team in the SEC. It would be a watershed moment of Auburn football history and John Murphy, an unknown player with enough courage, enough heart and enough confidence in himself to follow a dream, would contribute greatly to that moment.

A year later, Randy Campbell was the quarterback, Auburn was on the way to the SEC Championship and John Murphy was out of football, back among the normal student populace, riding his bicycle, eating lunch at The Grille. It is not known if he ever played intramural football again.

John Murphy now lives in Dublin, Ohio. Efforts to reach him this week were unsuccessful. His mother still lives in Birmingham, and she said John still follows Auburn Football. No doubt he is watching today's game, probably remembering how it was eight years ago today when, for one brief, shining moment, his dream came true.

And so, as Auburn and LSU are about to play again, let us pause to remember John Murphy and others like him. For their dreams are the stuff life is made of.

Here's to you, John Murphy, and others like you. Thanks for making our lives richer and more meaningful.

Auburn Football Illustrated
Auburn vs. LSU
October 14, 1989

Service Above Self

His name was not Petrie or Hare, but he was in their category.

His name was Ed Bagwell.

Officially, he was a geography professor, teaching geography for 38 years in Tichenor Hall, less than half a block up Thach Avenue from the stadium.

Unofficially, he was a keeper of the Auburn Spirit.

He went to North Carolina, but he found a home in Auburn.

To many of us, coming from dots across the universe, he was the first college professor we had. He set the tone for our college experiences. Some of us never had a better teacher.

Not only did we learn about the earth's geography and topography and the effects it had on mankind, we learned about truth and beauty.

One of the reasons Ed Bagwell loved Auburn was because of its values, values made evident in little things. Things like having streets named Magnolia, Camellia, Canary and Samford rather than second street, third street and first avenue.

As the Reverend John Jeffers said at his funeral, he not only cared that we learned what we were supposed to learn in his course, he wanted us to learn from the college experience as well.

Ed Bagwell was one of those people who put something back into the community where he lived. He made Auburn and Auburn University a better place.

It would be difficult to imagine a young person growing up in Auburn without coming under Ed Bagwell's influence. He was a Boy Scout leader and a leader in Dixie Youth baseball. He was a director of band camp. Wherever young people gathered, Ed Bagwell was there, working in the concession stand, standing behind home-plate or cooking for the masses.

Ed Bagwell was a Rotarian and no Rotarian ever lived up to that club's motto "Service Above Self" more than Ed Bagwell.

His father died when he was nine months old. Ed spent his life being a father to others and helping others.

Rarely did a week go by that a student did not call Ed at home needing help. It could have been needing someone to talk to or someone to sign bail. Whatever the need, Ed Bagwell was there, caring and loving, doing unto them as he would have their parents do unto his five children. Ed Bagwell never lost sight of the good in people and the tremendous possibilities in young people.

Auburn is indeed a better place because Ed Bagwell lived, worked and loved here.

He was a fixture at all Auburn football and basketball games. Many of you know him without realizing it. Ed was the small man who always sold programs just inside the front door of the coliseum. The friendly one who always smiled. That was Ed. His wife Sally and his son Edward were usually there with him. At one time or other, all of his family, girls, too, helped sell programs. Ed was Auburn's program vendor for years. People in Auburn really don't remember when Ed Bagwell wasn't selling programs. Many a young man saw his first Auburn game or had his first lesson in business because of Ed Bagwell. Auburn sells more football programs than any other school in the country—thanks to Ed Bagwell. But selling programs isn't what mattered most to Ed Bagwell. It was the opportunities selling programs provided to young people. That was what mattered most, a chance to learn, a chance to grow and a chance to have fun.

Ed Bagwell died Thursday before last week's Florida game, his gallant and courageous fight over. There was little thought given to having the funeral on Saturday. Auburn was at home and Edward Bagwell had to carry on his father's tradition of selling programs. The Bagwells were here, selling programs.

I saw Edward beneath the north end zone three hours before kickoff. We exchanged embraces of sympathy, and Edward said, "We're right where he would want us to be, doing what he would want us to do."

And Edward was right. Ed would have had it no other way.

I mentioned that a lot of people loved his Dad, that a lot of us were richer and more whole as human beings for having known his father. "We had to share him with a lot of people," Edward said. "At times it was hard, but looking back, seeing how many people's lives he touched makes it all worthwhile."

They laid Ed Bagwell to rest last Sunday, beneath a beautiful blue sky, a ribbon of orange and blue and a small American flag his son had placed on his casket moments before the service.

In the distance, not far from where Coach Jordan is buried, there was the sound of children laughing, playing, having fun. Playing football.

In Ed Bagwell's hand was a copy of an Auburn football program.

Auburn Football Illustrated
Auburn vs. Louisiana Tech
November 11, 1989

Dec. 2, 1989

The day we have loathed or longed for is upon us.

Whether we have loathed this day or longed for this day depends on what colors stir our souls, Crimson and White or Orange and Blue.

For Auburn this is a great day in our history, no matter what the outcome of today's game may be. This is the day we have longed for since 1939, the year this stadium was first opened. All of our Southeastern Conference brethren have now come to our house to play. Our circle is complete. For Alabama it is something else entirely.

Alabama has finally come to Auburn to play a football game. This is not the first time an Alabama team has run onto this field. Freshman teams from Tuscaloosa have played here on several occasions, but this is the first time a Crimson Tide varsity team has ever come to Auburn. It was said that this day would "never" come, but, as so often happens, "never" proved to be a very short time.

The emotional arguments about whether or not this day should have ever come could be outlined here, but it would serve no useful purpose. We have heard them all before, and our agreement or disagreement would depend almost entirely on whether we loathed or longed for this day.

I am man enough to admit that had I been born an Alabama man, had I been raised on the tradition of Wade, Thomas and Bryant, I would have loathed this day. I would have opposed my team coming here at almost any cost. Had I been born an Alabama man, I, too, would have probably said, "Never..." because it would not have been in the best interest for my school's football program to come to Auburn.

As an Alabama man, I would know that as long as we could dictate to our cross-state rivals where they played their home football games, we held the upper hand. We held the higher ground in image if not in fact. The cross-state rival could never be equal to us as long as we could dictate the terms on which we played.

And there are Alabama people here today who are man enough or woman enough to admit that had they been born an Auburn man or an Auburn woman, had they been raised on the tradition of Heisman, Meagher, Jordan and Dye, they would have felt exactly as Auburn people did.

As long as our cross-state rival could dictate where we play our home games, the rival held the upper hand, the high ground. There was no equality.

Today, for the first time, there is equality.

That is what I, as an Alabama man, would have loathed. It is not in Alabama's best interest to have Auburn as an equal. But equality is what I, as an Auburn man, have longed for. I owe it to my school to accept nothing less.

For Alabama, it was a matter of advantage. For Auburn, it was principle. For both of us, it was a matter of pride.

There is no reason to think that Alabama will not win in Auburn. The Crimson Tide, in its long and glorious history, has won everywhere it has played, and it will win here, too—we Auburn people just hope it won't be today, the day of our emancipation.

And there is no reason to think that Auburn will not win in Tuscaloosa. Auburn has won there before, 48-0 and 17-0, and the Tigers will win there again—in Bryant-Denny Stadium.

That day will come just as this day has come.

But this is 1989, and the time has come to welcome Billy Neighbors, Benny Nelson, Jay Morris, John Mosley, Kirk McNair, Cecil Dowdy, Bruce Graham, Barry Allen and, yes, even Ray Perkins to Auburn. Welcome to our home.

We know you didn't want to come and we understand the reasons why. We appreciate your loyalty to your alma mater and your support of its football program. We applaud you for your commitment to Alabama and what is best for its football program. Had we been in your position, we would have felt the same way.

We hope you can put yourselves into our position and appreciate the qualities in us that we appreciate in you.

Perhaps therein we can find the common ground this rivalry so desperately needs.

Forty years from now historians will look back at this day and wonder what all the hoopla was bout. Our game site issue—as real and as intense as it has been to both of us—will seem as silly to them as the reasons Auburn and Alabama not playing for 40 years seem to us—a disagreement over whether to have 22 players at a per diem of $3.50 or 20 players at $3.00.

The day we have loathed or longed for has come. It has not only come. It has come to pass.

Auburn Football Illustrated
Auburn vs. Alabama
December 2, 1989

Tiger Walk

It was a day "they" said would never happen.

They said Alabama would "never" play in Auburn.

But, as so often happens, "never" proved to be a very short time.

The story of this day is the story that only Auburn people know and understand. It begins 50 years ago, in 1939, the year Auburn first opened what is now Jordan-Hare Stadium.

For the first time, Auburn people had a home. After wandering the SEC like the Children of Israel wandering in the wilderness, Auburn people and the Auburn football team had a home. No longer would Auburn have to observe Homecoming in Montgomery. No longer would Auburn have to play all of its big games on the road because there was not a place to play at home.

The goal of Auburn Football has always been the same—to have a stadium as good as any in the SEC, to be as good as anyone in the SEC, to have all of the SEC brethren come to Auburn. To be equal.

With the opening of 7,200 seat Auburn Stadium in 1939, that goal became a possibility. But it took 50 years—and December 2, 1989—for that dream to become a reality.

It did not come easily and, until the very end, there were those who said it would "never" happen. In saying that, these prophets of doom, most of whom wore Red and White, were saying that Auburn would never be equal, that there would never be equality between Auburn and Alabama. They were saying that Auburn would never be in control of its own destiny. Others would dictate terms to Auburn. Others would dictate to Auburn when and where Auburn would play its home football games.

But it did not stop there. Auburn people were ridiculed. They became the object of scoff and scorn. From the state legislature to the corner cafe, Auburn and Auburn people became the butt of the now infamous Auburn Joke. Everybody had one and everybody laughed—except Auburn people. A seething resentment began to build among Auburn people. Somewhere, somehow, it had to end.

Year after year, Alabama fans laughed and made fun of Auburn. Through the years of domination at Legion Field in Birmingham, Tide fans laughed and laughed. Auburn people, for the most part, held their heads high, but deep within their souls there burned but one desire, one hope, one dream..."If we can just get them to Auburn, we can beat them. If we could just play them at Auburn, we would win...If we could just play at Auburn..."

The years went by. Alabama fans laughed when Auburn refused to get caught up in the rush to put down artificial turf. "Look at those country bumpkins," they said. And they were amused as Auburn kept adding seats "down there at Auburn." Cliff Hare Stadium became Jordan-Hare Stadium and grew from 34,000 to 44,000 to 75,000. They didn't laugh in the early seventies when Auburn Coach "Shug" Jordan suggested that Auburn might want to play its home games with Alabama at Auburn one day. "Never," they cried in chorus. "Never. Where would we sleep? Where would we eat?"

The City of Birmingham joined in, "Think what it would mean to our economy," they said, never pausing to think what it might mean to the economies of Auburn, Opelika, Montgomery and all of East Central Alabama. Thinking only of themselves, "Never" became the battle cry of Alabama fans and of Birmingham. "Auburn isn't big enough to handle the game. The game was meant to be played in Birmingham..."

It was almost as if God Himself intended the game to be played in Birmingham. But if God had spoken, He spoke only to the high and mighty. He had not spoken to Auburn. It was just another sign that Auburn was backward and country, that Auburn didn't understand. While Alabama—some Alabama fans at least—and the City of Birmingham spoke of Divine Right, Auburn went about doing good.

Georgia came to Auburn for the first time in 1960. Georgia Tech, which said it would never come to Auburn, came in 1970. Tech officials had predicted in 1960 when Auburn moved its home game with Tech out of Atlanta's Grant Field for the first time in 56 years, that the Tigers would "come crawling back to Georgia Tech begging" the Yellow Jackets to take them back at Grant Field. It didn't happen. Tech dropped Auburn in 1987 after Auburn had won nine straight. Tennessee came to Auburn for the first time in 1974 and came to stay in 1980.

It is worth noting that of all of Auburn's major "neutral site" rivals, only Georgia, time-honored, honorable ancient foe Georgia, came without a fight, proof once again of the deep respect the two schools have had for each other since the very earliest days of college football in the Deep South. Georgia alone came marching to Auburn with colors held high. All the others said, "No..." Alabama said, "Never."

When Auburn's Jordan-Hare Stadium was enlarged to 85,000 in 1987, the message was clear to Alabama, to Birmingham and to the college football world. Auburn intended to play all of its home games in Auburn—-Alabama included. The battle lines were drawn.

Contract negotiations regarding the game site began in 1987. Auburn said the current contract ended after the 1987 game. Alabama said, no, Auburn had agreed to a four-year extension. They cited as evidence a handwritten notation by former Alabama athletic director and head football coach Paul "Bear" Bryant on its copy of the contract indicating that the agreement to play in Birmingham had been extended through the 1991 season. Auburn had no record of a contract extension and there were no notations on the Auburn copy of the contract. The war was on.

Alabama threatened to drop Auburn. Auburn said, "If you kill the series, the blood will be on your hands...We will play in Auburn in 1989."

Alabama said Auburn should play the game in Birmingham because Alabama had never wanted to play Auburn anyway. Auburn "owed" it to Alabama, they said, to play in Birmingham. Auburn "owed" it to Alabama, they said, to let Alabama have its way.

All we are asking for, Auburn said, was equality. Equality for Auburn was what Alabama, understandably so, did not want. As long as Alabama could dictate terms to Auburn there would be no equality. Real or imagined, the playing field was not level.

The battle came down to four years, 1988, 1989, 1990 and 1991. Alabama said all the games were to be played in Birmingham. Auburn said it had the right to play its home games, 1989 and 1991, where it wanted to play.

Athletic officials at the two schools could not reach an agreement. Neither could the two Presidents. The "Game Site Issue," as it came to be called, went to the Boards of Trustees. The City of Birmingham filed a lawsuit against both schools demanding that all four games be played in the Magic City, a city that considered itself "Football Capital of the South."

Inch by inch, Alabama yielded. Not necessarily to Auburn, but to the rule of reason and to common sense. Game sites after 1991 would not be a problem, if Auburn would play in Birmingham in 1989 and 1991. Auburn said its 1989 game would be played in Auburn.

Alabama agreed to play in Auburn in 1991 if Auburn would agree to play its 1989 game in Birmingham. Auburn was determined to play its home game in Auburn in 1989. Auburn's stand became one of principle.

There were renewed threats that the series would end. There were threats that the Game Site Issue would go to the State Legislature, and there were proposals to put the game site issue to a public referendum. Finally, in the spring of 1988, a compromise was reached. Auburn would win its point in principle. Alabama would come to Auburn in 1989. In return, Auburn would agree to play its 1991 home game in Birmingham. As is the case with all good and fair compromises, both sides gave something and both sides gained something.

It should be pointed out that the game site issue was never more than an honest disagreement among honorable people representing two honorable state universities. It became an emotionally charged issue because of the overwhelming importance the people of Alabama place on the outcome of one game on one Saturday in November or December. Right or wrong—and there are many at Auburn and at Alabama who think it is wrong—that's the way it is—or was—in the state of Alabama in 1989.

The battle was over, but the words were not.

As the scoreboard horn at Legion Field sounded its last notes on Auburn's 15-10 victory over Alabama in 1988, Auburn's third victory over the Tide in three years, Auburn people began counting the days and the hours until their long held dream became a reality. Alabama coming to Auburn. Alabama playing at Auburn. Alabama at Auburn.

As they counted, they became aware of a new possibility so horrible and so terrible, they dared not utter the frightening words. But the words and the fear were there. "What if...What if Alabama won..."

With three straight wins over the Tide, two straight SEC championships and several outstanding recruiting years, there seemed to be little chance of that happening. But old champions die hard, and whatever else Alabama is or might be, Alabama was and still is a champion. For all of the pride Auburn people have in their Tigers, there is equal pride and tradition at The University of Alabama. And equality, true equality, runs both ways.

If beating Alabama in Auburn would be the greatest victory in Auburn history, beating Auburn at Auburn the first time the game was played there would be the greatest victory in Alabama history. It would spoil Auburn's greatest day. Nothing would be better for an Alabama fan. The worm turns both ways.

In anticipation of the Great Day, Auburn sold 75,000 season tickets, selling out of season tickets for the first time in its history. Special "First Time Ever" tickets were printed and tee shirts, bumper stickers and slogans about what Auburn was going to do to Alabama became the order of the day. Alabama and its football players put these things in their hearts and pondered them.

The season began with Auburn blasting outmanned Pacific and Alabama beating Memphis State. In the season's third week, Auburn was embarrassed at Knoxville, losing to Tennessee 21-14 in a game that wasn't that close. Tennessee gained 350 yards rushing, the most against an Auburn team in 14 years. The turning point came as it often does on the third Saturday of October. Alabama shelled Tennessee. Auburn lost again, 22-14 to Florida State. The Tide was rolling as in days of old, and in what was supposed to be a season of great promise, the Tigers were struggling.

Alabama clinched a share of the SEC championship Auburn fans had thought belonged only to them with a 32-16 win over LSU, a team Auburn struggled to beat 10-6 at Auburn. Alabama, undefeated and ranked No. 2 in the nation, was the SEC champion, but more important in this and every year, and especially this year, the Tide was the best team in the state—hands down.

To Auburn people, the unthinkable was about to happen. Their most dreaded, their most horrible fear was about to come to pass. After all those years, all those hopes and dreams, Alabama was coming to Auburn—and it looked as if the Tide was going to win.

It would be an event Auburn people would never live down. At what was supposed to be their greatest hour, could it be that they were about to be struck down once again? The ultimate Auburn joke was about to become the ultimate reality.

Alabama fans put it far more succinctly: "Your ass on your grass."

This book is the story of what happened on that long awaited day. It is a permanent pictorial history of the day Alabama came to Auburn for the first time.

It is the story of a *Tiger Walk To Victory*.

Foreword
Tiger Walk To Victory
Campus Spirit, Inc.
Auburn, Ala.
1990

Auburn won the game 30-20 and the day, the experience, was everything Auburn people dreamed it would be. That and more.

For Daddy

Many things can be said of Dave Housel.

One thing that can certainly be said of Dave Housel is "He was a good man..."

That has been said again and again as Mr. Dave, as he was known to many, turned toward the end of this part of life's journey..."Dave Housel is a good man."

To be able to say that about a man and really mean it as he crosses from the seen to the unseen world says a lot about how that man spent his time with us and the things that were important to him.

This church was important to him. He was a regular member of the Brotherhood Sunday School Class. He liked to go to Sunday School early so he could visit with class members and the men of the church. When his son David was a boy, David wanted to go early with his Daddy when Auburn won. When Auburn lost, David wanted to stay home, but Mr. Dave made him go anyway.

Every Sunday for almost 50 years, "Mr. Dave and Miss Estelle" would sit on the left side of the church about half way back, but Mr. Dave was not a man to wear his church, or his loyalty to it, on his sleeve. He was a man who believed in living a sermon rather than preaching a sermon. And he lived a good sermon to all who knew him, and especially to his sons.

When his church needed him, he was there, in big things and in small, he was there. Whether it was helping deliver all those Easter lilies and poinsettias his wife loved to sell, or serving on the Administrative Board or Finance Committee, when his church needed him, he was there. Dave Housel was a good man.

He loved his family and he set a good example. His father died when he was 18 years old and he spent most of the rest of his life caring for others, first his mother and later his wife. His sons learned about depth of love through his devotion to Miss Estelle after her stroke. It spoke of strength, commitment and fortitude. Here again, his life was his sermon.

He was especially proud of his younger son Raymond, and one of his great pleasures in his later years was working with Raymond at the store, "helping out," as he called it.

He loved his garden, too, spending long hours cultivating and nurturing God's green earth to bring forth a harvest as bountiful as the life he lived. He shared that harvest of peas, butterbeans, okra, tomatoes and corn with many of us here today. More importantly, he shared himself.

He loved this country. It was his home, and when called on to defend it, he did so with honor and without question. He was decorated for heroism after the Battle of the Bulge for leading his men to safety after they had been surrounded by the Germans. He was one of 65 to 100 American soldiers sent to contact the Russians at the end of the war, traveling unaccompanied through miles of German territory to complete his mission. He was a brave man, but he never would talk about his war experiences. What his family learned of them, they learned from others who had served with him or from magazines.

When Mr. Dave got sick for the final time, Raymond and Cindy called his commanding officer, a former superintendent of West Point. At the first mention of his name, his commanding officer said, "Dave Housel, a good soldier..." After all those years, he still remembered.

He loved this town. He loved Gordo and he loved the people of Gordo. He served on the city council and two terms as mayor, but that wasn't important to him. Helping people mattered to him, and that is what he tried to do, help people in the little things that affected their daily life.

Dave Housel believed in young people. Those who know him best know how proud he was of having had a part in building the new football field and especially the new Dixie Youth Baseball fields that have meant so much to young people. One of his greatest thrills was seeing his grandchildren, Matt and Erin, play on those fields and watching Raymond coach on those fields. It meant a lot to him that young people and helping young people meant so much to Raymond and Cindy.

Dave Housel was a kind man and gentle man. He was a good man.

We come here today, not to mourn his passing, but to celebrate his life with us and to thank God for sharing him with us and us with him.

As Christians, we take great joy in the fact that we are never far from Christ. Those who have gone before are with Christ, and because they are with Christ, and because we are near Christ, they are never far from us and we are never far from them.

The person of a man may go, but the best part of him stays. It stays forever.

So it is with Mr. Dave. So it will be with all of us.

July 30, 1990

Faith and Fortitude

When Auburn scored on its last offensive play to defeat Florida, 10-7, a year ago, some people saw it as luck. Others saw it as the culmination of all that Pat Dye believes in, as a man and as a football coach. And to Dye, the two, being a man and a football coach, go hand in hand.

Dye didn't see the touchdown against Florida as luck. Far from it. "I don't believe in miracles..." he said when asked about it in the post-game interview, "but I do believe in not giving up and having faith."

Not giving up, having faith and hard work have made Pat Dye the nation's fourth-winningest coach and Dye, in turn, has made Auburn one of the nation's premier football programs.

The victory over Florida was one of the biggest in a season in which Auburn won its third consecutive Southeastern Conference championship and its fourth in the nine years since Dye has been head coach. Since 1982, no school has won more games, more SEC games, more SEC championships or been to more bowl games than Auburn. Auburn is clearly one of the nation's premier football programs, and Dye is clearly one of the nation's premier football coaches.

When he came to Auburn as head coach in 1981, Dye made only two promises.

"We may not be the most talented football team in the country," he said, "but there is no reason we can't be the best conditioned and best prepared team..."

And, "We will give Auburn a football team Auburn people will be proud of, one that plays hard and plays with class and dignity..."

There is no doubt that the Pat Dye era of Auburn football has lived up to those early promises. It is the most successful era Auburn has ever known.

The Tigers have been to eight straight bowl games, six of them—including the last five—on New Year's Day. Auburn has been on television 53 times (36-15-2 record) during Coach Dye's tenure. In the 31 years prior to the Dye era, Auburn was only on TV 32 times.

And fans are attending Auburn games as never before. Last season, 985,951 fans saw the Tigers play—577,554 of them coming to Auburn—an average of 82,508 per home game. All three attendance figures are Auburn records.

When it comes to winning, Dye is quick to say, "There aren't any secrets out there." He knows that success comes with good players and good coaches who make them better.

Dye's players are among the most honored in college football. He is one of six coaches in history to have coached a Heisman Trophy winner (Bo Jackson, 1985), an Outland Trophy winner (Tracy Rocker, 1988) and a Lombardi Award winner (Rocker, 1988). Other coaches to have that distinction are: Fred Akers (Texas), Woody Hayes (Ohio State), Tom Osborne (Nebraska), Joe Paterno (Penn State) and Barry Switzer (Oklahoma).

Since coming to Auburn, Dye has coached 19 All-Americans, 58 All-SEC players, 38 Academic All-SEC players and 57 of his players have been drafted to play in the NFL, a number virtually unmatched in college football today.

Longevity has been a trait of many former Auburn football players in the professional ranks. Of the players drafted between 1981 and 1989, 35 are still on NFL rosters. More than half of those players still on active rosters have earned their degree from Auburn or return to Auburn during the off season.

Every player who has signed with Pat Dye at Auburn and has played at least four years has played on an SEC championship team. Dye is one of only four coaches in SEC history to win three straight SEC championships. The others are Paul "Bear" Bryant, General Bob Neyland, and Vince Dooley.

Dye, the only active coach to have won three straight SEC titles, is going for his fourth consecutive this year. Only one coach and one school have ever won four straight SEC titles, Bear Bryant and Alabama (1971-75).

Pat Dye has always been a winner. He was an undersized All-America guard for Wally Butts at Georgia in 1959 and 1960, and he was an Academic All-American as a junior. He played on Georgia's 1959 SEC and Orange Bowl championship team and was an alternate captain of the 1960 Georgia team which played in Auburn for the first time.

His coaching career began at Alabama in 1965 when Bryant hired him to replace current Alabama head coach Gene Stallings when Stallings left Tuscaloosa to become head coach at Texas A&M. While at Alabama, Dye was a part of five SEC championships and two national titles. Dye's recruiting and his coaching of the linebackers contributed greatly to one of Alabama's most successful football eras. He coached four All-America linebackers at Alabama.

Dye became a head coach in 1974, leaving Alabama for East Carolina, where he compiled a 48-18-1 record in six seasons and had the Pirate program on par competitively with traditional rivals in the Atlantic Coast Conference.

After one year at Wyoming in 1980, in which he led the Cowboys to a 6-5 record—their first winning season in eight years—Dye came to Auburn in 1981. The rest is a matter of record.

He has led—and is leading—Auburn to its most glorious moments in a long and storied history. Auburn tradition is being rewritten year by year.

Just as he believes there are no secrets to winning football games, Pat Dye believes there is no secret to success. There is only one way to succeed—work, hard work.

He learned the value of work growing up on a farm near Blythe, Georgia when he would get up before daylight to do his chores so that he could walk to school and practice football—work, hard work.

Auburn's values are Pat Dye's values. As it says in the *Auburn Creed*, written by Dr. George Petrie, Auburn's first football coach, "I believe only in what I earn, therefore I believe in work, hard work..."

Pat Dye and Auburn are a great pair, a matched set. Since they have been together, there have been many memorable Saturdays for Auburn football fans.

And there are many more to come.

Auburn Football Illustrated
Pat Dye Biography
1990 Season

Thrust Upon the Stage

Nine years ago today, Bob Hix was unwittingly thrust into the college football spotlight and into Auburn Football History.

Going into the 1981 season, Pat Dye's first as Auburn's head coach, Hix was listed as an offensive tackle. Some folks might say a "down the line" offensive tackle.

When Bishop Reeves, an all-star candidate at center, injured a knee in a freak accident the first day of fall practice, Hix was moved to center to provide backup help to Mike Shirey, a fifth-year senior, who moved to the starting position when Reeves was injured.

Hours before the season opener against TCU, a question arose regarding Shirey's eligibility. It centered around whether or not he had participated in a junior varsity game his freshman year.

The team had completed pre-game warmups and was in the dressing room awaiting Coach Dye's first pre-game talk at Auburn when the word came down. Shirey was ineligible. Hix, who had been a center less than three weeks, would start.

For Bob Hix, his great hour on the Auburn Football stage had come. Though he didn't say it, Hix, as Isaiah of old, must have thought, "Here am I, Send me..." He did not shy away from the challenge. The next day he remembered "not having time to be scared."

"If Coach Dye had told me I was going to start at eight o'clock that morning," he reasoned, "I would have been nervous. As it was I didn't have time to be nervous. I just started thinking about what I was going to do and went over my assignments."

Bob Hix played well that day and Auburn began what was to be a championship era with a 24-16 win over the Horned Frogs. He would start the rest of the year, but with the return of Reeves in 1982 and the advent of more talented players, he saw less playing time. When Auburn won the SEC and Sugar Bowl championships in 1983, Bob Hix was a reserve offensive tackle again.

But the important part of the story, the part that should never be forgotten, is that when Auburn needed him, Bob Hix was there. He was ready. He was prepared and he did the best he could do.

Nine years and four SEC championships have come and gone since that eventful day when Bob Hix was thrust upon the Auburn Football stage. Those nine years have been good to Bob Hix.

He married his college sweetheart, Ellyn, and they can frequently be seen jogging together near Chewacla Park in the wooded neighborhood where they live. He is an engineer for Ampex in Opelika, and she works for the University in computer services. Bob is on the Board of Directors of his neighborhood association, and enforcement of the speed limit for safety reasons is one of his big concerns.

Both are active in church and the community. They are youth counselors for the mid-highs at the Auburn United Methodist Church. Bob plays on the church softball team, and he and Ellyn coach a young girl's team in the Auburn City Rec League. Both are volunteers for Special Olympics.

Auburn is fortunate to have had many talented athletes come through its program, but in the final analysis the success of Auburn's program will be measured by people like Bob Hix, young men who have come through the program, got an education and gone on to make a contribution to their community and the world around them.

Nine years ago today, Bob Hix started at center and Auburn won. Bob Hix is still winning.

As long as Auburn keeps producing people like Bob Hix, Auburn will keep winning, too.

We all will win.

Auburn Football Illustrated
Auburn vs. Cal State Fullerton
September 8, 1990

Pass of the Eighties ————————————

Next week, we celebrate the eighties by honoring our all-decade team as selected by readers of *The Birmingham Post-Herald.*

In preparation for next week, let's think today about some of the greatest and most important plays in the Decade of the Eighties, pass plays in particular. There were many.

For drama, nothing could beat Lawyer Tillman's catch that won the Tech game in 1987, the last of the series. Remember Jim Fyffe, "Tillman, Tillman, Tillman, Tillman..." Lawyer's leaping catch with seconds left deserved every bit of emotion Jim gave it.

For sheer beauty of performance, Lawyer's touchdown catch against Tech in 1986 was exceptional, a 34-yard strike from Jeff Burger. He dove for the ball and, with his body extended full length, batted the ball toward his body with his right hand, catching the ball with his left.

He had several "Vintage Lawyer" catches against Alabama too, in 1987 and 1988.

What about Alexander Wright's 44-yard catch on third and five that set up the first touchdown against Alabama here in Jordan-Hare Stadium, the one down the Alabama sideline in front of our student section? It was an outstanding catch and a big, big play. It set the tone for the greatest moment in our long and glorious history.

Ed West made a critical fourth down catch against Florida State in 1983 to keep the game-winning drive alive in the closing minutes. Lionel "Little Train" James won the game with a fourth-down touchdown catch, and what a game it was, 27-24 Auburn, a game won and almost lost in the last minute of play.

Freddie Weygand had some great catches against Florida State the next year in Tallahassee in the 42-41 game. Let us not forget those. And how could we ever forget that game, 42-41 Auburn with three lead changes in the fourth quarter, almost as good as last week's Tennessee game? Almost.

And what about Shayne Wasden's catch against Florida last year? The game winner on our last offensive play, a 25-yard pass from Reggie Slack. Talk about drama!

But in this Auburn man's opinion, one catch stands out above all the rest as the most important, most significant catch of the decade, a catch on which turned our fate and present glory. It was one of those catches that alters the course of history and this one did.

Auburn-Alabama, 1986. Fourth quarter, two minutes, 18 seconds to play. Alabama 17, Auburn 14. Auburn's ball, fourth and three on the Alabama 49. Fourth and three. Would Auburn run or would Auburn throw? Fate and perhaps history hung in the balance.

After a promising start under Pat Dye, Auburn had lost eight games in two years, including two straight to Alabama. The Alabama coach, Ray Perkins, ever the warrior king, said Dye did not understand the Alabama-Auburn rivalry.

"He doesn't understand," Perkins said, "because he isn't one of us. He didn't play at Auburn or Alabama. He played at Georgia. How can he understand what this game means to us? It's the most important game in the world. Pat Dye doesn't understand that."

In the wake of a disappointing 18-17 loss to Florida and a 20-16 loss to Georgia, some Auburn people were beginning to listen to Perkins. Others were beginning to talk.

To his everlasting credit, Pat Dye chose not to respond. He would let his actions and those of his team do his talking and it had come down to this, fourth and three at the Alabama 49. Would Auburn run or would Auburn throw?

Jeff Burger dropped back and looked for Trey Gainous cutting to the Alabama sideline. The ball left Burger's hand when Gainous made his cut. He dove for the ball and clutched it to his and Auburn's heart just as he slid out of bounds in front of Perkins.

Brent Fullwood gained 19 yards on the next play and Tommie Agee thundered up the middle of the Alabama defense for 11 yards on the next play. The Tigers were homeward bound. Two plays later Lawyer Tillman scored on the reverse.

Auburn and Dye had spoken.

Auburn Football Illustrated
Auburn vs. Louisiana Tech
October 6, 1990

Decade of the Eighties ————————————

We pause today to honor the Team of the Decade, Auburn's best of the best as chosen by readers of *The Birmingham Post-Herald*. What a decade it was. It began in defeat and ended in triumph.

Auburn was supposed to compete with Alabama for the SEC title in 1980. James Brooks was a Heisman Trophy candidate. A 5-6 season, headlined by the worst home loss in Auburn history, 0-42 to Tennessee, brought about a coaching change and the dawning of a new era for Auburn, an era like Auburn had never known.

When Pat Dye was named head football coach January 3, 1981, President Hanly Funderburk said that Dye would build Auburn into a championship team of the eighties. The hiring of Dye and the vision he had for Auburn's football program may have been Dr. Funderburk's finest hour. Though he is no longer here, there is no doubt that he knew the score on Auburn football.

The Pat Dye Era began with a 24-16 win over TCU. The next week there was a 24-21 loss to Wake Forest, and though Auburn people did not know it, Auburn's future was about to begin. Bo Jackson committed that night. There would soon be hope again. The 1981 team finished 5-6, the highlight a 14-12 win over Florida and the tenacious manner in which the team played. You could call us Tigers again.

The next year was a bowl year, the first of what is now eight straight bowls for Auburn. Alabama fell for the first time in nine years, 23-22, and that old worm, long dormant, began to turn.

Auburn won the SEC title the next year and defeated Michigan 9-7 in the Sugar Bowl.

Disappointing years followed in 1984 and 1985, but there was a Heisman trophy in 1985. There was a rededication service in the dressing room after the loss to Texas A&M in the Cotton Bowl. Auburn beat Alabama and Southern Cal to end the 1986 season and began 1987 by beating Texas 31-3 before more than 80,000 fans in Jordan-Hare Stadium. Auburn had defeated Alabama, Southern Cal and Texas, all three in a row. At one time, that would have been a dream. Under Pat Dye, it had become reality.

Another SEC championship followed in 1987 with another in 1988 and a third in 1989, four SEC championships in the Decade of the Eighties, more than any other team. Another dream had become reality. Auburn won 81 games in the last nine years, an average of nine wins a year. We have won 10 games in three of the last four years.

What was Auburn's greatest win in the Decade of the Eighties? It is an appropriate question to ask as we honor those who made Saturdays to remember possible.

The first win over Alabama in 1982 was certainly one of the greatest. From an emotional standpoint and from establishing the competitiveness of Pat Dye's program, it may have been the greatest. The 13-7 win over Georgia in 1983 assured us of our first SEC title in 26 years. It had to be significant. The win over Alabama in 1986 was important in that it signaled the end of a temporary slump in 1984 and 1985. The solid win over Alabama in 1987 clinched another SEC title. It was big. Any win over Alabama is big.

There have been so many good and great ones, 28-21 over Florida, 1983, 27-24 over Florida State, 1983, 42-41 over Florida State, 1984, 16-0 over Florida, 1989, 20-10 over Georgia, 1988, 24-14 over Tennessee in 1982. Each of us has our own list of favorites for our own reasons.

But when all is said and done, when all the precincts are in, all the votes counted, there can be only one "Greatest Game in the Decade of the Eighties," and there is no doubt in this Auburn man's mind what that game should be: 30-20.

They finally came.

Auburn Football Illustrated
Auburn vs. Vanderbilt
October 13, 1990

Strong of Heart

This is a story about one of our own, Ron Stallworth. It is his story and his mother's story. As with most of us, these stories of a mother and her son are so closely intertwined it is as if they are one.

Ron Stallworth came to Auburn in 1984. *Parade Magazine* and *USA Today* named him National Defensive Player of the Year. He was a *Parade* and *USA Today* All-American. He had 60 tackles as a senior at Pensacola's Woodham High School, including three quarterback sacks and nine tackles for losses. He threw the shot and discus for the Woodham track team and he started at center on the basketball team. As a defensive lineman he was given credit for Woodham's 9-1 football season. In short, he was "All-World."

Ron entered a different world when he came to Auburn. The skills that had served him so well in high school, outstanding though they were, left something to be desired on the college level. There was a lot of work to be done, and Ron Stallworth had to be the one to do it.

There were some hard years and hard times, a redshirt year in 1984 and a less than sensational 1985 season when he made only nine tackles. Fans and the media were beginning to ask, "What's wrong with Ron Stallworth?" The term "bust" was being used as in "Is he a bust?" Ron Stallworth had to hear the whispers, but he did the only thing he could do in order to succeed. He kept working and he never lost faith, not in himself and not in his coaches. He just kept working and believing.

His sophomore year, 1986 was better, five starts, 61 tackles, including 10 against Alabama. Potential disaster struck in the spring of 1987 when Ron injured a knee on the first day of spring training. Major reconstructive surgery was required, but by now, no one at Auburn was writing Ron Stallworth off. They knew him too well. He was made of the right stuff.

He came back to have an outstanding 1987 season which included 13 tackles in the SEC championship game against Alabama. The next year was the same, another outstanding season, an All-SEC season, 13 tackles and four quarterback sacks against Alabama, one for a safety, the first in Auburn-Alabama history.

Ron Stallworth was a star on the football field, but he was a star in the classroom, too. He never made Academic All-SEC, but he was a star nonetheless. He did what every student-athlete and every student should do—he took his classwork seriously. He tried, he worked, he learned and he progressed in the classroom just as he did on the football field. He graduated with a management degree in five years, considered "normal" for a student-athlete.

On the day he was to have major reconstructive surgery, he surprised his professor by showing up for a test hours before he was to check into the hospital. Stallworth was in pain and the professor was willing to make other arrangements, but Ron said, no, "This is too important."

Ron Stallworth, now a professional football player with the New York Jets, is a good man. He was a good man long before he came to Auburn. Auburn only improved and refined the qualities that were already in his life, put there by his mother.

Maggie Stallworth never had the chance to get an education. From the time she was old enough, she had to work in the cotton fields to support the family. From the third grade on, she tried to go to school two days a week and work three, but it was inevitable that she would have to leave school.

She may have left school, but she did not quit. In 1983, about the time Ron was deciding where to go to college, she enrolled in an adult basic education course.

For the next seven years, she went to school four nights a week and worked full time during the day. This past June, almost 50 years after her dreams of an education appeared to be over, Maggie Stallworth held a diploma—her diploma—in her hand.

But she held more—much, much more—in her heart.

Auburn Football Illustrated
Auburn vs. Florida State
October 20, 1990

Thanksgiving

It's not Thanksgiving, not quite yet, but there are plenty of people and things to be thankful for anytime Auburn plays football.

I'm thankful for people like Ray McLendon at Downtown Gulf here in Auburn. He is a good man. If you break down tonight, Ray will come and get you. You don't find folks like him much any more.

I'm thankful for Mark Morgan and James Echols at Toomer's Drugs. They keep the the Toomer's Lemonade tradition alive. John Heisman, the man for whom the Heisman Trophy is named, drank lemonade at Toomer's when he coached at Auburn, and we can, too. That's tradition and I love tradition.

I'm thankful for small town barbershops and barbers like Larry, Jeanette and James at the Campus Barbershop on North College. They can make you laugh and brighten the darkest day. They rekindle the Auburn Spirit every day, as do Bobby and Sally Barrett at Flowersmiths.

I'm thankful for ministers like George Mathison and Lester Spencer who "dropped by" after the Florida game. They didn't say why they came, but I know—and you know—why they came. They came to see if one of their flock was all right after what happened in Gainesville. Auburn is a good town and Auburn United Methodist is a good church.

I'm thankful for Emma Jean Brooks' biscuits at the Auburn University Hotel and Conference Center. Auburn is known for good football and good lemonade. It is about to be known for Emma Jean's biscuits. Ron Franklin, tonight's play-by-play commentator on ESPN loves them. So does everybody else who has had them.

I'm thankful for young men like Dale Overton from Hackleburg, who came to Auburn without a scholarship because he loved Auburn and always wanted to be an Auburn Tiger. His dream came true, and I am thankful that it did. He is an inspiration to us all.

I'm thankful for the opportunity to work with good people in athletics. Roy Kramer, for example, an outstanding commissioner, and an even more outstanding man. A man of honor and integrity. An SEC kind of man.

I'm thankful for people like Claude Felton, Sports Information Director at Georgia. Yes, Georgia, our "enemy" tonight. When David Hardee, an Auburn student-assistant, had a diabetic reaction while in Athens for a baseball game, Claude took care of David as if he was one of his own. He was there every day. When my father died this summer, Claude was there, so was Ray Goff, Lee Hayley, Hootie Ingram and Steve Townsend of Alabama. The list could go on and on.

We are competitors, intense competitors, but we are not enemies. There is no hate. There is respect. There is often empathy and sometimes love. There are good people at Auburn and there are good people at Georgia, Alabama and all over the SEC. I am thankful for good people wherever they may be.

I am thankful to be a part of the Auburn family. When I needed you this summer, the family was there, from Coach Dye, the coaches, the staff, right on through you, Auburn fans and friends I have never personally met. You showed you cared. I thank you and I am thankful for you.

I am thankful for Auburn sunsets, for autumn leaves, for the chill in the air on football Saturdays, for the Tiger Walk, and for the roll of drums as another football Saturday at Jordan-Hare is about to get under way. I continue to be thankful for Coach Jordan and for all he has meant to so many. I am thankful for Coach Dye and all he is meaning to so many.

I am thankful for my family and all they have meant and continue to mean.

I am thankful for college football and for rivalries like Auburn-Georgia.

I thank God I am an American.

I am thankful He made me an Auburn man.

And I thank you, the readers, for reading for 24 years now. We've gotten to know one another pretty well.

Auburn Football Illustrated
Auburn vs. Georgia
November 17, 1990